COLE SAHIB
The Story of a Multifaith Journey

COLE SAHIB
The Story of a Multifaith Journey

W. OWEN COLE

sussex
ACADEMIC
PRESS

BRIGHTON • PORTLAND

2 4 6 8 10 9 7 5 3 1

First published in 2009 by
SUSSEX ACADEMIC PRESS
PO Box 139
Eastbourne BN24 9BP

and in the United States of America by
SUSSEX ACADEMIC PRESS
920 NE 58th Ave   Suite 300
Portland, Oregon 97213-3786

British Library Cataloguing in Publication Data
A CIP catalogue record for this book is available from the British Library.

Library of Congress Cataloging-in-Publication Data
Cole, W. Owen (William Owen)
 Cole Sahib : the story of a multifaith journey / W. Owen Cole.
 p. cm.
 ISBN 978-1-84519-336-2 (pbk. : alk. paper)
 1. Cole, W. Owen (William Owen) 2. Spiritual biography. 3. Religions.
I. Title.
BL73.C646A3 2009
200.92—dc22
[B]
                                                                    2009005826

Mixed Sources
Product group from well-managed
forests and other controlled sources
www.fsc.org Cert no. SGS-COC-2482
© 1996 Forest Stewardship Council

Typeset and designed by SAP, Brighton & Eastbourne.
Printed by TJ International, Padstow, Cornwall.
This book is printed on acid-free paper.

Contents

Foreword by
Charanjit K. Ajit Singh

Dr Owen Cole's autobiography, *Cole Sahib, the story of a multifaith journey*, is in every way a testimony to his extraordinary life experience as a pilgrim and as an academic in matters of interfaith. The title 'Cole Sahib' aptly applies to Dr Cole because of the respect he has gained, and by the very deep rapport he has developed with the people he met on his numerous visits to India since 1973. While reading the book, I was touched by the openness and generous sharing of his ideas and experiences and I feel that my own learning has been enhanced because of it.

I remember my first contact with Dr Owen Cole, when he joined London Borough of Ealing, which also covers the multireligious area of Southall, as a Religious Education Adviser nearly thirty years ago. Since then there have been many opportunities of exploring religious issues locally and nationally with Dr Cole.

In this memoir, Dr Cole describes his multifaith journey of over half a century in a way that engages the reader from the very start. We are enabled to walk the walk and experience the joys and hazards of his travels, which are gripping and absorbing. Dr Cole shares these adventures with us by telling us the stories of the hospitality of strangers, acquaintances and of course, friends, to harrowing encounters of staring death in the face, being called a spy and a revolver being pointed at him while visiting the subcontinent and Pakistan. Even after all this, he calls India his favourite country outside Britain.

Dr Cole is blessed with the particular gifts of insight and foresight and in this book he imparts his learning and experience of his study at a variety of Hindu, Muslim, Jewish, Jain, Christian and Sikh religious places and centres of learning in a meaningful and empathetic manner. In my opinion, it was his depth of knowledge about the Sikh faith that he was honoured as a non-Sikh to contribute to the *Encyclopaedia of Sikhism*, a reputable publication of Patiala University in India. For him, 'India is a country where many forms of spirituality are respected.' A person can be inter-religious in his or her daily life and that does not make that person any less in their commitment to their faith. Dr Cole also does not dodge what might be considered 'uncomfortable' issues, for example, caste among the Christians in South India.

His affinity with the Sikh community and his knowledge of Sikh history and practice are legendary. His close association and collaboration with the late Piara Singh Sambhi provided the inspiration and guidance for a series of publications on the Sikhs. There were also Sikh Christian Consultations under Dr Cole's guidance in the 1980s led by Dr John Parry; the first being in 1984 was especially poignant as it was soon after Operation BlueStar at the Golden Temple.

Dr Cole describes his passion for Religious Education in these words, 'I have lived and breathed RE since 1954 when I discovered its existence.' No wonder that he has used his energy, resourcefulness and influence in the shaping of Religious Education in the United Kingdom, through his writings, chairmanship of educational bodies, work on Agreed Syllabuses in different local authorities, as an examiner and on Shap (the Working Party on World Religions in Education). He has striven to make RE to be worthy of being regarded as an academic discipline. At the same time, he has raised his voice and written articles for the abolition of school worship. Having inspected schools, I know how many teachers in community schools feel about collective worship!

I share Dr Cole's broader definition of RE as 'the study of beliefs and values, many of which will be religious but which will also include Humanism and Atheism', with a view to helping the young 'to grow up to be critically aware of their human responsibilities and environment and capable of responding to global challenges'.

Furthermore, Dr Cole's quest goes on to pose questions about the religious gene, belief or otherwise of religious instinct, whether there are beings similar to us on other planets and then closer to home on our own planet, the issue of our own assumptions of our own religion as authentic. All these and many other questions need further investigation – hopefully through another volume from Dr Cole.

I have found Dr Cole's journey immensely fascinating as a man of faith, showing us how he has done it while being faithful to his own and with deep respect for the other, a true witness to interfaith. I strongly hope that other readers also find his journey of spiritual fellowship as transformational as I have found it to be for me.

CHARANJIT K. AJIT SINGH

Preface

Dedicated to Rhiannon and Ben our grandchildren for whom it was originally written in the hope that one day, many years from now, they might
ask what kind of things interested Ted Bear, (their name for me), and might
want to explore an interfaith journey as well as the pilgrimage of faith for
themselves. Whether they do so or not it is also written in the hope that they
and all their generation and those who follow them, of whatever faith or
none, may sit under their own fig tree and their own vine and that none
shall make them afraid. (Micah, chapter 4).

This story has three intertwining strands. One is my deep interest in
Religious Education from 1954 onwards when I discovered it, until now;
the second is the multifaith journey that I have travelled since about 1968;
and the third is my own continuing spiritual pilgrimage.

The help of many must be acknowledged. First, Sarah and Emily
Dyble who began the task of rescuing my manuscript when all seemed
lost; and then Heather Ballamy who completed what they had begun,
and Andy who repeatedly restores my computer to something approaching good health. Eluned and Siân, our daughters, have encouraged and
supported me during periods of self doubt that I have never previously
experienced and Gwynneth has been a continual source of loving
strength as my wife, and since 2003, as my Carer. Those who are named
and many unnamed in the pages that follow have been inspiring guides
and companions upon my journeys of faith.

Finally, no one should ever undervalue the efforts of publishers who
deal with writers like myself. Considerable gratitude is due to them.

W. OWEN COLE
28 January 2009

COLE SAHIB
The Story of a Multifaith Journey

INTRODUCTION

Cole Sahib

To be encouraged to write is a joy; ever since Mr Booth in the third year sixth at Heckmondwike Grammar School set us a weekly essay I have found it a source of great pleasure. Some people have even suggested that I have a certain fluency that results in me saying nothing but saying it well, as my archaeology tutor told me years after I had left Durham and when I began to know him in different circumstances as a friend. Over a pint he told me that he remembered my study of the town walls of Roman Britain very well because it read so easily. Had it been written hastily on the night before submission or was it the result of months of research? No one could be certain so the examiners gave me an A and that probably ensured my 2ii degree.

With short-term memory not what it was and Parkinson's turning reading and the holding of papers into an unpleasant experience I decided that the sooner I could write this memoir the better. Much could have been added that I might have thought relevant and even important, but tinkering is a skill that I have acquired and cultivated over time, and a point is reached when one must say write and be damned or blessed for brevity!

As a retired teacher I can now give more attention to this activity. I do not regret the fact that I could not give as much time in the past to writing than I did though sometimes an article could have been more comprehensive had there been a few days more before the deadline was reached. However, teaching has always been my vocation since I was sixteen years old and I have learned much from it, though whether my students, be they eight or seventy, have benefited to the same extent I do not know.

When I reflect upon the account contained in these pages I realise just how different Britain and the world are to that into which I was born and nurtured and yet note how little has changed. The sovereign is still the Defender of the Faith, our honours are still imperial, Order of the British Empire, and so on. Parliament is what it was after the 1939–45 war, and so is the Establishment in the UK and the United Nations. Part of my motivation in writing this book has been to remind myself and others that there is more to the living organism of humanity than what we trap in history and tradition, and to express the hope that our grandchildren may respond to it, though they live in Canada, perhaps a less trapped part of the fossilised world, though I am not sure about that.

This book is essentially the story of some aspects of my life from about the age of twenty-four until the present time, my seventy-eighth year. However, I begin with my childhood because the more I reflected upon my career and the evolution of my beliefs the more I realised how much was present in embryo whilst I was growing to adulthood. (If I had realised this sooner I might have made a better parent!) In me the child has certainly been the father of the man and the man has been his father's son.

My education took place during a static period of curriculum inertia as far as I was concerned. It had probably been taught unchanged since the boundary changes of the Treaty of Versailles at the end of the First World War required Geography to make at least some response to modernity. At university our course in modern history ended at 1878 and although some students would have liked it to include the Second World War and its consequences, we tended to accept the diet we were offered but realised that silent note-taking for about eleven hours a week for three years was not a good way to learn.

In 1954 when I began to train as a teacher I was well fitted to transmitting the knowledge of a former age without question. It was then that I also discovered that there was a subject called Religious Instruction. Though I had attended three grammar schools, in none of them had I come across such a subject, daily religious assemblies yes, but RI no. The Institute of Christian Education of which I formed the Harlow branch, described Religious Education as a three-legged stool, a partnership between church, school, and home, and this was a view that I was happy to endorse. The integration of RE with other subjects in the Humanities was my first distinctive contribution to the subject's development and even then the contribution was still Christian and sensible. I did not share the view of the Headmaster who told me he brought RE into Maths – cubits and spans!

It may have been a course taught by John Hinnells and the follow up discussions as well as the advertisement for a professor in Religious Studies at Lancaster which stated that applicants might be of any faith or none, that provoked me to consider and accept an open approach to the study of religions and with it, naturally, the rejection of school worship. Certainly it was not the presence of people of other faith in this country of whose existence I was scarcely aware. Multifaith RE began when I arrived in Leeds. I changed seismically from holding a traditional view of being British, one held by most people today it seems, to one who can still support Yorkshire cricket and Welsh rugby but has a vision of a nation truly democratic and secular in Nehru's sense with its equal respect for all faiths in which everyone may share as an equal stakeholder in a global society.

For someone who has a religious belief and who comes in contact with other faiths there may be two natural responses. One is for them to have no influence, to regard them simply as other religious phenomena to be studied. A classic example of this was a university lecturer in Buddhism who later became a bishop who once declared publicly that Buddhism was fundamentally wrong but did not provide any empirical proof to substantiate his claim. (He could not. Faith statements may tell us more about the person who makes them than about actual reality as readers of this book may discover.) On the other hand, one may choose the path of conversion to a new, more personally acceptable religion. This may seem an obvious solution but some converts have quickly discovered the idealism that they sought to be obscured by the reality of the street corner mandir or mosque as potent as any experienced in a typically British church. The third way, to which I responded, was to discover within my own tradition those things I came to value in others and to realise that any, if not all, faiths have sufficient inner riches to meet any needs, however peculiar, but it did require a considerable reconsideration of my views. (I almost used the word 'radical' but ever since Mrs Thatcher appropriated it I have been uncertain of its meaning and have had to look for an alternative.)

The remaining pages of this book tell the story of this threefold development. Thank you for being interested enough to read it.

1

Setting Out

To begin at the beginning to quote the opening words of my favourite play. (Will Chichester's Festival theatre ever stage it in my lifetime?) I am a son of the Manse but for many years that did not seem significant. Dad was very liberal in his views and my brothers and I seldom felt under any restraint except, in my case, I can't speak for them, when it came to education. When I hadn't the grades necessary for university I said I would leave school and find a job. 'No' came the reply and back to school I went, to captain the soccer and cricket teams, become head boy and, next time round win a county exhibition. Dad had left the pit in 1926. Like many miners he believed that a son's education was the key to a better life than that of his experience. But I have run too far into my future.

I was born in Sheffield on 22 September 1931 but was brought up in Bradford to which we moved in 1934; this was necessitated by the fact that the church in Brightside could not afford to pay dad £150 per year and that much of what he did receive was turned into pies by my mum to feed the unemployed. As my father told me later, we could either starve with the congregation or leave and cease to be a burden on them. Such was the situation that when a wealthy member of the church gave me a sovereign on the day I was born we had to use it to buy food instead of save it. Dad told me this very apologetically some months before he died. In 2001 our daughters gave me a 1931 sovereign to compensate for the loss! During the summer before I began at Dudley Hill in Bradford I went to stay with my grandma Coupland in Hull. One day she took me into the city. Perhaps as I had been misbehaving she told me that if I was not good 'that black man would get me'. Turning round anxiously I saw him standing on the other side of the road, looking quite innocuous and not in my direction! That was my first experience of a world that was not entirely white. During the same holiday I remember my beautiful black haired aunty Betty coming crying home to my grandma's. She had gone on a date but because she said she was not Jewish her fellow had stood her up. None of this made any sense to a four year old, but it stuck in his memory alas, much as his first day at school when he was taken on the tram by his mother and left until 3 p.m. because on that first day everyone had to stay for lunch. When she returned it was to face a crisis. After dinner everyone in the babies' class was expected to go to sleep on fold away beds which the school provided. Not only was this something I had not done for years but when the boy next to me wet his bed, made a little girl get up and swap places that was too much! Had someone wet mine on a previous occasion? Would I be the next child to whom he would turn? As I could already read fluently and tell the time mum and the teachers decided to move me into the second class immediately.

For some year's aunt Betty's tears meant nothing to me until, one evening Dr Fiddler and his wife came to supper and I was later told that he was Jewish. Some people on Tong Street would not let him treat them because he was a Jew, unless the other doctor in the district, a Scot, Dr Bremner, wasn't available. Then, Dr Fiddler was apparently acceptable. In the days before the NHS doctors seemed to fix their own fees. Both these men would ask my father about the circumstances of their patients and if he told them that they were unemployed, as many were, or were on low wages, no payment was asked but the better off might be charged seven shillings and sixpence to compensate for this generosity. The coming of the NHS seems to have assured many doctors of a secure and reasonable income for the first time. On the other hand, those who courted well-to-do patients may well have lost out. Dr Fiddler was obviously a very unobservant Jew, not that this meant anything to me as a child, but I was impressed later to learn that he was a doctor to Bradford Northern rugby league team, the one I watched.

Before the 1939 war began I learned that my father was collecting for Jewish refugees who were coming to the small community from Germany. He must have been taking them clothing as there was little money to spare where we lived. Unemployment was still high. Again I knew nothing about Jews, not even when I began studying German and was taught by the most sadistic man I have ever met who happened to be a German Jew. No one was spared his bullying sarcasm but it fell especially upon one of our set who suffered from four misfortunes – he had red hair, he was fat, he stammered and he was extremely clever. None of these attributes are very much appreciated by young teenagers and 'Shap' to give the teacher his nick name, relished stirring us up to ridicule his victim. My dad expressed a horror that a man who had endured what he had presumably had to face in Germany could behave in such a way. After a term in form three, we moved from Bradford to Newcastle but the memory is still vivid. I have had the good fortune to meet few people like him and certainly no one as unpleasant. Male teachers in those days were often brutal bullies. The primary school head master, a Scot, who followed the gentle but firm Miss Flathers when she had retired, had a taws, a thick rope's end that always stood on his desk and he was not afraid to use it. A teacher of top juniors, wounded in World War One, was given to throwing his walking stick at children but stopped when the boy in front of me, his target, ducked, and I was caught just above the right eye. Major Robinson, Belle Vue Grammar School's PE master, let me fall while going over the vaulting horse and only said; 'Kiss it better', as I lay winded on the ground. Another ex army man tried to make my best friend and I box one another. We refused and so I won yet another enemy!

My religious upbringing cannot be described as fanatical. I never felt at all uncomfortable with it, though one occasion, at least, my pals did! They asked me; 'Owen how is it that you are not dead'? 'What do you mean'? I replied. 'Well, when you go home you must go around with your hands together and your eyes shut. So you can't eat and must fall down the stairs'. Perhaps today the clergy is more aware of what those outside the culture of the church think of them, and maybe society at large is better informed about life in the manse or rectory, I hope so.

There were two features to my explicit Christian nurture. The first lasted about six years at most. Before getting into bed I was told to kneel beside it and say my prayers. This consisted of; 'God bless mummy and daddy, grandmas and grandpas, aunties and uncles, and cousins, and make me a good boy. Amen.' Then I got into bed with a goodnight kiss. When I was six years old and my brother Gawain was born mum had no time to supervise my devotions so I was told to say my prayers in bed, though still given a kiss.

A telling memory which I cannot place in time is that of visits to Mrs Kellett next door, the widow of a mill owner and member of our church. If only I could chat with her now but she must have been in her seventies when I was still under school age. She was a remarkable person, she taught me cards, gave me postcards of Chicago and other cities she had been to in America, told me about chief Sitting Bull whom she claimed to have met, and possessed a large refrigerator which she used to make delicious ice cream. Unwittingly she also introduced me to Tit Bits, a racy magazine with a green cover. In those days I would avidly read anything. One of the stories was about a white girl who was drugged by two Chinese men. I could not understand what they did but they left a pound note under her pillow. Mrs. Kellett was also rich enough to pay for my mother to go into a nursing home for the birth of my brother Gawain, and to offer to send me to Woodhouse Grove, a Methodist independent school; thankfully the war put paid to that idea, though I hope dad would not have favoured it. Mrs Kellett had friends for tea on some afternoons and I joined them. Using a metal triangular fire guard with a grill as a pulpit I conducted services whilst we all sang Sankey and Moody hymns. I still possess a Columbus half dollar from the Chicago World Fair of 1893 which she gave me. Perhaps my upbringing did have unsuspected consequences.

Every Sunday I ran alongside my swiftly walking dad to Holme Lane Congregational chapel where he was minister. Next to it was the Holme Lane pub which Mr Burnham, a neighbour, frequented and by it was Horniman Street, named, I was told, after a brand of tea that was mixed with the beer when men had drunk well and couldn't tell the difference. The street was built with money from the proceeds. In chapel I sat with other boys in the children's pew in front of the rest of the congregation; girls sat in one to the left of us. None of us wanted to mix at that age, of under ten. The service began when dad climbed the steps into the pulpit, gave a brief introduction and announced the first hymn. There was a reading from the Bible, another hymn and then the children's address, followed by the children's rather childish hymn, though to a pleasant tune so we quite enjoyed singing it. During the last verse we left, or at least the others did. I went and sat in the back pew with an elderly family friend, Miss Smith. Much later I discovered from her nephew that her brother had been killed on the first day of the Battle of the Somme. He wrote a letter before going over the top in which he left what money he had, five pounds, to Holme Lane. As far as I can recollect there was only one Sunday when my dad did not take me to chapel, that was in September 1939, the day when war was declared. He told me to stay with mummy and at eleven o'clock I heard Mr Chamberlain's broadcast. Mum said she was glad that I was too young to go and that the war would be over long before I was eighteen, though I didn't know what she meant. The back door was open and I can still see the steam coming from Lister's mill as the air raid siren wailed its warning before, only minutes later, sounding the all clear. The war ended many things such as going to watch cricket at a small field in the village of Tong with dad and some of his friends; if we were especially fortunate we might see a horse being shod at the smithy on the way. Most of the players had left to serve in the forces. The annual Whit Sunday service continued with everyone walking about two miles to a field down Bowling Lane where my dad and other ministers led a service from the back of a lorry. This, however, was really a secular event for most children played tag among the adults, and enjoyed the Salvation Army brass band's rousing versions of such hymns as 'O for a thousand tongues to sing', 'All hail the power of Jesu's name', and 'Jesus shall reign where're the sun doth his successive journeys run'. My love of brass bands, a feature of my Yorkshire identity, can probably be traced to this event. My last attendance at it was the summer before we moved to Newcastle; by now I was a bugler in the Boys' Brigade band. Going down Wakefield Road on the way to Bowling caused no problems but the uphill journey back was steep so I simply put the bugle to my lips and pretended to blow! I never learned how dad acquired some ability with the bugle but at holiday times when we would play in Toftshaw Woods he would give a sufficiently good rendering of 'Come to The Cookhouse Door Boys' to summon us the one mile home. The annual and much looked forward to trip to the seaside at Filey on Whit Monday was, during the war, replaced by a party and picnic in a farmer's field. A pity, I used to enjoy going to Dudley Hill station, finding the Holme Lane carriage, picking up other Sunday schools on the way and returning as night was falling. There were no hymns or prayers; this was just a good day out for the children whose parents, for the most part, could not afford such expenses themselves. These were secular occasions as much as Guy Fawke's night was; we enjoyed the big bonfire in a field down the lane, and, in school, enacting the story of discovery of Guy beneath the Houses of Parliament without ever thinking that they had anything to do with protestants and catholics, terms with which we were totally ignorant. Perhaps bonfire night and bananas were things I missed most during the war.

In school the only expression of religion I can remember from the primary school I attended until 1941 and three grammar schools was the daily act of collective worship, made legally binding from 1944 but commonly observed much earlier. It was nearly always conducted by the head teacher and at Dudley Hill had a set formula. We marched in from our classes, the youngest in front and the oldest at the back, accompanied by our teachers whilst the pianist played the famous march from Scipio by Handel. The Head then gave a talk and offered a prayer. There might be a hymn before the talk and another to end the service. We then went back to our classrooms for the register to be called. I later discovered that children exempted from the service could be given their attendance mark so long as they turned up by 9.30. In the nineteen seventies a student phoned me suggesting that I went to observe the act of worship in the primary school where he was teaching. It was last thing in the afternoon so I turned up at 3pm. The service was identical to my experience of almost thirty years earlier except for the fact that half the children came from Asian families. This was in no way represented or catered for by the school whose head later told me that 'they need to learn about our ways'. To hear Scipio again took my mind back to my own childhood!

One would not think that the Abdication Crisis of 1936 would affect a five year old boy in Bradford but it did. Just behind the boy's pew in chapel sat an elderly lady called Mrs Simpson. We lads all lived in fear of her as she carried a walking stick which she used to prod anyone who misbehaved. Sometimes dad had difficulty not smiling as a boy would suddenly stop talking or flicking through his hymn book during a Bible reading or the children's address, as he was poked in the back and sat bolt upright! When we got home, if I had been a culprit, he would laughingly tell my mother that Mrs Simpson had felt it necessary to call me to order. 'Oh Owen', mum would say, smiling.

Mrs Simpson bothered me in another way. Somehow I had some awareness of the Abdication Crisis but could not get my head around the notion that the King of England was in love with the old lady who sat in the pew behind us and was willing to give up the throne for her! We used to sing; 'Who's that coming down the street? Mrs Simpson with her sweaty feet'; that seemed much more appropriate! Dad sometimes took me visiting with him and one day we went to her house in Oddy Street. It was darkly Edwardian or even Victorian in décor, and there was no picture of the Prince. I was even more bewildered, but somehow didn't bother to question my dad or mum.

Cussedness set in at an early age. My first memory of it was when my pals came to see if I could go out to play when I had finished my tea. Mum said I could go so long as I ate everything up. I turned to my friends and said; 'It's egg sandwiches, I'll see you tomorrow'. They were placed in front of me as I sat at the table but some thirty minutes later I was allowed to leave the table with the sandwiches untouched! Egg sandwiches were definitely pre-war. I must have been seven or eight.

I suppose that these episodes in my early life prepared me for what was to come, especially my father's liberal attitude which I remember included inviting two men to supper who must, I realised many years later, have been gay. When I was about eleven years old I decided that I would like to go to the evening service and sit with Miss Smith. The first Sunday in the month included a communion service and naturally I took the small piece of bread and glass of wine brought around by a deacon. One evening he didn't give them to me but returned to the front of the church and spoke to my father to see whether I should be given the elements or not. A few minutes later he returned with them. Dad had told him that the Lord's Table was open to all who loved the Lord Jesus and he was sure that I did so he brought me the bread and wine. Some years later dad explained that the reason why he was not a Baptist like his family was that once, as a young man, he had taken a service in a Congregational Church. One of the deacons told him that a family had brought their baby in the hope that he might be baptised. Dad said that if this was the wish of the congregation he would perform the rite on their behalf. A few years later he went for an interview to be accepted as a student at the Bristol Baptist College where he was asked if he had baptised an infant. When he answered in the affirmative he was asked if he would do so again. He replied that he would in the same circumstances. The panel reminded him that Baptists believed only in believer's baptism and that a baby could not possibly make such a confession of faith, consequently he could not be accepted as a candidate for Baptist ministry. It was this event that resulted in him becoming a Congregationalist, training at a college in Bradford and meeting my mother who was a nurse in that city. He went to his grave unbaptised, something that worried none of our family. Surely he enjoyed the Baptism of the Spirit if anyone did.

Dad must have intended to become a minister when he returned from the war as he went to evening classes in Carmarthen to study Greek and Latin. The push came in 1926 in the form of the General Strike. The coal owners wanted to cut wages and increase working hours. To the slogan; 'Not an hour on the day, not a penny off the pay,' the miners walked out. The government suspected the influence of the communist party from Moscow, and my uncle Tom was certainly a communist. He and dad were among those who were told that when the strike was over there would be no work for them down in the pits. Tom left Wales to take his chance in the Middle East with an oil company and ended up as a miner in Australia; dad headed north to theological college.

The ecumenical movement scarcely existed in 1939, at local level anyway, but somehow it was agreed to hold an interdenominational service one Christmas at St John's Anglican Church. I remember it because dad insisted on the congregation singing Silent Night in German, *Stille Nacht Heilige Nacht*. This at a time when a local mill owner friend was having to get rid of his German Opel car, which dad pointed out, had been paid for before the war so it was not that Hitler was continuing to make money from the deal!

We seemed quite well off in 1939, I already had a clockwork Hornby train set with trucks, carriages and plenty of track. Santa Claus gave me more signals, points, tunnels and stations. To this was now added a fort with forty-eight lead soldiers. However, life was to change. My second brother, Raymond, was born in 1941. Dad's salary remained at £250 per annum and, one suspects, he was responsible for all heating and lighting expenses in our large four double bed-roomed manse, (which I considered to be haunted! I wish I had visited it in later life to discover whether other occupants shared my feelings). Added to which dad was a heavy smoker. The only rows in an otherwise very happy marriage were centred upon this subject. Mum would complain that he was smoking while she had not enough money to pay for groceries. Dad would get cross and throw the cigarette packet into the fire, he would then be miserable for days because of withdrawal symptoms, she would find money to give him from somewhere and tell him to buy some more cigarettes, he would do so and happiness and peace would return. (It may be significant that none of his three sons became smokers!)

Aware of poverty though not on the scale of a family with seven children and a father who never worked because he, Mr Burnham, had been crippled by a sniper's bullet, even though he had been a stretcher bearer, who lived across the road from us, I always felt reluctant to ask my parents for money during the war years and later. This had one important consequence. Periodically, to help the war effort, the government would declare such an event as a Warship Week when citizens would be asked to lend to defend the right to be free. Some people gave, most lent by purchasing savings bonds. In school the appeal was usually met by children buying saving stamps. I didn't feel that I could ask my parents for money so, at Belle Vue Grammar School in Bradford I found myself as the only non-contributory child. On about four occasions I was called to the front of school assembly by the headmaster, Dr Fisher, and told I was the one person who was preventing the school having a 100% record. This worried neither me nor anyone else apparently. I remember no bullying taunts, perhaps my fellow pupils sided with me against authority. When we moved to Newcastle, however, I decided that I wanted no more of this victimisation so when the first savings week was announced I was prepared. Finding a shilling in mum's purse I took it and bought a stamp on the Monday morning. On the way home I cashed it in at the post office and purchased another stamp in the afternoon which was cashed in the evening. This process was repeated each day until, on Friday, the shilling was restored to my mother's purse and on Monday at assembly I was publicly congratulated on having made the largest contribution to the war effort!

My bad feet, which mum felt would keep me out of the army if I was required to enlist, she and so did I, put down to wearing the hand-me-down shoes of a wealthy friend who enjoyed telling classmates and anyone else who didn't know that I was wearing his shoes! Not as noticeable, except to me. was that I may have been the only boy who wore pin stripped trousers. Dad came home one day with a suit of a man whose funeral he had recently taken, whose widow had given it to him. It was far too big to fit him but mum managed to make me a pair of trousers out of it.

The European war ended in May 1945; in the following autumn or winter a German pastor came to stay with us for a few days. I remember his surprise at being received hospitably and with friendship. Once the war was over ill feeling seemed to evaporate very quickly.

Identity is a popular modern issue. My awareness of being Welsh seems to have begun before my memory. Dad often talked about it though he had no accent, rather it was said that he sounded as though he came from Inverness, wherever that was. Perhaps his tendency to wake me up at 3 a.m. to listen to boxing matches from America on our fine Bush radio, through which we could reach the whole world, also contributed, especially the Tommy Farr and Joe Louis fights. My Welsh consciousness resulted in my first visit to Wales soon after graduation, in 1954, where I went to see my granddad and aunts and met my lovely wife Gwynneth.

My sense of Yorkshire identity developed soon after I moved to Newcastle in 1944. During the house cricket trials on the first afternoon of the summer term the teacher in charge suggested I should have a bowl, saying that being a Yorkshireman I should be good at cricket. I took five wickets for two runs with slow donkey drops and was chosen to be vice-captain! The next week I was brought on to bowl against the best cricketer in our year. After two overs of inhumane slaughter I was taken off. Next week I was relegated to the odds and sods, but I knew that I was a Yorkshire Welshman and eagerly read about the exploits of Len Hutton, Bryn Jones and men like Alan Edwards, Willie Davis, and Trevor Foster who played for Bradford Northern! Not long after we moved to Newcastle, I was joined by the great Len Shackleton, whom I had watched at Bradford Park Avenue, I was standing at the Leazes Park end of St James's Park when he scored his six goals against Newport County. Why had it to be a Welsh team?

Heckmondwike was an interesting woollen district town, originally strongly nonconformist to which the Church of England came only in the mid nineteenth century and the Roman Catholics later still. In 1947, dad became minister of the then famous Upper Chapel that had refused membership to the chemist Joseph Priestley nearly two hundred years earlier and still remembered it. The splendid building was the largest in the town and was used for concerts and school celebrations. Sadly the wealth of its builders had not been left to it in the form of legacies and most of its young people who joined the armed forces in 1939 did not return to it after demobilisation in 1945. It was a church in decline. Fortunately the grammar school was a thriving institution where my brothers and I prospered, though it had two shortcomings, only one of which really affected us. Its mission, if it had one, was to produce teachers. Friends of mine who wanted to become doctors or enter industry seemed to be given little help in preparing for their careers, but as we three brothers all intended to teach the school served us perfectly well. However, being fairly small it could only provide a limited curriculum. Thus, although I, who had to take the whole School Certificate examination twice, achieved distinctions in geography on both occasions though following different syllabuses there was no teacher competent to teach it at A level. I could have gone to Batley but three grammar schools were quite enough. Philosophy did not feature at all which was a pity in hindsight because this is the course that our youngest brother, Raymond, should have taken at university; instead he read Chemistry, not very well because he came under the influence of a Congregational minister and spent most of his time in theological and philosophical discussions. So radical did he become in his views and beliefs that, in later years, a Unitarian church where he occasionally took services said they could invite him no more because of his views. To be too radical for the Unitarians is, or was then, quite an achievement!

Close as I was to my father there was one exception to the supposed norm of like father like son. Dad had enlisted as a volunteer during the First World War. He and his brother falsified their ages after receiving white feathers through the letter box, so their older sister told me many years later. During World War Two he spoke on behalf of young men who, I much later realised, were conscientious objectors, and he worked with the British Legion, though not himself a member, to help soldiers or their widows secure (better) pensions. Long before the prospect of National Service became imminent I had decided to be a conscientious objector. One morning a friend who owned an air rifle decided that we might shoot some birds. One of my shots hit a male blackbird that fell dying at my feet. It squawked horribly for all of five minutes, though it seemed an hour, the rifle was returned to its owner, not to be used by me again. At the cinema a Pathe newsreel showed Australian soldiers using a flame thrower on a Japanese bunker from which three men emerged on fire. That memory remains undimmed sixty years later. Finally, I remember coming down the stairs in my grandmother's house to hear a news bulletin announce the dropping of the first atom bomb on Hiroshima. I was still in Hull on VJ Day and joined in the street celebrations at the end of which mum's eighteen year old cousin whose husband was serving in the army, asked me to walk her home. Grandma saw us departing, clipped my ear and ordered me to bed! At breakfast the next morning she accused me of being drunk.

When my time came to register for National Service, nearly a decade later, I joined the Friends' Ambulance Unit. Dad supported me though he said he could not share my views: my next brother, Gawain, enlisted in the RAF. Our different decisions regarding National Service caused Gawain and me no problems but did arouse the interest of the 'Sunday Graphic', a paper long defunct. It had run a piece on the worst dressed women in England and decided that they lived in Heckmondwike. A reporter visited the town to take some of its women out to lunch. Among them was our mother. During the meal families were discussed and the reporter learned of our different responses to military service. She wrote a piece to the effect that one brother was a conscientious objector and the other was in the armed forces but they were still speaking to one another!

2

Getting There

From Heckmondwike Grammar School the next step on the long road that eventually led to meeting with people of other faith had to be university. With hindsight, the only exact science, it is possible to advise young applicants to choose the course rather than the place, something that I wish I had known. After the headmaster's assurance that the ability to gain admission to Oxford or Cambridge was entirely lacking he encouraged an application to Durham to read history. An interview with the Master of University College, in the ancient castle, and a moral tutor who turned out to be an alcoholic, (later put firmly on the wagon by a lady he met in a pub and married!), and the history professor, though not necessarily in that order, I was offered a place on the spot, subject to obtaining a grant through a county exhibition scholarship or a county major.

The course turned out to be one in modern history that stopped at 1878 as it was deemed impossible to interpret the meaning of later events until the dust of time settled on them. Roman Provincial Administration was the most appealing specialist option when it came to making third-year choices. The foci of the degree were in economic and constitutional history to the extent that even when it came to the Reformation and Renaissance little attention was given to Martin Luther, religious events in England, or the Counter Reformation in Europe. My reading and essays written for tutorials tended to be on these subjects and did me little good when it came to the final examinations. Hence the advice given to those hoping to go to university to consider the content of the course not the location.

My first hall of residence was Lumley Castle near Chester le Street; in my third year I enjoyed a study in the Keep of Durham Castle overlooking the Cathedral Green from one direction and the courtyard of the Castle from another. Probably not many other members of the lumpen proletariat can claim to have lived in such style!

Some weeks after my arrival there was a knock on the door of my room. It was the college chaplain doing his duty in visiting all freshers.

Durham University was very Anglican but many members of Castle's community had no time for religion. In this knowledge I welcomed him and offered him a chair and a cup of tea. Even before he sat down he asked me if I was an Anglican; when I replied that I was a Congregationalist he turned and with no further comment left the room! Sad. How could one with such views minister to the college community? Incidentally, most students who did attend college chapel and support him were either low church evangelical Anglicans for whom denominationalism meant little, or Methodists.

I attended Claypath Congregational Church whilst I lived in Durhaam itself and, for a time, helped the minister run a club for boys aged about eleven from the locality. We decided that the evening should end with worship, the rest of the time being given to playing games. I went from the church hall into the church by the connecting door and invited one of the boys to help me carry in the hymn books. Never have I seen such terror on anyone's face, and I don't want to see it again. Surely, God – or Satan – must be hiding behind the pulpit. I said nothing but collected the books and, to his apparent surprise, emerged unharmed. The next Tuesday we left the connecting door open and the lights in the church on, just before the time of worship I asked the same boy to accompany me again. He refused, still looking afraid. A week later I again asked him. This time he agreed, gathered up a pile of books and fled back into the hall where his mates looked him up and down as if to make sure that he was alright. Eventually, we were able to hold our act of worship in the church itself but only after several more weeks. Do ministers and church goers appreciate how strange a place a church is to the majority of people who seldom attend one? At a recent baptism it was clear that most of the party and family, some thirty men, women, and children, had never been inside a church. Probably the parents had been married in a civil ceremony. Children and adults climbed over the pews to obtain a better view or find the best vantage point for taking photographs even though the rector had announced that no pictures should be taken during the service. Educational visits as part of the RE programme could perhaps help children come to terms with the strangeness of the building.

Choices followed graduation, stay at Durham or go elsewhere for the Diploma in Education year, or do National Service and then my Dip Ed, and what two method courses to choose if the decision was taken to remain at Castle? There was really no point in moving or deferring teacher training so I remained in the north-east. History must surely be the first subject choice, but what of the second? English did not appeal for the same reason that it had been put aside when choosing a degree course. It would probably be a naming of parts, dissecting and analysing much loved poetry for example. One of the lists had to be signed, but which? My eyes rested on Religious Instruction as it was called in those days. This could be the solution. Years of worship and participation in Sunday School Union examinations had resulted in a sound knowledge of the Bible, and I was also intending to embark upon the London University Diploma in Theology following a conservative London Bible College correspondence course as the guide to studying a theologically liberal qualification. However, in the three grammar schools I had attended since 1944 I had never had a lesson in Religious Instruction. It transpired that this was because I was either too clever, or not backward enough. Apparently it was part of the C stream curriculum, at least at Heckmondwike, together with woodwork for those boys who were deemed incapable of learning a foreign language! C streams were living proof, if any was needed, of the impossibility of selection at eleven plus. Few of them ever got O levels; none went into the sixth form, whereas some secondary modern schools had A level groups against all eleven plus predictions! This, then, was how I came to Religious Education, free from any awareness how, or how not, to teach it.

Our education tutors seemed to live with their heads in the clouds and their feet on a surface of unreality. They talked about Dartington Hall and public schools like Summerhill where students seemed to do whatever they liked. Then I was dispatched to a downtown secondary modern school in Sunderland. The experience was memorable for two things. The daily act of worship was dutifully observed by the headteacher who led it. During the Lord's Prayer, 'Hands together, close your eyes', he would pause periodically; 'Harris, your eyes aren't closed. Come out here. You know what you'll get when you come to my office', and then without a break in his voice continue the prayer. Other miscreants were picked out for talking or similar heinous offences. In such an atmosphere how could religious belief flourish? Fortunately, Religious Instruction did not seem to feature on the time table or, if it did, I was never asked to teach it.

My first taught lesson has always remained in my mind. Someone had warned me always to get my retaliation in first. Be firm, and later relax if possible. I was about to adopt this tactic with a boy who was not obeying instructions when another youth said he always drew pictures because he couldn't read. Thank goodness he spoke up on his friend's behalf; I allowed him to draw and had no further difficulties. This was my first experience of children with learning difficulties apart from two boys in Dudley Hill who were kept back a year to join us in standard three and proved to be very disruptive bullies because they were aware of being failures.

This teaching practice was otherwise fairly uneventful. The football playing card was used effectively in Sunderland, a breeding ground of soccer talent. My genuine enjoyment of sports, at which I had some ability, rubbed off on many children who accepted me as a human being and were therefore responsive. Later, in Harlow, an O level and CSE group attracted most of the year's soccer team to the surprise of the head who one day came into the classroom and loudly said that he thought RE was a subject for girls! Not surprisingly none of my tutors came to supervise me in Sunderland. My survival probably told them all they needed to know!

Back at Durham the group reengaged with our education tutor. We were told that we would marry people like ourselves, graduates or at least professionals. Two of us chose to argue with him. George Bennett, a fellow history graduate told him that his fiancée was the daughter of a porter at York station and herself a manual worker. Gwynneth, whom I was courting, was the daughter of a dock labourer now deceased and worked in an office. The don mumbled something about exceptions to every rule but maintained his general stance. At least he said no more about attitudes to class, fearing class warfare, no doubt. The first comprehensive schools were appearing and won my support over and against the grammar school system which now seemed elitist and unfair, relying as it did on doubtful selection procedures and condemning most children to a sense of failure and being taught by, for the most part, second rate, uninspiring, demoralised teachers, such as those in the Sunderland secondary modern school. This latter view was unfair, many of them, like my own brother, were strenuous in their efforts to enable their pupils attain some measure of success. Mr Millins provided hope in the context of otherwise total gloom. His interest was in social issues and he introduced a number of students to provision for children in care. A visit to a local foster home was transforming. The house parents were deeply committed and inspiring; the children we met were remarkable. Of course, the older ones were at school but those under school age impressed us by their conduct and attitude. One, when questioned about his favourite toy told me that they shared everything so he hadn't any toys of his own. This was not spoken in a spirit of regret but with a genuine feeling of cooperation and even mutual love. When it came to choosing a dissertation subject my choice was Family Service Units and my tutor Mr Millins. Some years later I met him at a conference and discovered that he was now a college of education principal in Liverpool.

Apparently he too found the air of the department of education in Durham stifling.

Darlington Grammar School was the setting for my final teaching practice. It was a well run school with a good academic reputation. Perhaps I was sent there to get rid of peculiar ideas about comprehensive education and a distaste of grammar schools, but this could not be as County Durham hadn't yet embraced the comprehensive system. They seemed to be confined to the isle of Mon, Anglesey.

A low opinion of the education department was reinforced by my tutor's only visit to sit in on a lesson. The subject was the Spanish Armada. A map was essential and was duly drawn on the blackboard from England westward instead of from Cadiz. By the time Spain was reached no room was left so it was bent southwards, towards Africa which did not need to feature on the map. The class made no comment and were well behaved, perhaps knowing why the man at the back of the room was there. He said nothing about the blackboard work or lesson content apart from 'you seem to be doing alright', as he left. Breathing a sigh of relief I thanked the boys for their cooperation.

Mr Lumsden ran a good RI department and was an excellent mentor, helping me to develop an enthusiasm for the unfamiliar subject. There may have been an over reliance on film strips but, at least he did not confine himself to the Bible as the only subject matter. He was also liberal in his approach, by which is meant that he did not attempt to persuade or convert his pupils; his aims seemed akin to those of the history department, namely to promote interest and encourage thoughtfulness. He turned out to be a former cleric and I discovered that most graduate teachers of the subject were either people like himself or graduates in other disciplines, who had made a subject change as, eventually, I did. Theology departments were geared to producing ministers or priests. He used the Sunderland Agreed Syllabus which I noticed had a section on World Religions at sixth form level. However, although it seemed to advocate the teaching of them it also suggested that pupils should be left in no doubt that anything good that was found in them was present to a greater and more perfect degree in Christianity. I pondered this in my heart though still being convinced that my task was to teach Christianity in a confessional manner.

We were required to wear gowns by the grammar school, something that I have never liked doing except on one occasion. Suddenly I felt a chill up my rear end and gently felt my behind to find out what might be the cause. My trousers had not split at the seams but frayed in the seat. Drawing my gown around me like a toga I got through the rest of the day with as little discomfort as possible. Back in my digs I changed into my one other pair, that belonged to my only suit.

One sometimes hears of strange or idiosyncratic staff room practices; at Darlington the deputy head had his own special chair in which no one else was allowed to sit, he also had first access to the 'Times' that no one else was allowed to read until he had completed the crossword – usually in a matter of minutes. What life would have been like for us had he not succeeded does not bear consideration. Thankfully, during my three month stay he was always victorious, throwing the paper gleefully upon the staffroom table with some sentence of appreciation for the setter's skill, or derision for the weakness of the challenge! Then, and only then, might someone else touch what was, to all extents and purposes, a sacred text.

The value of my Dip Ed year lay in the teaching qualification, of all my degrees and diplomas the qualification to teach is the one that I most cherish.

3

National Service
and Beyond

Decision time again. National service now lay before me as the next fence to leap. Heckmondwike was not far from local pits and the possibility of following in dad's footsteps seemed real and appealing but the Bevin boy scheme was terminated before it could be explored.

For my mother my being called up was not an issue. If I went for my medical my bad feet would probably lead to my rejection, if not I could join one of the forces as a graduate and get a commission by staying in for three years, and if there was a war, then, at that moment, I could say that I was a pacifist. Did I inherit her pragmatic genes?

Being a conscientious objector could be lonely, that advice was given by my dad and the Congregational minister in Durham who suggested I had a chat with Jack Dobbs, the church organist, a music don and a Quaker. He pointed me in the direction of the Friends' Ambulance Unit and gave me a contact address. Someone named Jack Norton replied to my letter and invited me to meet him at King's Cross station in London. The interview was brief; Jack's chief concern was how I would react to being asked to work on Sundays. There would be no problem in working in hospitals which he had mentioned or with refugees and other dependent people but forestry might be different. There seemed to be no pressing need to fell trees on the Lord's Day! Jack was pleased with my answers and invited me to turn up at Melksham at Lavender Farm in August to attend a training camp. We had a brief course in First Aid and attended a surgery in the village to be given jabs against various infections that might be picked up in places where we worked. The primary purpose of the camp, however, was to toughen us up. This was not necessary in my case as I had just finished working as a navvy for the Gas Board for six weeks, my usual summer job. In the course of acquiring some fascinating experiences I also learned some useful survival tips. One of these I now put into practice. A former FAU member was brought back to make us fit. He set a good example and was a hard task master but on one hot day his bullying and chivvying became too much. Someone who had been working in the kitchen produced a bottle filled with cold water. This was placed on the trench side next to David who proceeded to take several good mouthfuls. The bottle was replenished and he drank more. Soon he became water-logged and was unable to continue digging at which point I got into the hole to use the strength that I had kept in reserve. David said he felt sick and disappeared, never to be seen again! My conduct probably left something to be desired but it did save us from further pressure. From now on we could work at our own speed.

Conscientious objectors had to face a tribunal. These could be daunting experiences. We prayed that ours would not be at Fulham as it had a reputation for turning down most applicants. Most of us who were based at Melksham were required to go to Bristol which was said to be more lenient. During our initial training course several of us were summoned for our cases to be heard. My tribunal was chaired by a judge, not wearing a gown or wig, just a dark suit, but a judge nevertheless who had two companions to help him adjudicate, an army officer and a trade unionist. The applicant before me was a Jehovah's Witness whose plea was rejected on the grounds that he could not agree on the conditions that the court might impose. His father proposed to set him up in a poultry business by purchasing a small holding for him. Although agriculture was an accepted option it was felt that choosing something that might be a profit-making career opportunity was not what the tribunal had in mind. He was sent away to reconsider his future.

When my name was called I felt not at all confident after listening to the way in which the Witness had been treated, fair though it was. The judge read out my statement giving the grounds for my objection although his two assistants and myself all had copies. He also read a reference provided by my minister in Durham. The ground for my objection was that the Jewish and Christian scriptures stressed the need to love one's neighbour as oneself and I found that command incompatible with killing anyone, my neighbour being humanity irrespective of race or religion. (Gender was not yet an issue). Asked if I wanted to add anything I replied that I did not. The trade unionist asked what I gathered were fairly standard questions – what would I do if my mother was attacked by a burglar; would I have stood by and done nothing in 1940 if the Germans had invaded Britain? To my surprise I was required to answer none of these queries because the judge intervened to say that I was obviously sincere and my condition, to serve in the FAU, was perfectly acceptable. He went on to add that he had seldom read such a rubbishy letter from a CO in his entire career, but then pronounced a requirement to serve for two years and sixty days from my tribunal date. This was important. My contract with the FAU was two years from the day I became a member, my first day at Melksham, but legally it began only when one had passed a successful tribunal. Failure could have meant another three months, often the normal time between sittings. The sixty day requirement was explained by the government's decision that members of the armed forces should do fifteen days training each year after leaving the forces as a kind of refresher course. In the case of COs it was added to the basic two years.

Before the work camp was over two other graduates and myself were whisked away to St Wulstan's TB hospital at the foot of Malvern Hills. Our age meant that the NHS would pay us more than younger members fresh from school though we, of course, still received monthly pay of 28 shillings and six pence and a clothing allowance of 32 shillings and 6 pence, nor could we combine the two to make three pounds to be spent as we liked. Every group of members was known as a section with a section leader responsible to Jack and a Treasurer, usually a hard-nosed character. The one at Malvern was a member of a well-known confectionary family. One day someone went to him for money to pay for a hair cut only to be told he must produce a receipt. The tall member, a bus and truck driver in civvie street, bent down and invited David to look at his shorn hair, was not that proof enough? David still insisted on a piece of paper until we browbeat him into submission.

From Malvern I was dispatched to Jordan's Wood near Orpington. Washing patients and dishes had been among my main duties at St Wulstan's so my hands were very soft, not in a good condition for felling trees. We began work at 8 a.m. and within an hour they were red raw! Fortunately, after a couple of months I was sent to Germany to work with American Pax Boys, Mennonite conscientious objectors, on a house building project at Enkenbach, near Kaiserslautern. We arrived at Kaiserslautern at about 6 a.m.; our section leader asked me to look after the luggage whilst he and other members of the section tried to find the Mennonite offices. Gathering the cases around me I fell asleep, but only for a few minutes. The sound of pounding feet awakened me to the fact that Germans begin work very early in the morning. This was my first awareness of a hard-working nation that was quickly getting back onto its feet after a devastating war. A visit to Frankfurt some months later revealed something of the devastation that had still not been cleared, though I did find a newly built Marienkirche that remains one of the most beautiful modern churches that I have visited, far more inspiring than Coventry Cathedral.

My duty was to be responsible for work on the building site so a swift course in learning German was a necessity. If material was deposited in the wrong place valuable time could be lost having to move it elsewhere. The near completed house in which we lived, together with volunteers from France and Holland, had electrics for cooking and lighting, water for washing, but no bathing facilities, so once a week, on Friday evening we made our way to houses in the zeidlung, or small village, in which Mennonites from East Prussia, refugees from the Russians, had been settled. They provided food and drink and conversation, so far as was possible, as well as a bath. Eyebrows were raised quizzically one evening when Ken, our section leader came downstairs, holding his dictionary in his hand and said, 'Ich bin rein'. Our hosts tried not to laugh while gently telling him that 'rein' meant pure, the word he should have used for clean was 'sauber'!

My German, now mostly forgotten after over fifty years of non-use, was good enough to understand the Sunday sermon in the local church and German radio broadcasts, by the time we left after a four-month stay. I also had a minor altercation with the head of the Mennonite community and it was good enough for me to realise that my American Pax boy translator was not doing a faithful job, so I took his place!

Life was demanding but enjoyable, the work was hard, the diet was strange; the Americans seemed to mix everything together – mashed potatoes with rhubarb – for example, but the companionship was excellent. Our small FAU contingent was frequently supplemented by short-stay workers of various nationalities. Two in particular deserve mention. Bart was a Dutch carpenter, a young man of secondary modern school ability as far as I could judge. We discovered that he had not only the ability to play chess against two of us at a time and win both games but that he could hold conversations in English, French and German, as well as Dutch, at the same time. The grammar might be far from perfect but the general linguistic ability was remarkable. In England language learning was usually confined to the grammar school and it was possible to gauge a person's ability, and it still is under the comprehensive system, from the number of languages they studied. Show me someone who took three foreign languages at A level and I will show you a very high flyer. Bart explained his position very simply. Holland was a small country with a large population. Often it was necessary to find work beyond its borders. Germans, French and Belgians were not going to learn Dutch so it was up to them to learn the languages of their neighbours. British insularity and the international dominance of the language have meant that we are reluctant to become linguists.

Marie, aka Flossy, was a pretty, vivacious and generally attractive young Dutch nurse. She too spoke several languages but pretended to know only her own 'water pipe language', as she called Dutch. We taught her to say: 'Snow me again, I didn't get the drift,' if she couldn't understand something and to say, in response to the question: 'How are you?' 'I'm a bit of alright'. Many were the middle-class gentlemen who blushed to the roots of their hair!

The Pax boys were big and strong and usually well to do compared to us Brits. I came across a few cast-off shirts and a jacket that I decided to liberate from a pile of discarded clothing and was able to wear them for a few years. Soft ball was their favourite summer game. We compared it to rounders and tried to teach them about cricket but did not get very far, having no bats or balls; Jack refused to send us any from HQ. One thing I could do was demonstrate our superior fielding ability. Whereas they caught the ball in a gloved hand and threw it with the other I caught the ball in my bare hands. At the end of an evening my hands might be bruised but the point had been proved!

We had an international song book which must have included some hymns as we always closed the evening with: 'Blessed be the tie that binds true hearts in Christian love'. It also contained the Yorkshire national anthem; 'On Ilkla Moor baht 'at'. One evening I heard David, an FAU member and bishop's son, explaining it to an American. It meant 'on Ilkley Moor at about eight o'clock in the evening', he said. When I told him it was a warning about going on Ilkley Moors without a hat he refused to believe me, preferring his prep school teacher's explanation! This taught me a lesson that I was to relearn several times in my career, namely that the teacher's word has amazing authority. Even worse were the times when our own children would come home from school and inform us that Hadrian's Wall had been built to keep out the Scots, for example. My attempts at a more sophisticated and accurate explanation were met with a blunt; 'No. Teacher says'. How should one try to guide children to the truth without damaging the child's trust in teacher?

Life was not all hard work. We had some drivers among us and managed to visit Worms, Heidelberg and Frankfurt in the lorry loaned to us by the Americans. Ken and I also hitch-hiked along the Rhine one weekend to see the famous Lorelie. During this visit we slept in an outbuilding and disturbed the owner who called the polizie. Somehow we managed to escape in the woods. Once, after work, a group of us took the lorry into the dense woods near Enkenbach to collect blue berries, and lost it. Some of us made our way back to the village and reported the loss to our section leader, Ken, whose reply was, 'Have a cup of tea!' The Americans were not so phlegmatic when we told them what had happened!

Bradford Royal Infirmary was my next posting, only a dozen miles from home in Heckmondwike, which I headed for every weekend. As section leader I had the duty of liaising with Jack Norton, the General Secretary. Two of the six of us were very young and I was surprised to discover just how overawed they were by him! They feared the imminence of his coming just as much as evangelical Christians looked forward to the Parousia! As he was a Bradford man perhaps there were grounds for expecting him to descend on us.

This was the time of the Suez crisis and the only time I felt discriminated against for my pacifist beliefs. Ward ten was mainly for male heart cases; in those days they were put on complete bed rest for up to a month and many had to be fed. One patient spat his food back in my face saying he supposed I would let Nasser invade us. Most of his lunch fell back onto his pyjama top!

Sister's attitude and behaviour was more serious. She had served as a Queen Alexandra's nurse during the Second World War and been in London when the anti-Suez demonstration took place. The following Saturday I was on a long duty, till 4.00 p.m. She ordered me to tidy the linen cupboard with her. This was a large room, as big as most lounges in normal houses, and stacked from wall to wall and floor to ceiling with sheets, pillow cases, towels, blankets and other items. Once in the room she began to tell me what she thought of me and other similar cowards. How she had been ashamed of being British as she saw the London demonstrators, and contrasted me with the heroic wounded she had cared for when she was a young nurse during the war! Whenever I tried to reply I was reminded that she was the sister and was required to listen in silence. She then sent me to help with the tea round and left the ward.

Some months later my dad had a minor heart attack, again on a Saturday when I happened to be on a late duty; sister would not let my mother speak to me when she phoned but said she would pass on the message. When I asked if I might be allowed to go to see dad in Batley hospital I was told that his condition was not life threatening so I could complete my shift. When she disappeared soon after three o'clock the staff nurse in charge gave me leave to go. In hospital dad's main concern was with the Sunday services which he asked me to take. Saturday evening was spent preparing for the morning and Sunday afternoon after lunch for the evening. I had to leave mum to reassure my father that I had done a satisfactory job while I returned to Bradford where, on Monday, the sister didn't even ask about his well-being!

One day a black kitchen maid came onto the ward to help with cleaning and washing up. This was only the second black person I had ever seen and the first one I had met; the year was now 1957, and the city Bradford. How much things would change in the next decade! For the moment what I noticed most was her reaction to snow which had begun falling and was lying on the ground. She opened the glass door onto the balcony and stood catching the flakes in her hands before scooping up a handful and eating them. I was reminded of her when, twenty years later, I would stand outside our daughters' school with a crowd of Asian mums waiting for their children, shivering in their sari or shalwar kameeze, despite their thick overcoats.

Hospital life is never without its lighter moments. I drew the line at visiting all my previous section leader's girl friends to give them a kiss and a cuddle every morning. It would have meant rising at five o'clock to catch an earlier bus and having to explain things to my fiancée! One afternoon I noticed that some of the wafer biscuits intended for patients' tea were missing. When I mentioned this to the friendly staff nurse she felt in the pockets of two nurses who had told us they were going to the cinema and found them. She injected each of them with something and put them back. Next day we asked how they had enjoyed the film; not greatly apparently as they had had to spend most of the time going to the toilet!

One of the section was a chemist so he worked in the hospital pharmacy and only put in an appearance at 9.30 a.m. when us ward orderlies were taking our break. One day someone put a pill used to check on urine flow into his tea, which resulted in pea green pee. He came into the breakfast room in a very agitated state, took a male staff nurse to one side and explained his concern to him. The nurse said he feared that John might have a heart attack and had to spoil our trick. Less personally directed was the pleasure each one of us had if we could find anyone taking a body to the mortuary in the basement. By pressing the button at the right moment they could be kept going up and down for five or ten minutes. More than one emerged shaking with terror!

From Bradford I was sent to Hednesford immediately; this was also the time of the Hungarian uprising in 1956. I had been put on standby to go to Budapest but when the Russians closed the frontier with Austria I was directed to the major refugee reception centre, a former air base mainly used for square bashing, putting airmen through their initial six weeks training. It was a bleak spot some two miles from Hednesford station, on the edge of Cannock Chase. The Hungarian refugees travelled across Europe and onto the camp by train, usually arriving in the early morning while it was still dark. It was manned by a naval commander and other members of the senior service, all of whom, as far as I could discern, treated the refugees humanely and with respect.

Most of the refugees were young people with children. A school already existed, set up by a South African lady who was reputed to be a member of the Black Sash Movement, which, I was told, protested against apartheid. There were two other FAU members, both part of the pool of car and lorry drivers. My duty was to help with the school but once it became known that I was a qualified teacher I was put in control and the lady vanished! But not before she had given me something of a briefing. One thing she emphasised was that Lady Mountbatten made fairly frequent visits and enjoyed listening to the children singing Clementine. Just think of its words for a second! 'twas a miner, forty niner'; 'and her shoes were number nines'; 'orange boxes without topses sandals were for Clementine.' As soon as I took charge I decided that the children should greet visitors with Hungarian songs and dances, and that, as a matter of principle, they should not be deprived of their own cultural heritage, whilst acknowledging their need to learn English and know something of our ways.

I formed a football team and discovered that many boys had the skills of their idol Ferenc Pushkas, but one thing they lacked. If they took the lead their opponents had little chance but if they went even a goal behind their heads dropped and it was very difficult to revive their morale!

After an appraisal of the situation I went to the camp commander and suggested that Staffordshire Local Education Authority should formally establish a school. The present voluntary arrangement was inadequate in terms of staffing, general organisation, provision of books, and such things as writing materials. The local authority responded quickly, appointing the retired headmaster of Rugely Grammar School, who held a Belgian Croix de Guerre, to be in charge, and myself and some Hungarians to be assistant teachers. Jack was very pleased as I became the highest paid member of the Unit, having a good honours degree and a teaching diploma! The genial and very competent adviser in remedial education was charged with liaising between the LEA and the school. At this time besides not wishing to teach clever grammar school pupils I was thinking of working with slow learners or Educationally Subnormal children so I had a number of conversations with the adviser who suggested that I should teach for three years in a primary school and three in a secondary and then apply to take a diploma in special education. This determined the course of my career during the next six years or so.

Many Hungarian undergraduates had escaped to Britain; one told me how he had been imprisoned for attending Mass. When the uprising took place his cell door was opened, a machine gun was thrust into his hands and he was told to join the resistance. Others confessed that they were still communists, but anti-Russian. Most of them wanted to go to the USA as Ford scholars. I wondered what America which still had its fear of reds under the beds would make of them. My duty, however, was to help them on their way by giving lectures on British history and culture and helping them develop their, already pretty sound, command of English.

Almost all the refugees were Roman Catholics, as was the camp commandant. One day members of the camp committee came to him to ask him to invite the speakers they had heard a few weeks earlier to return. He made enquiries through an interpreter and discovered that the popular visitors had spoken about birth control!

Hednesford was closing, its inmates were being successfully dispersed, and my two-year contract with the FAU was also coming to an end. This left me with the requirement to serve sixty days from the date of my successful tribunal, effectively the 17th of November 1957. About thirty primary school age children had arrived at Drake Hall, formerly an emergency teacher training college and open prison, though not at the same time! They were Italians expelled from Egypt by President Nasser; being Roman Catholics, they were to be educated at a Roman Catholic school in Swynnerton, a pleasant Staffordshire village near Stone. I was asked if I would like to be their teacher. This was a neat solution to my difficulties, my only problem was resigning from the FAU as Jack wanted to keep his highest earner and I needed to save up some money for my marriage to Gwynneth which was originally fixed for Easter 1958 but might as well be brought forward to Christmas 1957 if I was going to be living on my own somewhere. Jack reluctantly accepted my resignation.

Membership of the FAU had been the most worthwhile experience of my life so far. Its members were not all Friends and those who were included free thinkers and a few spiritual atheists, as well as many agnostics. One belief that everyone shared was that there is that of God in everyone, though they dispute the meaning of the word 'God' which is the way of Friends! 'That of God in everyone' explains why Quakers sit in a circle or square facing each other during their meeting for worship. That is where God is, in all other people besides themselves. Hence too their opposition to slavery, war, gender discrimination, and an ordained ministry. Anglicans and Roman Catholics face the altar; Baptist and similar denominations place the Bible in a focal position, Muslims in Britain face east towards the Ka'ba at Makkah, Sikhs who also believe in the immanence of God, have a scripture, the Guru Granth Sahib, as their authority, and it is the focus of their worship, whereas Hindus face towards the murtis and Jews towards the Torah. 'That of God in every-one' may be a belief that I had held implicitly throughout my life, inherited perhaps from my father. My time with the FAU made it explicit. Holding such a view meant that feminism was not new when its time came.

Advices and Queries, frequently used at Friend's meetings, or by indi-viduals in their devotions, express the view mentioned above more fully: 'Do you respect that of God in everyone though it may be expressed in unfamiliar ways or difficult to discern? Each of us has a particular expe-rience of God and each must find the way to be true to it. When words are strange or disturbing to you, try to discern where they come from and what has nourished the lives of others. Listen patiently and seek the truth which other people's opinions may contain for you. Avoid hurtful criticism and provocative language. Do not allow the strength of your convictions to betray you into making statements or allegations that are unfair or untrue. Think it possible that you might be mistaken'. (Number 17).

Race and religious and gender differences have never meant anything to me, my brothers, my wife or our children. Women ministers came to our house as guests and preached from my father's pulpit. In fact I would go so far as to argue that it is possible to be unaware of these differences to a significant degree. Siân, our younger daughter came home from infant school one day complaining that she had been pinched. Her sister asked whether the girl who had done it was white or black. Siân replied, 'I don't know but she was a good nipper!' Some years ago my wife and I were staying with friends in Connecticut who took us to see a perfor-mance of Romeo and Juliet given by a racially mixed company of actors. By the time the play was over I had long ceased to notice the ethnicity of the person playing Romeo or Juliet, or any other member of the cast; my problem was becoming attuned to the accent, and that only lasted to the end of the first act.

Apart from the behaviour of an Anglo Catholic sixth former during a school anniversary service that was held in my father's church, Upper Chapel in Heckmondwike, because it was the only one large enough to hold the whole school and invited guests, (she decided to eat sweets noisily and read a novel, and sat during the singing of hymns, because she could not participate in schismatic worship), the Durham chaplain who fled my room in Lumley Castle when he learned that I was not an Anglican, and membership of the FAU, I had as yet little knowledge of denominational differences. At Swynnerton this changed. The Catholic School held an act of worship on two mornings in the week, followed by religious instruction. At the same time the Anglican vicar came into the school to meet the needs of the rest of the pupils and he invited me to help him. The vicar and I were welcomed cordially by the school's Roman Catholic staff but I couldn't help thinking that the village was predominantly Roman Catholic and eyes were cast at the beautiful Norman Church with the hope that it might some day be restored to its pre-Reformation status. This would be unlikely to happen. The Establishment works on the principle of authority not numerical superiority and the Church of England is the form of religion established by law in England. This division lasted, and I felt, blighted school worship and the teaching of my subject until Vatican II when, almost overnight, withdrawal became a thing of the past and Roman Catholics positively opted into both with enthusiasm; a large number of my best students came from this denomination.

It was time to move on. The sixty-day requirement of National Service was almost at an end and the number of Suez children was falling as their families dispersed to other parts of the country. Where, I knew not because those who could speak sufficient English were fond of telling me that their parents owned hotels in Egypt and expected to be provided with positions of equivalent status by the British government which they regarded not so much as deliverers as nuisances and meddlers who had disturbed their idyllic existence.

Gwynneth and I decided that I should apply for posts in pleasant parts of England not too close to either of our families so that we could enjoy our marital independence. The school to which I was appointed was Regis primary school at Corsham, near Bath. It may be that my work with the Hungarians helped me to be short-listed because, whilst we were awaiting the verdict the deputy head teacher asked me whether I would like to teach at his annexe if I didn't get the job for which I had applied as he had a number of Hungarian children there. My reply was negative because during my interview the governors had noted that I had not yet taught 'normal children'.

We spent three happy years in Bath, though as soon as our honeymoon and visits to our respective parents were over Gwynneth had to take work in the office of a very uncongenial camera shop whose owner seemed to keep his staff by deducting large amounts from their wages as holiday pay and telling them that even if they left a week before the holidays they would lose entitlement to any of it. Though we needed her weekly wage until my monthly salary was paid she left as soon as possible.

School worship was regularly observed on a daily basis by a headmaster who enjoyed sung services and preparations for Christmas. As that season drew nearer he would smilingly encourage us to go to our classrooms to mark books or prepare lessons. No child seemed to be withdrawn, though a Roman Catholic teacher who remained in the hall at the side of her class excluded herself from the hymns and the prayers. We came to an arrangement that I would take her Religious Instruction lessons and she would teach needlework or craft to my class. No children were withdrawn from my lessons. One teacher who was an atheist observed the requirements of the 1944 Education Act by following the Agreed Syllabus requirements for his year punctiliously, asking children to read the Bible aloud round the class until the forty minutes of lesson time had been completed! My childhood at Dudley Hill now came in useful. Curriculum inertia was such that I needed only to teach what I had been taught, with the exception of Physical Education. Here there had been a revolution. Instead of stretching, running on the spot and playing team games, twisting and curling seemed to dominate the syllabus. One day the county adviser for PE came to Regis and watched every teacher in turn take their class; when I had finished my lesson she simply said 'Thank you', but in a manner that indicated that she had not been enthused by my performance. Later, Mr. Pearce told me that she had asked if I had been secondary trained. When he replied in the affirmative the adviser simply sniffed and made no further comment. The head leant me a book on twisting and curling PE.

As a child I had enjoyed Robin Hood; indeed, it was the second film that I saw after Snow White. I decided to use it at story time. I began by saying that 'Robin Hood' was not the hero's real name and asked if anyone knew what it actually was. To my surprise every hand shot up. And I was told it was Richard Greene. This was not correct, I retorted, only to be shouted down by an otherwise well behaved class. Of course, Richard Greene was the name of the actor who took the part on television, but not being able to afford a set, even to rent, I did not know this. Five years later we did rent a television, to help me compete with my secondary pupils who were all authorities on Top of the Pops, though the real reason was that the England versus West Indies Test series was being shown!

Gwynneth was an Anglican and I was a Congregationalist. One day, not so long after we met, I heard her mother mentioning this to Mr Wilkie, owner of the corner shop whilst I was waiting to catch a bus into town. He sagely replied that; 'It could be worse, he might be a Roman Catholic, Mrs Bowen!' Denominational differences did not trouble us but with the prospect of having children being discussed I felt that matters of belief would one day emerge as they asked who was right – mummy or daddy. We attended confirmation classes conducted by the kindly Dean of Bath who became a personal friend and I became an Anglican, though years later an eminent person in the interfaith movement, the Methodist Kenneth Cracknell, said: 'Whenever you hear Owen you must remember that it is a Bradford nonconformist speaking!' can the leopard really change its spots?

Christmas in primary school was a nuisance from the very beginning and things did not improve when I was teaching in a training college, especially at Leeds. The Corsham staff held back the season for as long as possible but by the end of November, at latest, and if we were lucky, one of our number would enter the staffroom very apologetically and tell us that one of her children, usually a girl, had brought in a bag of last year's trimmings which she would let the children put up during the lunch hour. We knew that we would receive similar discarded remnants on the next day!

At Leeds the final teaching practice fell between half term and Christmas. There was a good academic reason for this, it gave the students a two-term run in before their final examinations but in the days before the National Curriculum it resulted in such things as my Religious Studies group coming to me and asking me not to be annoyed when they told me about yesterday's school visit. Most of them had been told to forget maths and reading. What was wanted was a Christmas card and calendar for each child and learning carols to go with the class or school play. (No wonder our smaller daughter Siân came home at the end of her first term telling us that there was no point in going back in January, she knew it all!) Perhaps I should have been pleased that religion was receiving so much attention but actually I was keener that the final teaching experience before going into schools as qualified professionals should be a good one. Also opportunities to integrate RE with other subject areas did not exist. All I could do was address practicalities, such as the fact that the Bible nowhere mentions three wise men, only three gifts, so the whole class could be wisemen, who may have brought their wives, if they were truly wise! Everyone too could be a shepherd and the gifts could be things that might better be given to needy members of the community, but first of all teachers needed to discover what might be appreciated. (I have known children taking tins of food only to be told by the recipient, 'That's the third lot today, I don't know where we'll manage to keep them, never mind eat them', and childish enthusiasm is destroyed instantly). Blue Peter type collections that can be turned into money to be distributed in February or March when the needy are forgotten might be a solution preferable to taking gifts at Christmas. Gatherings such as Christmas should not be occasions when the unreliable children are hidden away in the secretary's office! In the multi-religious context there are specific questions to be considered – should it be held in a church, what role should the vicar have and what about the place of other religious leaders who might be willing to be involved or should we have a Muslim Mary, for example? Answers need not be doctrinaire but the result of dialogue among and between the teachers, parents, and religious leaders.

In my three years at Corsham I taught three very different junior third-year classes, always under the eye, (benevolent) of the head teacher who knew that by the end of term one in year four most of the eleven plus selection would have been decided. The first class was normal, if such a word is appropriate, unstreamed with Intelligence Quotients, whatever they are, ranging from about 130 to 80. The second class was composed largely of clever but unruly children who had seen off their previous teacher. The head told me I could do almost whatever I liked as long as I didn't kill anyone. It may seem strange that in a village like Corsham ten-year-olds could be so difficult but there were some 'problem families' in the housing estate and when six or seven of their sons were gathered together trouble could be found in their midst. That small group infected another five or six and there the difficulty began. It took until half term in October to settle everyone down, by which time I learned that a number of parents from owner occupied homes had enquired of the head what manner of man I was. He was quite protective and shielded all his staff from irate parents. My third class occupied an annexe fifty yards from the main building and consisted of fifty percent children who could not be trusted to cross the main road to another building and fifty percent who were judged to have no chance of success in their scholarship tests, that is pupils of IQs of 100 or less. Among the least able was Richard whose dad was a farmer, when I asked each child to select a subject that they would like to tell the rest of us about he chose pheasant rearing. Apparently he did this every spring and summer. No one else's presentation stays in my mind almost fifty years later, but his was interesting, informative fluent, and erudite, despite his IQ of 85! It increased his self esteem, his standing in the opinion of his classmates, and taught me a lesson that I have never forgotten, namely that most of us have greater potential than is usually recognised but that it takes some particular circumstance to release it. I felt increasingly interested in teaching children with special needs, especially as two children in the class, Adrian and Christopher baffled me entirely. Each day I would find time to listen to them read and each day they would forget even the page that we had read the day before! Adrian was orally bright, perhaps we might diagnose him as autistic today; Christopher was a quiet, smiling little boy, who made no progress in any area of the curriculum during the whole year. Our special needs teacher had no success with him either.

IQ tests were supposed to be objective and accurate but seemed to be capable of manipulation, not by many percentage points perhaps, but by enough to make the score unreliable. This seemed true of the other tests in maths and English. Children who scored over 125 or 130 could be predicted by their teacher's knowledge of their abilities, so could those who fell below, say, the 110 level. But what of those between 100 and 125? How could they be graded with any accuracy? Wiltshire had introduced parental and pupil interviews and these appeared to be very useful in borderline cases. If a parent was interested in their child's education, chances were that s/he would succeed in the grammar school. Some, however, were only interested in the cap or hat or blazer, if Mavis or Freddy had won a grammar school place, heads could be held up high, but they did not encourage them to do their homework and get O levels. There was also the little matter of being able to gauge one's ability at fifteen or sixteen from tests taken at ten or eleven. From my own limited observations in Heckmondwike and Darlington I was aware that A and B stream pupils would probably do well enough at O level to go into the sixth form and probably make it to university. But what of the percent who ended up in the C stream? Were they not living testimony to the inadequacy of selection at eleven plus, not to mention the 10 percent or more who went on from secondary modern school to do well through apprenticeship schemes, or in nursing, and later through the Open University? I still believe that a grammar school with an intake of, say, one hundred children per year should be judged on the totality of its achievements as well as the demoralisation of those children who feel themselves to be failures at the young age of eleven. That is the Cole test!

Sports days were interesting occasions. The head stood at the winning line giving each girl a hug. This was a perfectly innocent act in days when no one gave such conduct a second thought, but it could mean that we could miss our bus back to Bath. I was given the starting pistol and as soon as the children in a particular race were gathered, I fired it. Soon the head was sending back messages to slow down. He couldn't get things processed at the other end. Somehow my colleagues didn't pass the message to me and his problems grew the nearer 4.10 came. I also learned how fickle children can be. A group would walk with me to the bus stop each day and wait with me till my bus came. At the beginning of the next academic year they melted away, all but one; a colleague pointed out that they were now in the top class and that I reminded them of a bygone year.

I must have been on a course; such things have a lot for which to answer. One day I decided not to praise members of the top group, children who seemed to have PhD potential, so I marked their books and told then to choose work cards with no further comment. The least able children received praise almost for breathing. By the end of the day they were performing tremendously well while the top group were doing and behaving badly. I never repeated the exercise but had learned from the experience the importance of valuing every child at the same time.

It was time to build on my three years or more in primary education with at least three years in a comprehensive school. Where we might move depended on councils or housing corporations providing rented accommodation for teachers as, hard though we saved, the possibility of us putting down the deposit on our own house kept receding as prices kept rising. Before we left Bath I had decided to become an Anglican and had been confirmed in the Abbey. Gwynneth was not enthusiastic and did not see a need but I thought that belief was difficult enough in the sixties and beyond without children having to ask who was right – mummy or daddy. The decision was not easy but was helped by the fact that the Archdeacon of Bath was such a warm and generously spirited man. Whenever we visited Bath in later years we enjoyed seeing him and his wife, and he pushed our children around his garden in a wheelbarrow. Interestingly, both our daughters became Quakers, but that is their story.

4

Harlow

On a cold day in winter, 1960, I walked across a muddy field to Passmores School on the southern edge of Harlow New Town. The school was rectangular, built around a courtyard, with a hall and offices at the east end. Only one-third of the buildings seemed to be complete and a playground reached from a path running from the road on the south side. The headmaster, a Scot, welcomed me by apologising for the state of the site and his secretary, the only other person on campus apart from builders, gave us a cup of tea. Mr Hart explained that the school, Passmores, would open in September to accommodate first-year pupils who were presently at Latton Bush, the last school to have opened, plus a handful of children whose parents had not expressed a desire to stay at that school. It was assumed that I would take the post and we discussed what duties I as head of History and 'scripture' as he always described the subject now beginning to be known as Religious Education, would have. His main concern seemed to be that I would supply him with a term's school worship material in advance. At the end of quite a short interview he formally offered me a post, told me how to apply for development corporation housing, gave me instructions for the best way to return to Harlow station, shook hands, and said that the deal was that I would give him three years service, at the end of which he expected young people like myself to move on, and he would give me his support followed by a good reference. With that I left. At the station I found a letter box into which I placed an envelope turning down an interview to another comprehensive a few days later, and tore up one accepting an interview!

Passmores was a humane institution, children were usually respectful and so were teachers – friendly in the context of professional relationships. At the end of the first year the headmaster asked me whether I would prefer to be in charge of History or Scripture, pointing out that History would carry an allowance of £230 pounds per annum whereas RE might be worth £160 in a year's time. I was already beginning my career long love affair with the latter and so became number two in the other subject. The head held the view that no one should teach scripture full time so my weekly timetable was about two-thirds RE and the rest History, with Thursday afternoons given to helping in the sports department, an arrangement that suited me well because I had a natural ability at games and took charge of football and cricket. One afternoon, a group of boys came to me telling me that they were going on a cross-country run and enquiring about the weather. It was likely to rain at the bridge they had to cross at the half way point, I told them so, and it did. From then on my reputation sometimes won me awesome respect. I was God's paid employee, according to one boy who challenged me one day, asking whether he could believe a word I said because I was paid, and even, perhaps given an allowance, and if I lost my faith I would have to resign, but I enjoyed a prophetic reputation; I didn't make it known that I had been home for lunch and had heard the weather forecast on the radio! I remember my leg spin bowler once asking me why we had to spend a year on the Old Testament as none of us was Jewish. He set me thinking about the whole content of the syllabus, but without coming to any conclusion, just an uncertain feeling of dissatisfaction even though the new Bristol Agreed Syllabus of Christian Education had just appeared and seemed to endorse the prevalent view that RE was a partnership in Christian nurture, a three-legged stool of church, school and home. At one time I had four colleagues all qualified in RE, one being a Swedish theologian who graduated from Upsala. Classes were streamed to a limited degree; on one occasion when I was attempting to convey the idea of commitment to one of the less able first year forms a boy challenged me by saying that he did not think much of a missionary who had gone to Africa and within a month or so had buried his wife and two children who had died of fever, 'I don't think he was a good man, he shouldn't have gone there,' he said quietly but firmly and with feeling! The same child asked me whether my wife and I had children; I replied that we were waiting until we could furnish our house sufficiently well to provide a good enough home. He said that I was talking about a house not a home. I learned more from some students than I have ever taught them.

One advantage of being head of two departments was that I could arrange the timetable so that I taught, say class 1A both subjects. They only had one period of RE to two of history, so I have to admit there were days when I used history time to complete something begun but not finished in the RE lesson. Occasionally a child would ask me whether we were doing history or RE! Here it might be added that the head said I could have as many periods as I liked with the least able children, as he didn't want them to injure themselves in the workshops or laboratories, and their morals might benefit from plenty of scripture! At the end of year one I discovered the secret of the timetable. He and the senior mistress would use wooden squares to sort it out and give teachers those that they couldn't allocate. I realised that by going in to help them in mid August I could sort out the timetable to suit my needs!

An unexpected advantage of giving up the history brief was that the head of department kept me informed about matters such as homework, examinations, and the allocation of money for resources. He would simply say, 'Owen, there's a head of departments' meeting this evening at four o'clock to discuss homework. See you there.' I would then see the head as soon as possible and say that I would be at the meeting, suggesting that he probably hadn't got round to inviting me! He would then reply; 'Homework in scripture? Well, alright. You will have to do the marking!' We had the same terse discussions about examinations and resources though on this matter he assured me that I would be given an allowance in year two and a smaller one in year three and no more. But he did agree to review the situation if I had O level candidates. The Gideon Society provided us with New Testaments. There was a certain satisfaction to be had from seeing prefects patrolling the corridors and reading their Bibles or exercise books just before an examination. Teachers also expressed pleasant surprise with the exception of the head of English who often sent one class to me five or ten minutes late. When I suggested that they might think my subject less important than his, he said that perhaps it was, and he was an Anglican lay reader! At this time there was a disagreement as to whether or not RE was an examinable subject. I firmly believed that its credibility with pupils, colleagues and management depended on it being treated like any other subject and was rather pleased to find that students wanted to do well in it so their average exam marks would not suffer. Where there were no exams teachers told of being given one lesson a week or of heads who tried to claim that the act of worship was a legal substitute, and of surviving because of their vocation to spread the Gospel.

As I have already stated, my chief usefulness to the head was providing him with material for school worship for the following term. He expected it to be on his desk a week before term began but didn't usually look at it until the service had begun. I knew this to be a fact from, for example, the day that the theme was caring for people in need and I selected as the Bible reading the story of the lame man who was healed by Peter at the Beautiful Gate of the Temple. The prefect, whom I had rehearsed, was ready to begin once the head had given his introduction which was the well worn sentence: 'The story of the man who asked for alms and got legs.' To give him his due the head did not bat an eyelid and said, with the briefest of pauses; 'The story of the healed cripple'. Afterwards he asked me if I thought it was right to be facetious when reading the Bible.

Roman Catholic children were excused from school worship and RE so long as they brought a letter, as required by law, seeking to be withdrawn. At worship they were supervised by a Roman Catholic teacher who led them in prayers and pupils were visited once a week by the local priest. We were both emphatic that this was not a time for catching up on any uncompleted homework. On a shelf at the back of my classroom was a pile of pamphlets published by the Catholic Truth Society. These I took home and read before my first September term began. They were, for the most part, distortions of Protestant Christianity. Somehow I managed to contact the Catholic priest, probably through the teacher who was responsible for the withdrawn group, and he visited me in school, looked through the literature and shared my feeling of horror, agreeing at the same time to produce more ecumenically acceptable material.

We did have one Jewish pupil, a clever and delightful girl. She joined us in year one and said that she would like to take part in the *Old Testament* lessons that dominated that year's syllabus but would withdraw from the *New Testament* and church history courses. This was perfectly acceptable. Apart from being a good student and relating well to the other girls in her class and house I have only one regret. Some years later, in Leeds I trialled a unit on Judaism produced by the School's Council with a class of Jewish fourteen-year-olds. They were friendly and polite but very critical in the proper academic sense of the word. From them I learned much about festivals and home life and worship in the synagogue, as well as an understanding of the *Torah*. How I wished that I might teach in schools or colleges where members of different faiths could sit side by side and share the riches of their traditions. Instead, after the lessons I would return to the Leeds staff room frequently to hear a language teacher complaining about the 'dummies' in the C stream to whom she had to teach French. One day it became too much for me and I reminded her that next year the school was going comprehensive. She needed smelling salts or something stronger to recover! I, on the other hand, received further confirmation that selection at eleven plus cannot be achieved, and came to support the Leeds comprehensive scheme of transfer at nine and thirteen. Unfortunately, teachers did not seem to be given much preparation for their new roles, primary school teachers suddenly found themselves having to teach thirteen-year-olds and some who had good experience of fourteen-year-olds were expected to teach children of eight if their school had been reclassified as a first school.

Returning to my one Jewish pupil at Passmores, during the daily act of collective worship she would sit in her form room or my classroom if, for some reason, this was more convenient. Occasionally I would not take my place in the hall but chat with the duty prefects, visit the Roman Catholics, or Judith. She was always to be relied upon to be studying Hebrew, a copy of the *Torah*, or some other book on Judaism. She would tell me things about her faith and so began my understanding of what it meant to be a Jew. People may be surprised to know that the Holocaust scarcely seemed to feature in conversations at this time or later when I lived in Leeds, even though, as I was to learn from my next door neighbour, scarcely any family was unaffected by it.

Upon reflection I wonder whether Judith should have taken part in the *Old Testament* lessons. Although we studied the scriptures without adopting a Handel's *Messiah* approach, that is implying or explicitly stating that the *Hebrew Scriptures* can only be understood from the standpoint of the *New Testament*, the course paid little attention to the *Torah*, the first five books of the Bible, other than the Joseph saga and stories of Moses and the deliverance from Egypt, examples of divine providence. Its focus was the ethical teachings of the prophets. However, Judith seemed happy enough; when I left Passmores she gave me a collection of prints of Jerusalem which I still possess. Sad to say I never met her parents.

Authority can transform us, not always for the better. An amiable head of department was promoted to deputy head. Immediately his attitude to junior staff became one which required them to call him by his surname. He also became a cane wielding Wackford Squeers. Christmas was approaching and I was given the task of organising the carol service with the music teacher. Readings were scriptural and from poems or passages of prose using authors such as Dylan Thomas. Readers came from a variety of backgrounds from well spoken young girl prefects to Terry who managed to work out the combination of my cycle lock in less than two minutes. (I keep looking for a sighting of him in *Crimewatch* or as an adviser to *The Bill* or some similar programme!) The deputy walked into one of my rehearsals and dismissed the boy readers on the spot. When I complained to the Head, not so much about his interference but his overbearing attitude and thoughtless undermining of my authority I quickly found that he was upheld. The sacked boys took it better than I did saying: 'Tough sir, we're used to him.'

My reason for choosing these three boys as readers was to give some little boost to their morale, and possibly encourage their mates to believe that there were people who could trust them. Seeking new ways to develop self respect and respect for others have always been important features of my educational philosophy. I can never forget Edward, a boy from a foster home who was in 1E in our loosely streamed system. He was polite and a pleasure to teach but was stagnating, going nowhere. The music teacher auditioned him for a role in a production of Benjamin Britten's *Little Sweep*. Even during the rehearsal period one sensed a more positive approach to his studies. The performances lasted for three nights and Edward was a great success, being publicly praised by the Headmaster. A few weeks later Edward was promoted to 1D. Leapfrogging over 1C, in summer it was decided that he should enter 2B. Opportunity, responsibility and respect seemed to have changed his life. If only class sizes were smaller so that proper attention could be given to all children. Once, whilst attending a conference at Westhill College in Birmingham one of Her Majesty's Inspectors of Schools asked me what single thing I would do if I was secretary of state for education. There was no need to give the question any thought: 'Reduce class sizes,' I replied. 'And if you can't have that?' he answered. I said that I thought class size was the most important issue, only to be told that it was the one item not on the government's agenda.

Being a form teacher gave me the opportunity to watch and support the progress of boys like Edward and girls like Sheila who was bright and gentle and wanted to do technical drawing, a subject not for girls. It took some persuasion to get the head to allow her to take it and when she did she immediately became top of her group. There could, of course, be another side to my position. One Sunday the rather elderly parents of Agnes approached me after church to tell me that they were worried about their daughter. She had been demoted from 2B to 2C without telling them. They did not take kindly to such deceit especially as they had given her five pounds more than the school allowed her, when she went to Belgium, with instructions to buy herself a watch but not to tell her teachers or declare it to customs officials. They failed to realise that twelve-year-olds cannot always discern who to deceive and who not.

One day the Head asked me to come to his office; there he asked me if I would be interested in mentoring two Scripture students. Of course I was thrilled at the prospect as were my colleagues in our large department of five. Their tutor came to see me after school one day to discuss their timetables. When I suggested that he would pay supervisory visits I was met by a reply that both surprised me and made me consider changing course from special needs to training intending RE teachers. He told me that he had never been in a classroom from the day he left his public school so he would certainly not be visiting them. Supervision would be my responsibility. He also asked me whether I believed in the priesthood of all believers, put simply, the doctrine that any Christian might conduct a communion service; it did not have to be an ordained priest as in the Roman Catholic or Anglican traditions. When I told him that I did he said it was a pity because he was looking for a colleague and that academically I would have been most suitable but was doctrinally unacceptable.

I began to look in jobs pages of 'The Way Out', the name often given to the *Times Educational Supplement* by teachers. An interview for a post in Wrexham confirmed me in the view that I might be heading in the right direction, even though I didn't get the job which went to a woman who was a musician and had no qualifications in RE. Another candidate was a Baptist minister who greeted us all in Welsh and told us of his theological qualifications, all part of his one-up-manship device for undermining our morale. For the only time in my life I said, as he proffered his hand to me: 'My name is Cole and I'm English.' May I be forgiven! He was the first person to be called for interview. Twenty minutes later he rejoined us, pulled out a packet of cigarettes and chain smoked for the rest of the morning. Apparently one of the panel had suggested that he had lost his faith and another that it might be money that had encouraged him to leave his calling as a minister of the Gospel!

The most important event in our life in Harlow was the birth of our first daughter Eluned. She should have been born on St David's day but in that extremely cold winter of 1963 she decided to enjoy the warmth of her mother's tummy until St Patrick's Day. At least he was a Celt and, according to my reading of his life, was born in Wales. I had been called for interview while Gwynneth hung about waiting for something to happen. On Friday I caught a train to Goole to spend the weekend with my parents. On Sunday I received a phone call from a friend to tell me that after a protracted labour and generally unpleasant experience Gwynneth had given birth. On the Monday I continued my journey to Newcastle eager to return to Gwynneth and Eluned who were in hospital in Epping. (Harlow, the pram town, boasted a crematorium but not a maternity hospital! The people of Epping were somewhat angry at us taking up their maternity beds). Another candidate was staying at the same hotel in Newcastle so, on the Tuesday morning we travelled together to the college in Benton. He must have been fifteen years older than me and was saying how much he needed this job – it might be his last chance. It was tempting to withdraw and leave the field to him, but there were other candidates so it was not possible to be sure that he would be appointed. In fact, he was. As we journeyed back to the station his eyes welled with tears. On my way home I visited the hospital and met Eluned for the first time. She, and Gwynneth, came home soon afterwards.

This was not the end of the Newcastle story. Apparently the other interviewee had also applied to a college in Hull, a senior lectureship. Against every rule of professional etiquette he had left Newcastle, attended the interview and been appointed. I had dismissed Newcastle from my mind when I received a letter offering me a lectureship in RE and History. I had one more thing to learn at Passmores. One morning I turned up in the staffroom to find two of my colleagues and several other people sitting there in their go to interview suits and dresses. When I asked the Head why he had not consulted me on the short list he told me that it was nothing to do with me as I was leaving!

CHAPTER
5

Newcastle

The college to which I had been appointed had previously been a pud school, that is an institution whose purpose was to train young ladies to teach Home Economics. It had been expanded to become a general training college with an HE wing but attitudes had not changed. The HE staff were usually old students so much so that when I was asked to have a word with a former student now teaching and living next door, who said she had only a year's experience in schools, I was told to tell her that the vice principal whose messenger I was had only taught in schools for two terms before taking up her post in the college many years earlier. Another lecturer made the mistake of enquiring after the well-being of the head of the Art department, who asked whether she really wanted to know. When he said; 'Yes'. He told her 'Bloody awful' and the lady screamed; 'I knew it would be like this when we got men here!'

We lived about two miles from the college and close to what is now the Metro line which gave us easy access to the city and the coast, an ideal location. The parish was divided into two parts, that where we lived, largely owner occupied, and served by a church school and parish church, and the council estate whose houses were rented, served by a maintained school and a daughter church with a curate. A teacher in the denomina- tional school and a near neighbour suggested that we would, of course, send our daughter to the church school, which made us elect to take the council option, perhaps not a very good reason for making such an important choice on behalf of Eluned but such an assertion of class differ- ence was more than we could accept, especially when we were told that even choir boys from the daughter church were not admitted to the denominational school as they would not feel happy there!

I had been licensed as a Lay Reader in Harlow by the bishop of Chelmsford who invited me for interview at Liverpool Street station. It lasted ten minutes. I remember comparing it, in my own mind, to going to a soccer match to enjoy half time as the journey was forty-five minutes each way. However, it took the ingenuity of the curate and a reader attached to the parish church in Benton to enable me to take a service in the parish church itself (I had already assisted in the council estate church). When the month's services were being arranged the vicar found that he had to be elsewhere, and so had his two colleagues. The vicar asked what could be done and was reminded that I might be available. After some thought and with no enthusiasm he said: 'Very well, I shall not be here anyway!'

Eventually we got to know each other better and were fairly friendly, to the extent of him telling me that he had been a Baptist minister and that his only son had died at the age of twenty-three. I can still hear him saying that no parents should have to stand at the side of their child's grave. Eventually, he allowed me to take services at the parish church. One Sunday during the Rhodesian crisis I was preaching, probably against white colonialism, when one man rose from his pew and walked out of the church. I wouldn't have minded but I never saw him again to discover whether he left because he needed to go to the toilet, he had remembered that his lunch was burning in the oven, or he disagreed with my views. Whatever the explanation for such an action I think it should always be made clear – at least I wouldn't still be worrying almost forty years later!

People Next Door was an ecumenical venture which I helped organise in our parish. Our vicar played little part in it and was mostly negative about it. One Sunday evening all churches in the district were invited to a communion service at the Presbyterian Church. On the previous Sunday our vicar had said: If you go you will not take communion, of course, because you will already have taken it here, and we don't take communion twice on one day.' It seemed prudent to stay away. A lesson I learned from this incident and ecumenical activity in general is that the response of hierarchically organised denominations such as the Anglicans or Roman Catholics depends very much on the attitudes of parish clergy and perhaps bishops. Several parishes of my acquaintance have become enthusiastic on the arrival of a new incumbent, or have ceased to be involved if he is not supportive. One reason why I eventually turned my attention to interfaith activities rather than interdenominational ones was my feeling that ecumenism had gone as far as it could until church leaders accepted such things as intercommunion, probably the first expression of union in the early church and the last one today.

An organisation concerned about the welfare of people with disabilities, both physical and mental, wanted to buy a house at the end of our road. A public meeting was called to be held in the church hall. Most people were opposed to the idea. 'They would not really be happy round here; access would be difficult or unsuitable'; these were the kind of arguments put forward. No one said that they didn't want them, but clearly this was the main reason. Leaving the hall I spoke to the Methodist minister and told him that half the opponents attended the parish church, to which he replied that the other half were from his congregation. This was my first experience of what has come to be known as NIMBYISM – not in my back yard!

College life was memorable for two things, the first trivial and completely secular but it remains very much in my mind! One term I took a course in RE for students who were going to teach in infant schools. The room was a banked lecture theatre. The winter had been extremely cold but the young ladies; mostly teenagers had regularly worn their mini skirts. At the end of the last session I felt that I should express my appreciation. Word got to the principal who, at coffee break the next morning, asked whether I thought I had acted appropriately. I replied in the affirmative and told him that I felt their courageous conduct should not have been allowed to pass unnoticed. No more was said.

Everyone was expected to take the RE college course and in over twenty years only two students raised objections, apart from Roman Catholics, who withdrew under the 1944 agreement which applied to colleges as well as schools. This may be because each was provided with a prospectus explaining the content and containing an assurance that the purpose was to inform and prepare them for work in the classroom not to challenge their beliefs or try to convert them to mine.

The first challenge came from a mature student, a county councillor, who failed to submit his first piece of coursework. My head of department did not want to make a fuss and the principal was minded even less to take on such a student for what was only a college method course, one of about six including PE, English, science, and history for example. Where he succeeded others might follow so I remained obdurate. He was given the approaching holiday period to complete his assignment, at the end of which he handed in nothing and began missing classes in his main subject, science. This was altogether more serious. After a number of warnings he decided to withdraw from college; it emerged that he had not been a very satisfactory student at all, but as if he was a member of a Kiwi second row, no one wanted to tackle him head on. My stand had been vindicated. I breathed a sigh of relief as I knew authority would not support me against the councillor, though my head of department did.

Somehow a head teacher named Mrs. Dobson got in touch with him. Why she chose Noel Smith, my head of department, or our college I never discovered but Noel kindly invited me to join him in a visit to the primary school that was situated in a mining village some miles north of Northern Counties. The head was a no nonsense person, firm but kind and deeply committed to her children who thrived in her care. The school was remarkable. There were classroom doors but. like that to her own office, they were seldom closed. Many pupils arrived at about eight o'clock in the morning and did not depart until 6 p.m. It was no place for faint hearted and clock watching teachers or caretakers. In the Humanities area of the curriculum each child was encouraged to work at its own pace and on its own topic, in consultation with the class teacher, of course. It was more usual than not to see children heading for the well stocked resource centre or library to borrow items to bring back to class. What became of these pit village children we did not discover, ours was not a funded research programme but a response to a request for help. In the sixties timetables were subject based, as they had been when I was at Dudley Hill, with Maths till playtime and then English till lunch. This was considered to be the time when most children were wide awake. Afternoons were given over to the rest of a curriculum that seldom included science. In history a class might be studying the Anglo-Saxons, in Geography voyages of discovery and in RE the miracles of Jesus. There was no integration. Mrs. Dobson was not satisfied with this situation but had not come up with any solutions. Noel and I agreed to give the matter some thought and to return a week later. Integrated humanities seemed to be the solution. Perhaps our thinking was influenced by our Northumbrian context. What could be more sensible than looking at its geography, including industries, the coming of the Anglo-Saxons, and the Northumbrian Saints for a start? Similar topics suggested themselves, mostly centred upon Britain or the world from our own perspective, for example, voyages of discovery, in geography and history and the journeys of St Paul, and their purpose, in RE. As yet the Empire had not reached these shores in any numbers and a multiracial or multireligious approach was something of which we were unaware. Still, what we had to offer attracted some interest, an article in the University of Newcastle *Journal* and an invitation to give a presentation at Carlisle Cathedral, my first RE public lecture, I suppose. Journeys to Bedlington continued even after Noel had become a vice principal in Liverpool; his successor Alasdair McKenzie shared his enthusiasm and kept in touch with the school after I had moved to Leeds. We even planned a primary RE book focused on our approach but publishers were not interested.

The second objection came from another mature student, a woman whose main subject was Mathematics. She came to my study one day to say that she did not wish to take the course. I pointed out that RE was something which she could withdraw from on conscientious grounds but she told me that this was not really the problem; she simply did not wish to take it. We discussed the fact that she would probably work in multi-faith schools and that it would be advantageous to know something about the beliefs and values of Muslims and other children. She insisted she was going to teach only Maths; if any counselling matters arose she would refer them to the form teacher. When it was suggested to her that she might have such responsibility she affirmed that she was only interested in teaching Maths. Apparently her main course tutor also had difficulties with her attitude and she also withdrew from college. Again it was a pity but all teachers are teachers of children first, second and third and only then subject specialists.

The Roman Catholic Church's Second Vatican Council had an amazing impact upon Religious Education. One afternoon a Roman Catholic student came to see my head of department and myself and told us that he was interested in taking RE as his second subject. Knowing that Roman Catholics withdrew from anything to do with religion we suggested that he spoke to his priest. To our surprise the priest contacted us and informed us that not only was he happy for Alan to take the course but that, in the spirit of Vatican II he would encourage other Catholics to do the same. Since then, many of my best students have been members of that denomination. The Bachelor of Education degree was being introduced at about the same time and this encouraged interaction between colleagues who had previously led separate existences and may have been rivals. We exchanged visits with the local Catholic college at Fenham where we acquired interesting ideas about RE and child development whilst discovering that their biblical resources were exclusively protestant, Professor C. H. Dodd was probably the most popular. My vicar once said, of Vatican II: 'The Romans are just getting to 1662'. I felt they were nearer to two thousand! If only the spirit of Vatican II had been encouraged after the pope's death there can be no guessing at what might have happened, but as has frequently occurred in the story of Christianity since the first Pentecost, the church has made strong and often successful efforts to stifle the effects of the Spirit. The same is true of other faiths; sociologists may use the term 'institutionalisation' but people for whom faith matters might be more concerned at these attempts to put the geni back in the bottle by those who believe that so long as God is kept in his heaven all will be right with the world. Ideas may hit the ground but vested interests prevent them from running!

My colleague, Alasdair, a Scottish Baptist minister, and I were becoming increasingly dissatisfied with developments in RE. Their main focus was on content and was very necessary. The old syllabuses worked on the kind of principle that stories about little people in the Bible would be more suitable for the younger children in our schools. A popular example was the story of Samuel being taken by his mother to the Israelite shrine presided over by Eli, and being left there. In the darkness he hears the voice of God calling him and replies: 'Speak, Lord for your servant is listening'. Just the tale to tell a small boy whose mother only a few minutes earlier may have left him at the school gate! Or even the story of Jesus in the temple at the age of thirteen, intended to impress believers with his precocity and devotion. Is it surprising that one child said; 'I don't think much of that mummy, my mummy won't have let me go by myself'. However careful the storyteller may be, if the material runs counter to a child's experience s/he cannot be expected to make sense of it. The West Riding of Yorkshire Agreed Syllabus addressed some of these matters and also mentioned other religions but took the possibility no further. Herein lay our solution if we had only recognised it. Ronald Goldman's work on religious readiness seemed very persuasive.

Our students tended to be suspicious of our approaches to RE, not so much its integration with other subjects in the primary school, or with the idea of being experientially ready for the content of the material being used, for they could see the sense of not talking about weddings with children who had no idea what a wedding was, for example. Where they parted company with us was when we suggested that RE should be open ended; most of them were still at the stage of thinking that I had been in Corsham and Harlow and had only recently left. Alasdair had been a student of the famous Professor William Barclay and had persuaded him to giver a lecture at the college, even though his diary was always booked up three years ahead. When the time came to ask questions a student had the temerity to ask what he thought of open ended RE. I can hear his thunderous reply now, given in a broad Glaswegian accent, 'The only thing I know that is open at both ends is a toilet roll!' Our students looked at us and laughed, and gazed at him with admiration. Thank you, Professor!

A lecturer, John Hinnells, newly appointed to Newcastle University's theology department, advertised a course in world religions which Alasdair and I attended. With Donald Butler we began to meet in a Conservative Club, because of the quality and cheapness of the beer in order to discuss the implications of the study of world religions, for schools. We discovered that some syllabuses already advocated teaching it but, as in the case of the Sunderland Agreed Syllabus, only at sixth form level and for the purpose of asserting the uniqueness and superiority of

Christianity. Our concern was that the study should be fair, objective and balanced, aimed at helping children understand what it means in terms of belief and practice to have a religious faith. As yet non-religious stances for living, such as humanism and atheism, were not on the agenda, though at this time I did meet a humanist who was a city councillor to canvass his views. John's enthusiasm, influence and contacts resulted in a residential conference being held at the university's adult education centre, the Shap Wells Hotel, in Cumbria, just off the A6, in the winter of 1969, at which it was decided to set up The Shap Working Party on World Religions in Education (Shap). Those present came from all levels of education and included the famous Humanist, Harold Blackham, but most of us were Christians as RE and its higher education kinsperson, religious studies, were generally regarded to be the concerns of Christians at this time, Christianity being the sole content and nurture into the faith the main purpose. Shap has been a major influence in my life as a religious educationalist. Through it I have met many fine people and developed my own ideas about the purpose of my subject. It has challenged and inspired. Its influence has extended beyond England and Wales to Scotland and continental Europe and ideas which were often resisted by some members of the RE establishment have now become the norm. It publishes an annual calendar of religious festivals and an authoritative book to help teachers understand and teach about them. It also produces a volume of essays each year and, most recently a pictorial calendar. With hindsight at the end of almost forty years of activity it might be appropriate to say that its great strength has also been its weakness. It members are all engaged in education at one stage or another, responding to the day to day demands of their jobs and serving Shap in their spare time. If we could have employed a full- or part-time executive officer, a specialist in religious studies, we might have made an even greater impact than that which we have achieved.

At some point during or after the course that introduced me to world religions, a group organised People to People week to provide citizens with opportunities to visit one another's places of worship and meet adherents. This was my introduction to a mandir, gurdwara and mosque. Other commitments prevented me from going to the synagogue and Orthodox church but I had experienced enough to enable me to realise that the RE I was struggling towards would not only include a study of sacred texts, as the existing syllabuses advocated for Christianity, it would also find an important place for the study of worship in the different faiths, including Christianity. So often it was assumed that school worship covered that aspect of religion, or that children would experience it on

Sundays when they went to church, and in the celebration of festivals. How frequently have I heard teachers give thanks for the Easter holiday saying that it is difficult enough coping with the Crucifixion, for it would be impossible to tackle the Resurrection with six years olds!

I probably owed my appointment to Northern Counties College to the government's intention of making teaching a graduate profession, the first step towards this goal being extending courses from two to three years. Our department responded by adding certain courses in the intertestamental period of the Bible, covering Jewish reactions to the Greco-Roman occupation of Palestine, some church history, and giving more attention to the teaching of RE in schools. We were aware that some other colleges simply spread the same amount of butter over three slices of bread instead of two, claiming to increase the depth of study, of which examination results provided no evidence. When the time came to plan the Bachelor of Education courses each university, being autonomous, followed its own inclination. The Newcastle Theology department summoned college lecturers to a series of meetings and imposed upon us, rather than discussed with us, a syllabus that was largely biblical. We argued that it would not meet the educational needs of students who were going to be teachers but the dons replied by saying that anything to do with schools must be left to the education area of the degree. Thus it was that B.Ed. undergraduates were to receive no training in the delivery of their specialist subject, Religious Education. Meetings were sometimes acrimonious but time was pressing and decisions had to be made. Almost the last words of Professor Boobyer were to the effect that perhaps we had not produced a course that would meet the needs of potential teachers – but as he was retiring, it would be up to his successor to sort out the situation. At least what we did achieve was better than the original intention that our students should be taught theology by the university staff. However, if we were to be the tutors, they must look at our qualifications and decide what aspects of the course we might teach. My head of department. Alasdair, having a Ph.D. was allowed free rein; I was restricted to New Testament introduction, John's gospel, and church history. Each college library was visited by members of another college to see that its resources were adequate, for the university was fearful of college students using their facilities and so depriving them of books. In this way I discovered that a vicar, who was employed for half a week by another college, actually, in his Monday to Wednesday lunch time stint, taught more than full-time lecturers were required in the whole week.

The most important family event whilst we lived in Newcastle was the birth of our second daughter, Siân. If I do not mention it I shall never be forgiven. At about 3 a.m. Gwynneth broke the news that the baby might be born that day. With a little more warning she could have been encouraged to spend the previous day walking up and down the Forest Hall flyover. April 5th marked the end of the tax year and children born on that day received a full year's tax rebate. This would have been £40, about the amount of my first month's pay as a teacher. Instead we received nothing! Eluned told me that the baby would be a boy so she got that wrong, and the nurse at the hospital said there was no point in waiting around as nothing would be likely to happen for some time. In fact Siân was almost born by the time I arrived back home, so I didn't see her birth either.

By 1968 I was ready to run my own department even though I was the best of friends with Alasdair, and Gwynneth with his wife, and we both liked Newcastle and visits to Northumberland. During our house hunting we saw a semi in Rawdon where Hedley Verity may have lived, the great Yorkshire spin bowler who was killed in the war, and I may have held his bat. Religious relics have never meant anything to me but this experience helped me to understand what they might mean to believers.

CHAPTER

6

Leeds

Leeds seemed much more cosmopolitan than Newcastle but this may simply have been that we lived on the edge of Chapeltown where our daughters went to school and because the Asian and West Indian communities, to use the terminology of the seventies, seemed larger as a consequence.

Sholebroke Avenue was a wide street with once elegant houses on the left-hand side. They were probably built for mill owners in the late nineteenth or early twentieth century. Now they were multiply occupied mainly by West Indians. The area between Chapeltown Road and Spencer Place or Harehills has been settled in turn by Jews, Irish, East Europeans, Asians and West Indians and some poor whites who had been unable to move away.

Reasons for migration varied from group to group and often within them. The building of a dam in Mirpur, or Amin's expulsion of Asians from Uganda, for example, were factors even greater than the desire for a better life, the motivation of many. As one Jamaican put it: 'We didn't come for your climate, Owen, or even for your cricket, even though this is Yorkshire! We came to share your wealth.' She was thinking of education and social services, as well as employment. These were the days when advertisements were being placed in West Indian newspapers informing readers of the needs of the transport and health services. British unemployment was comparatively small and those unfortunate enough to have no work were often unwilling to retrain as road sweepers or hospital cleaners or porters.

When the phrase 'third world' was coined I don't know, or by whom, but I have never used it, preferring to talk about the 'recovering world', for most of the countries covered by this expression are ones that were ruled by colonising European powers which, after exploiting them, reluctantly gave them their freedom but seldom with adequate political or economic preparation and education. Most migrants came to the places where they were needed. Few of them headed for the pits of south Yorkshire, for example, but I do recall the black comedian Charlie

Williams, at a multicultural concert in Leeds, say how much he approved of the National Front's offer to pay his passage back to his birth place. They would give him a thousand pounds, he said, and it was only a fifty pence bus ride back to Barnsley! He also said he had worked down the mines but was a safety risk. No one could see him! But there were few Charlie Williams' because they knew that there were not many jobs in coal mining, an industry on the wane. Instead they might settle in nearby Rotherham or Sheffield and work in the iron industry. A Sikh group, called Jats, are traditionally farmers in the Punjab, but I have only seen one Sikh working on a farm in England; they know that land is too expensive for them to buy and often, as in their own homeland, kinship among farming communities is involved. Being landless in the UK they had to find whatever work they could in cities such as Leeds.

Jews were the first settlers to arrive in Leeds, after the rural migrants who created such cities as Leeds and Bradford during the industrial revolution. They came at the turn of the nineteenth and twentieth centuries because of pogroms in Russia and other east European states. But when one asks why Leeds the answer can be a little more complicated. Jews have traditional practical skills. A rabbi, for example, might also be a craftsman or a dentist or merchant. Tailors travelled to the houses of wealthy Russians carrying cloth, threads and needles, and clothed them, returning home only occasionally. Leeds was a textile town where Jews might hope to find work. However, other Jews spoke of it as a half way house between Hull where their passage by ship had ended and Liverpool from where they might be able to continue their journey to America. Some told tales of paying for passage to the USA and being made to disembark at Hull which they were informed was New York! Their tendency to be self employed or to set up Jewish firms seemed to partly the result of painful experiences of being let down by gentiles, or ingrained tradition, or, perhaps more often, because it left them free to observe the Sabbath and other holy days without depending on favours from employers. It should be remembered that until after World War Two the working week usually ended at lunch time on Saturday whereas Shabbat began on Friday evening. Leeds also had its share of refugees escaping from the anti-Semitic policies of Nazi Germany.

By the time my family arrived in Leeds most Jews had left Chapeltown for more northerly suburbs such as Street Lane and Alwoodley. They were well established with at least eleven synagogues, and community centres. In reply to someone who once said, in a somewhat anti-Semitic tone; 'You never see a poor Jew', one of my friends replied, 'No you don't. We see them first and do something about it'.

Muslims have similar needs to Jews but for different reasons. Dietary needs require them to live near their own butchers shops, for example, though the ownership of motor cars has enable dispersal to take place. The tradition of walking only a mile to the synagogue on the Sabbath has encouraged Jews to live in its vicinity, though I have met Rabbis who took a more relaxed view of that injunction arguing that they would prefer their congregants to drive to schul by car rather than not come at all. Muslims need close-by prayer facilities on Fridays at least and many men wish to be able to pray in the mosque daily for all five prayers. Education, especially in an alien environment, is important and Jewish and Muslim children often attend schools attached to their place of worship. Perhaps finally, and sadly, one should note that all immigrant communities can feel vulnerable and may have been victims of racial attacks. Only in a society where settlers can feel safe can they be expected to forsake the protection of the ghetto and many do not yet regard the UK, even in the twenty-first ceentury, to be somewhere that is secure

I have often felt that British Asians might learn much from the Jews who came before them and have overcome the difficulties faced more recently by Muslims in particular, but we all like to be independent of each other and perhaps in religious and social matters we have to make our own way. Come to think of it, Christian denominations have often preferred to stand on their own feet rather than be willing to learn from the Anglicans and Baptists down the road!

The Hindu mandir was situated in another part of the city as was the Hindu community; the fact that they came from Gujarat rather than the Punjab might provide much of the explanation for this. Leeds was, to some extent, unusual in having a specific place of worship, as congregational worship is not essential or necessary. Each house has its puja room or shelf, or alcove, set apart for this purpose where family members will offer their private prayers and grandma will teach the grandchildren, by following her example, what to do and how to it, and what to say. Frequently, a sad feature of life in the UK was the lack of the older generation who passed on religious traditions and the stories associated with them. In Britain the mandir fulfilled a function that was social to a large degree, enabling families to catch up with the gossip from home. This was a time when phone calls were expensive and many people living in India did not have telephones.

Congregational worship is at the essence of Sikhism. Their pattern of migration, not unique to them, was for men to come first and then for them to bring over their wives and children. Meanwhile in Leeds they bought a small terraced house to be used as a gurdwara, a Sikh place of worship. Strictly speaking this is a wrong way to describe a gurdwara; it is the presence of the scripture which gives it its status. Remove it and the house, room, disused hall or former church simply becomes a building that can be put to any use. No consecration or deconsecrating is need. Sanctity is provided by the scripture, the Guru Granth Sahib. This means, among other things, that Sikhs will be unable to point their grandchildren or local historians to important sites relating to their origins in the UK as they may well have left them and moved on. In India it can mean the almost total rebuilding of an historic gurdwara, that is one linked with a Guru or an incident in Sikh history to the extent that not one wall or foundation more than twenty years old remains standing. Secularly this may be a sign of affluence, socially it may be an indication that a certain family has been very successful in the UK or North America; religiously it is, to use a Christian statement, an assertion that the Sikhs have no earthly abiding city. In the days of Mughal harassment it is said that the Sikhs carried their scriptures on horse-back and read them where and when they could, so today, it should be a faith that plants no restraining footprint but is constantly moving on, everywhere being hallowed ground.

The Sikhs came from the Indian Punjab, sometimes from Muslim dominated areas of what is now Pakistan from which they had been evicted in 1947, or from east Africa to which they had gone in the 1890s to build the infrastructure of empire directed by white settlers and administrators. As Africans gained their independence there was no place for Asians; those with British passports came to England preferring it to jostling for position in an India that no one knew and where it was said corruption was rife.

In his Newcastle course John Hinnells gave one lecture on the Sikh religion in which he dispelled the view of a contemporary scholar that it was a recent and intentional form of synthesis of Hinduism and Islam, and that it was polytheistic, he also challenged the notion that it was a militant faith, and stressed its teachings on the gender equality and the rejection of caste. I had also visited the gurdwara during People-to-People week. Now provided with some accurate knowledge I could now begin my own excursion into the religion. All Sikhs do indeed enjoy theoretical equality; there is no function in the life of the community from which anyone should be excluded save, sometimes, performing the rite of initiation, and only those who are themselves Khalsa Sikhs can bring others into its community, a perfectly understandable rule and one that has it parallels in other religions. Also most gurdwaras have rules about the quality of person who may be elected to its committee and who may have the right to vote. Names, since the rise of feminism, have been problematic; I suppose our daughters could have rejected my surname and choose that of their maternal grandfather but their surname would be have been of male derivation. Sikhs have cracked the problem; daughters take the surname 'Kaur' meaning princess, and sons, 'Singh' lion. Even the given name can be non-sexist, 'Jaswant' may be a boy or girl, so may many, if not all, others. In England I have come across the nonsense of a woman named Singh, usually a nurse, who had to give her father's name when she began training and, when she completed it, was told that it had to be the name on her certificate. If she argued she was told she could begin her course again but the outcome would be the same, she would be staff nurse Singh. Fortunately the British Nursing Council has come to its senses, so there are no more women called nurse Singh! As in all communities Sikh women may have to struggle to gain equality, but it is an integral part of the Gurus' teachings and world view. Socially, they may be the heads of the families.

Between the Jews and Asians had come the Irish over a century ago, and east Europeans who had fled the Nazis or post-war communism, Poles who had been given permission to settle in England after the war by Churchill as a reward for supporting Britain during the war, or our daughters' friend, Stana's father who had come from Yugoslavia where he had fought as a partisan only to find himself on the opposite side to Tito who dominated the country after the Nazis had been defeated. Sikhs originally met in a house in Leeds but had bought a redundant Christian church by the time I arrived; it had a baptistery which mystified them until I explained the idea of believers' baptism. Trying to discover the origins of its first worshippers I spoke to a group of elderly white people in Chapeltown one evening only to learn that they were from Lithuania and could not help me. The year 1923 and Independent Baptists was the best answer I could come up with but I wouldn't trust too much to this conclusion.

Immigration is seldom out of the news. Britons might remember with some pride that most groups and individuals have come here to escape oppression, though their history in the last century or so does not support the view that the British have always been tolerant; indeed, the first recent Act of Parliament, late in the nineteenth century was directed against Jews. Those anxiously looking for solutions to the possible threat of our islands having a majority population that originated from overseas by the year 2030 should realise the simple truth that we live in one world and that people who see our affluence on television, whether they come from Poland or Africa, will want a share of it, in the same way that those ancestors of ours who could went to carefully selected parts of the globe often to do good, just as east European economic migrants, Asians or Afro Caribbeans have done in the UK. At the heart of migration lies the greed of those who are rich and the wish to recover from greed on the part of those who have never had it good. Migration is as natural to humans as it is to swallows, with this difference, we do not need to react to it instinctively. We can reason and plan; likewise we can to solve threats of famine and war.

Incidentally, a Hindu friend smilingly suggested another reason for migration. There were two Indian villages, the inhabitants of one were lively, busy, innovative people, those in the other were very traditional and set in their ways. One day storms and floods destroyed the homes of the busy people and they were scattered to the four corners of the world while the rest remained untouched and unmoved. Someone who had noticed this event and was puzzled by it went to a holy man in search of an explanation. He, in turn, spoke to God who told him there was no point in moving the traditionalists, wherever they went they would contribute nothing to their new environment, whilst the others would bring fresh ideas and energy to communities that were in danger of stagnating. 'This is what we have done,' he added, with a grin. The story provided me with much food for thought.

Surrounded by so much wealth in the form of human resources it is surprising that in Leeds University, Hinduism or Islam might be studied from their expressions thousands of miles away or as concepts and Sikhs not at all, unless it were in the sociology department by academics such as Roger Ballard. Changes came with the appointment of Ursula King, her student Kim Knott's work on the Hindu community of Leeds and the Open University course, AD208, Man's Religious Quest, which encouraged visits to local places of worship. Until then I was the only person with his students, beating a path to such buildings and inviting faith members to come to college to meet with and speak to my students.

I must admit that I would have accepted the head of department post anywhere so long as it was congenial and accommodation affordable. The line was drawn around what is now the M25 and an interview thrown at a college when I discovered that I would teach Religious Studies for two years after which they would learn RE method with tutors in the education department whom I knew to be evangelicals and opposed to the teaching of world religions.

It was not that I seized Leeds but that it grabbed me! At a failed interview at Bretton College I had a long conversation, during the weary period of waiting for the panel to make up its collective mind, with Derek

Webster, the candidate who was ultimately successful. He told me of James Graham College, Leeds, named after a Director of Education for Leeds, and before I left encouraged me to apply for the post he was now about to vacate. It was a college for mature students, situated between Leeds and Bradford, not very far from the Moravian village of Fulneck and Tong where I had seen my first cricket match. As I write these words I am surprised to recollect that I never took the students to Fulneck, though we visited as a family. It is so easy to forget that the diversity of religion can be ignored or that some of the mature students had never been inside a place of Christian worship since their own weddings or some other family event. At least, when running in-service courses I tried to be more inclusive.

An organisation named the Yorkshire Committee for Community Relations, (YCCR), already existed when we came to Leeds. The driving force behind its Religious and Cultural Panel and women's work was Peggy Holroyde, Roedean, Oxford and Harvard educated, an activist as well as a visionary. The Religious and Cultural Panel was already established by the time I arrived in Leeds and had published a book, *East Comes West*, which included contributions by local Hindu, Muslim and Sikh authors. Peggy asked me to take over the chairmanship of the panel which I did enthusiastically. Before long we were working on a publication which appeared in 1973 under the title of *Religion in the Multi-faith School*. How much of what I did from about 1967 to 1979 can be attributed to my position at James Graham College and how much to my membership of YCCR it is impossible to say, and anyway attempts to unravel the two strands may not be worth the effort. Somehow Peggy was aware of my move to Leeds almost before my first term at college had begun and from meeting her I became indebted for her encouragement and practical support as well as friendship.

It was through YCCR that Peggy and I met Piara Singh Sambhi who was to become my close friend until his death in 1992; our families continue to be friends, so much so that I was staying at Jaswant's home in Birmingham when Saran was born in 2005 and was the first person after Jaswant and his mother to see her in hospital on the morning after her birth.

The richness of James Graham lay in the variety of its Religious Studies students. Most were Christians of one kind or another, from the major dominations, or from the Levant or continental Europe, or lapsed Christians or Christian atheists or agnostics. One atheist told me he couldn't possibly accept the Christian beliefs about Creation or the Fall of human kind, or the Resurrection of Jesus, as though these were the only options. When I introduced him to Indian thought about enlightenment, admitting as it does in some forms of Buddhism for example, atheism, he began to realise that his western perspective might be limited. Whether he gave the matter further consideration I do not know. Sadly, in my decade or more in Leeds I only had two Jewish and two Muslim students, and just missed out on an imam who went to Bradford. These were not days when mature members of religious minorities looked upon teaching as a good career move.

I quickly learned never to ask candidates who I interviewed why they wanted to teach. They were street wise enough to give the answer that they thought I would like. This became shockingly obvious on two occasions; one when I was sitting with a student having a cup of tea.

'You know Owen, I told you that I had always wanted to teach ever since I began to take a young people's class at church. Well, that was only part of the truth. You see my husband has beaten me and committed incest with our two daughters. He's a professional person and if I reported him to the police, even if they believed me, it would only ruin him and not provide us with a roof over our heads. When I qualify as a teacher I can leave him and start a new life with the children.'

The other student told me that her husband was only in his forties, that he had suffered three heart attacks, and the next would probably be fatal. She hoped to complete the course and so be able to provide for their young children before that happened. Fortunately she did!

Once we had moved into our house in north Leeds the summer was spent exploring the countryside, visiting friends in York or my widowed mother in Goole and discovering how to find the college by car. On the one side of our house lived our delightful Jewish friend Len and on the other two elderly unmarried ladies named Winifred and Eleanor. On our first day they invited us to tea and asked us to call them by their Christian names. Both came originally from Liverpool. Winifred had taught French at the University and Eleanor music in various schools. She had also taught the famous comedian, Arthur Askey, in Sunday school. Not to be outdone but with no hint of competition, Winifred said she had sung duets with Tommy Handley perhaps the most famous comedian of the Second World War period and the possessor a fine tenor voice. Both ladies had been suffragettes and gave to sailors' charities. We wondered whether they might be one of the one million women, cruelly called surplus, whose young men had died during the First World War. Winifred drove a 1934 Austin which she called Poppy and Eleanor, hatted, sat in the rear seat looking extremely regal, a lady to her gloved finger tips. It was always wise to give Poppy a wide berth and not to put too much trust in Winifred's ability to see zebra crossings on Fridays when they drove to the parish church for the Eucharist.

We also had to find a school for our older daughter. Standards in the local church school were good but for some reason we sent her to the council school where she found herself one of about six white children in a class of thirty black or Asian children. This was the way the world was going and we felt we should be part of it. The headmaster was a Jew, a man of considerable humanity, but someone whose policy it was to treat all children the same. Although I understand what he meant, they are not the same and their diversity and distinctiveness should be recognised and valued. This was actually done once a year when children were encouraged to attend school in their national dress. The West Indians wore for the most part their going to meeting clothes except for those with Rastafarian links; Hindus, Muslims and Sikhs dressed in saris, or shalwar kameeze, and our daughters in their Welsh hats and capes, with aprons; sadly the English seemed unable to make any response but perhaps being in a majority raises no issues of identity. I know it was not until I visited Pakistan that I gave any thought to what being British was.

I prepared for the term ahead by reading the Qur'an and the Bhagavad Gita. In vain I looked for a commentary of the Hindu scripture only to find that first, there was none of the kind I had used when studying John's Gospel, and secondly, this was not the way that Hindus used their sacred texts. They were concerned with overall interpretation not verse by verse analysis; an approach which I have come to believe has much to be said for it. Not long afterwards a scholar named R. C. Zaehner published the kind of commentary that I had in mind. Significantly he was a Roman Catholic Christian!

I joined James Graham in September 1968 when the first cohort of Religious Studies students was passing into year two. My students had eventually to be told plainly that I was not my predecessor. Some of them never forgave me for his departure. I had heard church members say of my dad, 'He's not a bit like our old minister', but I never expected to suffer in the same way. When the first course work essays arrived on my desk I was amazed to find that they weighed in, on average, at about twelve thousand words, the results of diligent work that could not be commended too highly. However, I realised that in going for length they had avoided the challenge to use their powers of discrimination. They had given me the whole carcass and invited me to pick out the bones – to take what I wanted. When the marks ranged from an A for excellent to C for satisfactory there were complaints from those who had written the most and achieved the least. I stipulated that in future the maximum length of a study should be about 2,500 words, which caused further grumbles because they had to be critical, analytical and evaluative.

I have never been greatly in favour of unseen examinations; so much can depend on circumstances on the day, a person's health, some domestic upset, nerves. It is argued that life is an examination; maybe – but how does a three-hour paper on Hinduism prepare one for the crises that probably come to our minds? Colleagues in other colleges in the Leeds Institute area alleged that I might coach my students to write good essays. I discovered that they told theirs what was on the unseen question paper. In my attempt to find approaches that were new to the examination systems experienced by my students, I introduced a one-hour seen and previously prepared essay to be written in class; the subject was the church in Rome during the first century AD, preparation time was two weeks. During this period I was peppered with questions which were finally reduced to the following: can we bring notes into the room on the examination day? Yes. Then can we bring text-books? Yes. When the day came every student had a clean note pad and a ten-page long essay which, when they were told to begin they began to transcribe. All had engaged in a practice run at home so they finished with a few minutes to spare. They left the room muttering about the stupidity of the exercise and, I suspect, the tutor. Next time I met the group I returned the essays duly marked. The best had received an A, the poorest a C. They asked for an explanation as they had all used the same books. We looked for reasons and agreed, more or less, that it was rather like cooking, not a subject that I can say much about as my wife is excellent in the kitchen and has not passed her skills on to me; we might all use the same ingredients but one Yorkshire pudding might be more successful than another. It's not what you do; it's the way you do it! By common agreement we decided not to use seen essays as a method of assessment, though it has much to commend it, if only tutors and students don't play silly games. Much later, in Chichester, a seen essay together with multiple choice questions, formed part of the assessment for BA degrees.

My new world in Leeds seemed to be an ocean without any horizons. There were new vistas as far as the discerning eye could see. How it was that tutors in other colleges did not appreciate the richness that lay around them I could not understand, yet when we discussed world religion syllabuses and the B.Ed. world religions paper at the university, they insisted that it should be left until last and usually made their excuses to depart leaving the world to university teachers of the subject, the professor and to me. Fortunately, my own students, whatever other diffi-culties we had, were persuaded of the need for a broadly based approach to RE; my task was to help them change theory into practice. Ironically, fourth year students in their B Ed year from all the colleges in the Leeds Institute elected to take the world religions option of Hinduism, Sikhism and Islam, and came to me once a week! How different it was to Newcastle. In Leeds there was a Principles and Practice of RE paper, and all tutors were trusted to teach on the degree programme in which the professor, John Tinsley, was keenly interested.

One afternoon I was visiting Jean at the school that Eluned and now Siân attended. After playtime came story time; Jean had decided to tell the story of the Good Samaritan. Thankfully she did not dramatise it as a student in Newcastle once had. A potentially riotous situation developed, I was about to try to take control of the class but did not wish to undermine the student's authority, when the bell rang for playtime. All fighting ceased as the children made a Pavlovian response and lined up at the classroom door for break! Jean simply came over to me and quietly said: 'That's it. I've dried up – and there are ten minutes left!' I asked if I might take the class which was the response that Jean was hoping for and with her agreement began to tell the story of the Sikh Good Samaritan, as the Sikhs themselves have called him, Bhai Khanaiya. During battles between Sikh and Muslim armies in the seventeenth century Khanaiya, a devotee of the Tenth Guru, could be seen going around the battlefield with a waterskin over his shoulder. When he came across wounded men lying parched he gave them water to drink. A group of Sikhs took him to their Guru, Gobind Singh, and complained that he was giving succour to the enemy. The Guru demanded that he should account for his actions. He replied that he saw neither Muslim nor Sikh, friend or foe, but only God's face in each of the men he helped. The Guru gave him a jar of ointment and some bandages with the instruction that he should not only quench their thirst, he should also tend their wounds. (Sikhs have honoured the sevadar by calling him 'Bhai', brother, and point out that this event took place two hundred years before the European engagement that resulted in the establishment of the Red Cross!).

Of course I pitched the story at the level of nine year olds, but what amazed me was the response it drew from the eight or nine Sikhs in the class. Not only were they attentive, sitting up straight, but I swear they each grew by about a foot. They looked round the class at their peers with pride. Someone had told a story about them! How long the occasion made an impact on them I don't know, but it is one of the most precious memories that I possess. One of the downsides of being a visitor is that such experiences are one offs, but it is still fresh in my mind and confirmed me experientially in what until then was theoretical belief based on the conviction that every child, so far as possible, has a right to hear their own story and that in a country like the UK we should learn one another's stories, otherwise we shall not only continue to live with a false sense of superiority based on ignorance, but on ground fertile for belief in racial and religious superiority.

Students and many qualified teachers were enthusiastic to teach multi-faith RE, all that was lacking was knowledge of the different faiths. Here one came up against the usual difficulty though less so during the students' three certificate years than in the fourth B.Ed. year, namely that academic courses are less related to helping students acquire material for use in the classroom and more, say, to what they should know of Islam or Christian theology, to be considered academically literate. Very little of what I studied in my history course at Durham was ever of use to me in the classroom except when I was teaching sixth formers on teaching practice or Roman Britain to undergraduates in Newcastle. My task was to quarry the uncut stone for students to shape and turn into material for use with children from five to sixteen. A few examples of many successes stand out for one reason or another.

A Batley infant school had a large influx of children from Pakistan, the student decided to explore Eid and Christmas both of which fell at about the same time in that year. The children being young had to be helped. All too often teachers seem to think that they are well informed resources when in reality they may know as little as the average six-year old Caucasian child, and therefore, presumably Christian knows about Christmas. They therefore avoid a topic for fear of 'getting it wrong' as they are wont to say. Marjorie's solution was to acquire as much knowledge as she could so that she could act as a resource; to encourage the children to tell one another what they did; and to persuade the children that some may do one thing while others did something else that is equally valid, and to accept diversity. Thus, for example some 'Christians' might eat chicken and others turkey, some 'Muslims' might send and receive cards or visit relatives whilst others did not. Parents were made to feel that they could come to the school and make a contribution. The local church was well known by everyone as the school had links with it, but not with the mosque. This was because the Muslim children were too young to attend the madrasa after school lessons in learning Arabic and reading the Qur'an. When the teacher showed them a photograph of the mosque, they recognised it and were pleased that she had mentioned it and knew about its use and other aspects of their religion. As with Jean's experience, it gave children a feeling that their culture and values were worthy of attention. Not many had Eid cards. The sending and receiving of cards and the commemoration and celebrations is not a universal phenomenon. (Until I met my wife, Gwynneth, I did not give my parents Christmas or birthday presents, or cards). Children from the subcontinent have often been upset when an alert head teacher has noted that it is Iqbal's or Surinder's birthday, called them in front of the school to be applauded by their peers, asked them how many cards they have received and been told none by a crestfallen child. Marjorie provided Eid cards to supplement those brought by children. The Muslim children were absent for two days at Eid and this had to be explained to the rest of the class some of whom wondered why they didn't have a holiday on Jesus' birthday! Marjorie proved to be a missionary in two ways. First, other teachers in the school saw what she had done and realised, to use a term not current in those days, that it was not rocket science, secondly a Muslim father popped into school, walked round the classroom, saw the display of the children's work, asked about Eid cards, and then took a sweet out of his pocket, gave it to Marjorie and said: 'You very good!' she didn't realise what an accolade this was. For a Muslim man to speak to a woman outside his family was probably rare and to a non-Muslim exceptional. Marjorie was a vicar's wife.

One Friday afternoon I took some students to Batley boys' high school to observe Muslim prayers in the PE hall, which was used to accommodate the one hundred and fifty of them. In the past, I was told by their Muslim teacher, a friend of mine, that they all went to the mosque which was not far away. However, some of them disappeared into Batley market on the way so it was decided, as my friend said, to bring the mosque to the boys instead of taking the boys to the mosque. The teenager who called the faithful to prayer had a memorably beautiful voice. After prayers we met the head teacher who talked about the number of immigrants in the school. When I suggested that most were Yorkshire born and asked when they would cease to be 'immigrants', I was told 'When their English is good enough'. At the mosque we were shown a coffin and told the story behind it. In Pakistan the body would be covered in a shroud and taken to the cemetery and so the custom was naturally followed here but local people were offended. The community therefore put the shrouded body in a coffin, carried it to the cemetery where they removed and buried it bringing the empty coffin back to the mosque. What the folk of Batley made of that practice I never discovered. From the mosque we could look down into the valley and saw a row of about eight houses in a terrace; as we watched a Muslim lady entered the first house and a few minutes later emerged from the last one.

This reminded me of something I later saw in Pakistan, the extension of a house by adding rooms to accommodate a newly married son and his bride.

Helen decided to do a topic on Sikhs with her nine year olds, all white, potentially racist, and not above using a few expletives when they felt like it. She equipped herself with artefacts and photographs from the college library, but then asked me if I could help her arrange a visit to a gurdwara. I approached my friend Piara Singh Sambhi who persuaded a number of members of the community to act as guides and hosts. The children knew that they must take off their shoes and cover their heads and bow towards the scripture, the Guru Granth Sahib, because it was special. Off they went and behaved well. Their guides were friendly and typically hospitable, giving them biscuits and a glass of orange juice as they sat on the floor at the end of the visit and telling them that no one should leave the gurdwara hungry, such was the teaching of their Guru. As they left Helen was pleased to hear the children say to one another: 'Ee, weren't they luvely fellers!' Back at school they were inspired to produce some fine written work and pictures and a model of the gurdwara.

There could be anxious moments. A head teacher in a church school felt that it was only right that the assembly, that was usually Christian, should focus on Islam one day. She spoke to the vicar who agreed and then to one of the boys whose father was an imam. It was decided that he should make the call to prayer, that someone should read from the Qur'an and that some Muslim children should demonstrate the prayer positions. All went well until it was almost time to go into the hall, and then the head teacher noticed that Iqbal was missing. Had he taken fright? What could be done? He was to play a key role. Then he appeared. He had been to wash his hands; after all he was going to handle the Qur'an, removing it from the cloth in which it was wrapped. The teacher made much of this event, asking the children how they looked after things that were special to them. At the end of the assembly she suggested that she might take care of the Holy Book. Iqbal looked around her office, dusted the top of a high cabinet and placed the Qur'an on it, saying that it would be safe there; no one would turn their back on it. A fascinating lesson for everyone, especially for Christians who might treat the Bible as casually as they handle other books. Some time later I was told about an assembly in a secondary school with a large number of Muslim pupils. The RE teacher was talking about Bible translations and versions and used six or seven different English New Testaments to illustrate his point. After reading from each one he put it on the ground at his feet. The Muslim boys were horrified that a sacred book could be treated in this way; to reassure them and save the face of the Christian, their Muslim teacher told them that the original New Testament was written in Greek so these were only copies and perhaps were not regarded as quite so holy! The scriptures that I possess, of whatever religion, have been treated with greater respect since that day and stand on the higher shelves of my study.

Manjeet had very recently and conveniently given birth to a baby girl. A student who was doing a topic on homes and families thought it would be a good idea for her class of six year olds, and all white, to meet an Asian family so it was arranged that mother and baby should go to the school. Of course it would be necessary to arrange transport, something that teachers can be in danger of forgetting. Manjeet turned up with baby, a plastic bath, a clean nappy, change of clothes, and all the other things that mother and baby need. Helped by the girls and some of the boys, she proceeded to bath Maninder, dress her and give her a feed. The fact that she had brown skin seemed not to concern anyone. What they commented on was that such a tiny baby already had ten toes. Presumably they thought children developed like tadpoles!

These examples, and others that could be added to them, illustrate the good sense of beginning where children are at. Christian RE had been the telling of Bible or heroic stories or examples of caring and sharing devoid of any explicit Christian reference or material, often because teachers were no longer believers and did not wish to put themselves in a position where a child might say: 'Do you believe that?'. The use of input from other traditions enabled them to deflect the focus from themselves and their imagined Christian children to a broader interest in what others do and believe, without, I would argue, avoiding big questions of life when it was appropriate to consider them. However, there was also a need to provide story material from the different faiths: what Alan T. Dale did with his *New World Testament*, Hindu, Sikh and Muslim friends and I did with material from their faith traditions. My own decision to become a writer began with addressing teachers at in-service courses and encouraging them to begin using material from other faiths in their RE lessons. The challenge took the form of: 'Alright, you've convinced us but where can we find stories to use?'

Whilst I was trying to respond to this demand, I attended a conference on multicultural education and found myself sitting next to a man who had written *A Hindu Family in Britain*; from him I learned how to go about the task of interesting a publisher and decided to write *A Sikh Family in Britain* as I had already met Piara Singh Sambhi and knew that I could work with him. The book contained material that could easily be adapted for use in the junior classroom. Still there was much persuasion to be undertaken. One evening I was waiting to be introduced by the chairperson at an in-service course when I overheard two teachers on the front row say: 'I suppose he's going to tell us to teach transmigration. Well I've enough trouble teaching my seven year olds the Resurrection!' They had presented me with my opening gambit. I assured them that I was not going to encourage them to teach transmigration or the Resurrection to seven year olds. Instead I concentrated on what Hindus do when a baby is born or when they marry, or worship, and the celebration of festivals, rather than what they believe. Something that I realised was that we had never taught Christianity. We had assumed that every child goes to church and knows what worship is for example, that they have been to baptisms and weddings, to Christmas and Easter services and to Eucharists. Instead they had been told Bible stories and some church history. The daily act of collective worship is supposed to have given them all they need to know about worship – I wonder what ideas a Muslim, for example, gets about Christian worship from what happens day by day in school, even if it is well done? My concern has always been to encourage teachers to approach Christianity in the way that I ask them to teach any of the other religions. Of course, there is one particular obstacle to this being done – most teachers have a relationship to Christianity that they do not have towards other religions. It may be the religion they believe in and base their lives upon. It may be the one that they have rejected and regard as a form of superstition. This also goes for the children. Once I overheard a student put it succinctly, in a nutshell. He said; 'It is easy to teach Buddhism. Everyone knows that I'm not a Buddhist so no one will ask me if I believe it, and I know none of them is a Buddhist so I shan't be afraid of getting it wrong!'

To teach about one's own tradition, whether we believe it or not, is the most difficult task of all, probably harder than the challenge facing a history teacher seeking to defend her nation's past. The production of reliable information and the encouragement of teachers to use it in an open, critical manner have been two of my main guiding principles throughout my career.

Just as my Christian studies had to be self-taught, though with help from correspondence courses, so had my religious studies. I have always regretted lacking the opportunity to be an undergraduate in Religious Studies, and envied my own students, though not for the quality of the tuition they received! A moment of great significance for me was the Sunday morning that I first visited a gurdwara. We had been to church as a family and after elevenses at home I drove to the Sikh place of worship that was only about a mile away in Chapeltown. As arranged Piara Singh was waiting at the entrance to greet me and when I had covered my head with a large handkerchief which he provided, and taken off my shoes, after which I washed my hands, he led me into the Diwan or worship hall. Following his example I walked to the front of the congregation, bowed towards the Holy Book, placed some money in a box, and went with him to sit among the men. For some time I let my eyes travel round the hall taking in the bright colours of ladies' clothes, shalwar kameezes and saris, the Christmas-like decorations, everyone seated on the floor, some older Sikhs with their shoulders against the wall or a pillar, the portraits on the walls, the canopy over the scripture, a man holding a fan over it made of animal hairs or nylon embedded in a metal holder and groups of musicians, one playing a harmonium and the others what I took to be Indian instruments. Then I began quietly to question my friend: there was none of the silence that I had experienced in my own church and had expected here. Children moved within the room from mum on one side to dad on the other or to children their own age, sisters, brothers, cousins or school friends. Families came and went. Same sex relatives or friends chatted quietly to one another. It might seem irreverent or rude, but it was not. There was naturalness about it to which I soon became accustomed. Occasionally one reader was replaced by another, man or woman, who would wave the chauri, to give the fan its correct name, and might read from the Book or comment upon the reading. The ragis might then chant the words that had been read. I began to ask questions that might range from why did women and men not sit together and why did they remove their shoes to why is a chauri held over the Guru Granth Sahib, or why is everyone seated on the ground. Very occasionally Piara Singh said he couldn't provide an answer other than it was always done that way; he would try to discover the real reason and tell me when we next met. Sometimes there can be more than one answer all of which can be correct. For example, I asked why Sikhs take off their shoes in a gurdwara and was told that as worshippers sat on the floor it was important to keep the carpets clean. Some years later I visited a gurdwara in Cardiff with a friend. At the end of the service we went to the food hall for a meal but he picked up his shoes and carried them with him across the room where we had been worshipping. Sikhs shouted at him and demanded he replace them in the shoe rack. Clearly ritual pollution not cleanliness was the issue. The first religious studies lesson that my introduction to Sikhism taught me was never to try to be clever by suggesting, for example, that many Sikhs are vegetarian because meat is so expensive in India. 'Yes', will be the inevitable polite answer, to contradict is rude unless a friendship is old and firm. If one is fortunate, as I was with Piara Singh, sometime later one may be told that many Sikh extended families have Hindu members so out of respect for them meat is not eaten, and later still one might be that the product of the sheep or goat might be eaten by not the cow, or that meat, because of the blood it contains is polluting. The second lesson was to enquire openly, listen and observe, but be slow in jumping to conclusions or being clever.

When I went to my own Anglican church on the following Sunday I found myself asking questions about things I had previously taken for granted, such as why is there a lectern and a pulpit, why is the font near the church door, did we always have pews, why does the priest always eat the remaining bread and drink the remaining wine after communion? (Dad and granddad poured the wine down the sink and threw the bread to the birds). Now that I had begun to ask questions I found myself doing so in mosques, synagogues and mandirs, and also churches, (why do Quakers sit facing on another?). Soon Piara Singh was asking me why the Chapeltown church that was now a gurdwara had a hole in the floor. (It was a Baptistry). Curiosity can be catching and should be at the heart of Religious Studies and Religious Education, not to mention education as a whole. From this time on until his death, question and answer became a way of life between my friend and me.

On some evenings when I visited Piara Singh he was chatting to other Sikhs in his front room as if it were a counselling session which, in fact, it was. He was a discreet man who never discussed these conversations with me but when I asked him why they didn't go to one of the statutory services he mentioned the word, 'Izzat', pride. Issues should be dealt with inside the extended family and to involve teachers or the social services was to bring its opposite upon the family and community, disgrace and shame. Izzat is a fundamental concept among all Punjabis and probably most inhabitants of the Middle Eastern world. We ignore it at the peril of not understanding their cultures; it explains the crisis that arises when a son or daughter will not accept an arranged marriage or the practice of forced marriages and honour killings to a large degree. Repugnant as these things are, and I have never heard any Asian approve of them, when family pressure says, 'What is wrong with you that you cannot control your children?', it is hard not to buckle, especially when it is followed up by blunt statements that news of failure will spread among the community so that no one will want to marry into that particular family.

One evening my friend announced that he had to go to India to settle some property issues. To my surprise he asked me to visit his wife and children every so often and phone them at least once a week. Then he would know they were safe. He had, he said, many cousin brothers but I was his true brother and more reliable than them. Only gradually did I realise the honour that was being conferred on me by asking me to visit a lady when her husband was not at home. On the evening before he left, Piara Singh had an endless stream of visitors bearing gifts and money, as much as 200 pounds in one case. Men he dealt with, couples were sent into the living room where Avtar, his wife, took what they brought and noted it in a book. I was told that these were relatives and friends to whom he had lent money over the years, they knew that he would now need it for legal and land fees and were reimbursing him. Again one saw the importance of the extended family and the wish not to be dependent on banks, though Piara Singh had a mortgage and insurance policies.

Cousin brother is a strange term that I had not previously heard but my friend would use it frequently and rather dismissively to describe a person who was not a close relative. 'He's just a cousin brother'. One evening a young Sikh, Leeds born, came to see his friend Jaswant, Piara Singh's son. As apparently he had nothing better to do he began to tell me of relationship terms. After mum and dad, grandparents, uncles, aunts and cousins, most of us become lost in the realm of second cousins and cousins twice removed, if they are not the same thing. He ran through sixty-eight with different names for an older brother than a younger one, others for older and younger sisters, for an uncle who was older than his father and for those who were younger. Jaswant seemed as perplexed as I was, but it was reassuring that a second generation Sikh was still so involved and informed about his culture.

Sometime after Piara Singh had returned to England, his wife and two children went to Punjab leaving him to fend for himself. A memorable consequence of their absence was that he had to make the tea; whenever I went to see him, normally Avtar obliged. One evening I came home and told Gwynneth that something had not been as it should have been that evening, but I couldn't think what was the matter. Next day I realised that I had not been given a cup of tea. When I visited Piara Singh later in the week he said, 'Am I glad to see you, come in and have the cup of tea that I forgot to give you last time, my rudeness has been worrying me ever since you left the other evening, then later we will have today's cup!'. And we did! Such is Asian hospitality. I have always warned students not to visit a family unless they have time for a cup of tea or evening meal. 'Sorry I can't stop!' is not part of Asian vocabulary or etiquette. If one were to ask, however, whether Izzat and hospitality were part of the Asian religion or culture, one would be met with a quizzical look; these are western questions to which there is no eastern answer, unless second and third generations have become so westernised that they are dislocated from such aspects of their parental tradition.

Mavis ran an excellent school in that village between Leeds and Bradford, sacred to Herbert Sutcliffe, Len Hutton, Ray Illingworth, and now, I don't know why, Pudsey Bear, (pronounced Putsey as Bratford in Bradford) and had been one of the panel that prepared the recently published West Riding Agreed Syllabus. My students and I would visit it often because it was well run and took the responsibilities of its pupils seriously through a student council. They were invited to make suggestions and decisions on most aspects of school life other than those over which the head teacher and governors had legal responsibility; such things as what clubs might be offered and when they would meet and what they would do, likewise, the planning of assemblies, school outings, rare cases of bullying, a school tuck shop, and the charities to which collections might be given. I was asked to speak to her staff about RE but not to say much about teaching other religions than Christianity because, 'we don't have any here'. At least I could try to persuade them that there was more to it than caring and sharing, the usual aspects taught by many teachers, especially if they were a bit shaky regarding their own religious position or anxious about that of the children and their parents. The session seemed to be successful and I persuaded them to accept principles that could be observed whatever the religious content might be, Hinduism or Christianity. It came as a surprise to me to receive an urgent phone call from Mavis during the next summer holiday informing me that twenty Sikh families had moved into the area, they would be bringing their children to school in September and could I tell the staff something about the Sikh religion! Such invitations are fairly rare and when they come must be received with alacrity! Taking my box of Sikh artefacts with me I went to Pudsey on the agreed day and tried to assure them that what they obviously regarded as a threatening invasion could be an enjoyable experience. This they accepted, not being the kind of teachers for whom the word 'problem' is most prominent in their vocabulary. An added bonus was the fact that most of these children who came from Uganda were expected to know some English. I popped into the school fairly frequently and found that the children were settling in well and Mavis and her staff found them a joy to teach, but she had some difficulties responding to them in curriculum terms, amending the integrated day and RE to meet their specific needs.

Religious Education in England must be taught in accordance with an Agreed Syllabus, sometimes drawn up by a local authority, often borrowed from another. Once it was fairly easy to produce such a syllabus as the content was confined to Christianity but even this could have its difficulties as the various parties to the syllabus had to be in agreement. Four groups are represented on Agreed Syllabus panels: the Church of England, other denominations, (to which Jews, Muslims, Sikhs and other religions found in the area in such numbers as to warrant attention, have now been assigned, sometimes to the distaste of nonconformist Christians), teachers' organisations and the local authority. Each panel may exercise a veto and all must agree before the syllabus can become a legally approved document, hence the place of the word 'agreed' in the title. (The important West Riding Syllabus of 1967 contains one or two sections about which, it is understood, the men who masterminded it were uneasy, regarding them as beyond the religious understanding of children of particular age groups but, I am told, they had to accept them because one of the free church representatives would not otherwise have agreed to the syllabus and could have wrecked the whole enterprise).

In 1974 Bradford published a supplement to the West Riding Syllabus, Guide to Religious Education in a Multi-Faith Society. It could only be a supplement because it was not produced by a duly convened conference as outlined above, being more a working party of interested people and experts in multi-religious RE. It was, nevertheless, the first document of its kind to be drawn up by any English local authority. Three meetings relating to it stand out vividly in my mind; the first and second were panel meetings; the third was a talk on Judaism given by a Bradford rabbi. One afternoon most of the teachers involved in the project met with four other faith representatives, a Jew, a Hindu, a Muslim and a Sikh. The dual purpose of the gathering was to improve our own knowledge and to decide what material might be put in the Supplement. During the discussion the other faith members were sidelined completely; instead the teachers asked me what they believed. After only a brief time I reminded them why the Jew and the others had been invited and assured them that all spoke excellent English, they should ask them. This they did, but why had there been such reticence in addressing them in the first place? A number of answers suggest themselves. They might not have known what questions to ask and no teacher likes to appear ignorant. Teachers in those days, if not now, were expected to be authority figures, both in status and in understanding. 'Do you believe in God?' might have seem far too simplistic; 'What kind of God to do you believe in?' an admission of ignorance. We have to play a game when we are questioning people on all sorts of matters; media interviewers realise this well, we are not asking our question but those of the men and women we are representing. 'If a child asked you what kind of god you believe in, what answer would you give, and are there any scriptural verses you might quote?' The teachers might have been, and in fact were, almost completely ignorant of the four religions which were entirely new to them. At a basic level these reasons combined in this probably being the first time they had ever met a person who was not of their religious persuasion. The meeting was ultimately fairly successful but I came away from it realising how much more preparation was needed, both in briefing the teachers and also the members of other faiths.

The second meeting was a disaster! A gathering of secondary school heads of RE was convened at the city library with me as chairman and a Muslim imam and scholar from London was to be our speaker. I met him at Foster Square station, a small man, elderly with a long white beard and white robes but with good English. He was clearly fazed from the moment he entered the room, probably having never met any women outside his own family at any time in his life. When I introduced the ladies to him there was no hand-shake or even a glance of awareness. They all felt suitably snubbed and rightly so from their cultural perspective. He gave a fairly conventional talk on Islam and there were no questions. I was rather pleased to bring the meeting to a close and take my guest to the home of a local Muslim. At least it saved me from being savaged by five angry teachers until next time we met, by then they might have cooled down, Inshallah, though I rather doubted it. They had not.

The preparation of the Bradford Supplement provided me with an interesting learning experience. In future I needed to realise that other participants might not be as far down in the inter religious road as I was. They might never have met a person from another faith. The imam needed to be prepared for the fact that his audience needed to be helped to respond. Some thirty years on things are much easier, but in those days there were few Jews or Muslims, for example, who were used to sharing their religion with such people as the Christians on the syllabus panel. An important principle in my approach to multi-faith RE has always been to involve people of other faith as much as possible, but these experiences made me realise that I might still have a preliminary role as an interpreter or go between, assisting teachers especially in making initial contact with a religion. It was with this in mind that I accepted invitations from Huddersfield librarians to talk to them about Islam, some months later, an exercise made more daunting by the premature presence of a Muslim who was taking me home for a meal afterwards turning up almost as soon as I had begun speaking. He still took me home. Muslims are very polite and forbearing!

Soon after I met Piara Singh and his wife, their family was struck by tragedy. Their two little girls were crossing a zebra crossing on their way to school when a car, overtaking a bus that had stopped to make way for them, knocked them down. The amazing number of mourners from their community shocked me and I shared Piara Singh's grief at not being able to arrange the children's funerals. In Punjab they would have been cremated on the day of their deaths unless it was too late in the afternoon when the ceremony would have been carried out on the following morning. Here they had to wait almost six weeks for the post-mortem, less commonly used in India Each time we met he asked me; 'Why must we wait?'. Surely this is an important example of a custom and a sense of feeling to which officials must and can respond.

There was an inquest and a court case and I understand that Piara Singh walked across the court before proceedings began to tell the driver that he had been praying for him; perhaps not many men could have adopted this proper Sikh attitude, but my friend was not typical and accepted what had happened as God's will. When the funeral was over the family gave donations to a number of children's charities in England and in India, Christian as well as Sikh. Some days later he told me that he had deposited the children's ashes in the river Aire not far from Goole; many Sikh families take them to Kiratpur on the river Sutlej where the sixth teacher, Guru Hargobind, had lived, not far from the town of Anandpur Sahib, associated with the ninth and tenth Gurus.

The five hundredth anniversary of the birth of the first Sikh teacher, Guru Nanak, in 1969, was celebrated universally and was the occasion when a number of people then and later became more closely involved in Sikh studies. In India my friend and academic supervisor attended a conference at which Geoffrey Parrinder, who was later to be examiner of my MPhil and PhD, was also present. The Albert Hall conference stimulated the interest of Eleanor Nesbitt and Christopher Shackle of the School of Oriental and African Studies and was a gathering at which Hew McLeod heard a passage from his remarkable study, *Guru Nanak and the Sikh Religion*, only recently published, read by a Muslim speaker at the gathering. In Leeds I was invited to be a member of the planning committee that was arranging a major event in Leeds Town Hall. I was given the date and place of a meeting and asked to turn up at eight o'clock which I did, to be shown an empty room by a lady who spoke no English. At 8.30 I sneaked to the door to check that I had come to the correct house number; the lady of the house spotted me, smiled and signalled for me to return to the room. Half an hour later the Sikh members of the community arrived. Next time I turned up at 8.30 and was still thirty minutes early, so on the third occasion I decided to present myself at nine o'clock only to be greeted by a room full of Sikh men who hoped that everything was alright. What had made me late; they had been waiting for me for an hour! Never take Indians on when it comes to timing. In Punjabi, the word 'kal' can mean yesterday or tomorrow depending on the tense that is used; (kal I will go to work, or kal yesterday I went to the gurdwara. It is said that once a Sikh was asked whether they had anything like manyana in their language, when he was told it meant tomorrow he replied: 'Oh no we haven't anything as urgent as that!').

The college music department composed a rendering of the Mul Mantra which was much appreciated and the event was very popular with the Sikhs but less so with such local politicians as the MP Denis Healey. They are usually treated with respect on these occasions, but children ran up and down the few empty rows of seats and families rose and walked out noisily if they had other things to do.

A number of important Sikh scholars visited the UK to take part in the celebratory events. One, Dr Gobind Singh Mansukhani, came to Leeds. In the August, 1969 I had an urgent phone call from Piara Singh informing that Dr Mansukhani was intending coming to Leeds before attending the Albert Hall event, and wanted to address a non-Sikh audience. I knew I must do something to save my friend's pride, loss of face, as already stated, is very important in Middle Eastern societies; fortunately the new academic year was about to begin at James Graham in a few weeks time. Certainly he could speak to my students who had a two-hour session late in the afternoon. It also happened that the first part of Monday afternoons was given to student matters, police might come to talk about drugs or social workers might discuss truancy, or the students' union might hold a meeting; on this particular occasion, as it was the first Monday in the term nothing was planned. I was told that Dr Mansukhani could have the hour but, of course, an audience could not be guaranteed. As it happened about two hundred students came to listen to him, a photograph showing them sitting attentively was produced in a booklet, *Guru Nanak World Teacher*, that was published by the Leeds Gurdwara; such was the success of the event that I was never able to put a foot wrong in the Sikh community, and when I went to India four years later Dr Mansukhani was my first host.

The prospect of ever managing to visit India was a remote pipe dream never to be realised, especially as I did not smoke! Suddenly, however, round about half term in February 1973 everything changed.

7

Setting Foot in the Subcontinent

The Department of Education had the wise idea of sending teachers, HMIs, college lecturers and advisers; in fact most people involved in multireligious or multicultural education to the Caribbean or subcontinent, areas from which new Commonwealth migrants has come or were arriving in the UK. Obviously Idi Amin's Uganda was not included. Arrivals exported from the country had no prospect of return and the sooner they realised it the better. Most did before they boarded the plane clutching their few belongings and the ten pounds they were also allowed to bring. Although I was consulted by HMIs organising the visits my LEA, Leeds, turned down my application to be considered for one of the journeys; an adviser was sent instead. This was initially disappointing but turned out to be for my good in a number of ways. First, although a friend deeply interested in Buddhist studies was able to disengage himself from his group and go to Sri Lanka, I would probably have had to remain with mine and I much preferred the prospect of doing my own thing to a guided tour. Secondly, I had counselled against only going to villages and towns from which migrants had come, but I knew that these might constitute the bulk of the experience. It was, I acknowledged, important to go to some of these places but I rather likened it to walking down Lumb Lane in Bradford but not seeing York Minster. Lumb Lane, incidentally, when I was at Belle Vue Grammar School, was one of the more unpleasant streets in Manningham, a dirty slum where one might be mugged. When migrants from Pakistan moved into it they quickly made it clean and tidy and a respectable neighbourhood, though parts of it, to their annoyance, were still used by prostitutes and pimps. I strongly felt that the legacy of Islam or Sikhism and the richness of Hinduism should be recognised by spending time at the Taj Mahal, the Red Fort in Delhi, the Golden Temple in Amritsar and the most ancient city in the world, so I had been told, Varanasi. Instead many teachers returned with photographs of villages with mud huts, these were in fact kuccha houses of unburnt brick, not unlike the thatched cottages of England to which some of the more successful town dwellers aspire. They are more satisfactory than the red burned brick houses that have sometimes replaced them, thanks to money sent home by Asian settlers in the UK because in the winter they are warmer, retaining the heat, and in summer cooler, not absorbing the power of the sun. One Brahmin I visited showed me a kuccha annexe he had retained next to the brick house paid for by his successful sons and told me that this was where he came to meditate and study the scriptures because of its acceptable climate.

Peggy Holroyde proved to be my guardian angel, the person without whose aid the visit would not have been possible. She contacted the Rowntree Trust which gave me a travel grant and she also put me in touch with Jamila and George, friends in Delhi. Piara Singh Sambhi, arranged hospitality with Gobind Singh Mansukhani, an internationally known Sikh living in Delhi, and Dr Muhammad Iqbal of Huddersfield College, contacted his Sufi teacher in Pakistan. I tried to learn some useful phrases and especially how to say 'please' and 'thank you' to the mystification of friends. Only in the subcontinent did I discover that instead of actual words the inflection of the voice conveyed the meaning. In England, I have heard Asian children described as rude for not using these terms! I had also been warned against offering money with my left hand, a problem being left handed, but no one ever seemed to mind, perhaps they were too well mannered. After a birthday meal for Eluned and Siân I set out for Heathrow where I planned to fly Air India to Delhi, surely the only airline to choose for such an adventure. At the airport I was relieved to discover that unlike travelling on a train I did not have to carry all my cases with me onto the plane but that I was free of them from checking in to collecting them at my destination. The walls of the cabin were decorated with scenes from Hindu mythology and the women members of the cabin crew wore saris. I felt I was already in India. My seat was by a window so I slept very little preferring to look at the scenery, especially the brown deserts of Afghanistan where it was impossible to believe that anyone would want to live even if it were possible.

As I left the plane in Delhi I was pleased that I had not heeded my mother's advice to take my heavy overcoat because it was only March and the weather could still be very cold, she warned. The hot air almost knocked me over. As I joined the queue at passport control I was relieved to see a group of Sikhs on a balcony with Dr Mansukhani in the middle, waving at me. Few simple experiences can be more enjoyable than that of being met by friends, relatives, or even a stranger holding up a placard with one's name on it when one arrives at a never before visited destination, or even one's home town. Long before I had collected my luggage and cleared customs they had raced downstairs to greet me. Soon I was enjoying my first Indian meal in India, vegetarian of course.

That evening after I had rested I was taken to one of Delhi's main gurdwaras. Through Dr Mansukhani's connections I was able to visit all the principal gurdwaras of Delhi and was also taken to the Guru Har Krishan College where I spoke at morning assembly and observed a number of lessons. Like many Sikhs Dr Mansukhani rose early in the morning to bathe and read the scriptures. After taking my shower I would take a walk around the neighbourhood while breakfast was being prepared. February and March 1973 were already very hot with people dying of heat stroke in some parts of the city. Hopes were being expressed that there would not be many power cuts in the coming summer, something that seemed strange to me until I realised that instead of using central heating to keep warm, Indians who can afford them rely on fans and air conditioning to keep them cool during the summer heat. Once we had taken breakfast we would follow the plan that my host had devised for me. On leaving the house he would always open at random a gutka or prayer book containing the main passages used by Sikhs in their devotions and ceremonies and read the vak or command or advice which God gave him for the day. We were usually chauffeur driven which meant that I could be given a conducted tour during the journey. On days when my host took the wheel I was sometimes rather anxious because, when we came to a roundabout, he might well take a right turn of 45 degrees instead of the legal 270; what was the point, he said, in driving further than necessary? However, he did give way to such vehicles as buses and lorries.

I would not want to drive a car in Delhi or most other parts of India even though people drive on the left as in the UK and I always am wary of Indian motorists in England! Although I have never seen a serious accident in my dozen visits to the country, I still regard every journey as hazardous. Everyone drives on the horn which must be the most worn part of any vehicle. As for the least worn, it must be the handbrake or headlights. Seldom do I seem to have seen a driver park his car on the flat and use the handbrake, on a hill recourse is often made to a couple of bricks kept in the boot and placed under the rear wheels. Use of lights is sparing because, I have been told, the dynamo will wear out. This can lead to all kinds of terrors as one travels along the Grand Trunk road from Calcutta to Lahore and beyond, presumably to Kabul, at night and suddenly comes across an unlit parked or broken down lorry, a buffalo pulled cart of hay or straw with its load extending over a metre on either side, even a heavily burdened camel, or a car coming in the opposite direction on a dual carriageway, because its driver wants to turn off to the left and why should he go an extra couple of miles to the next round-about? Much easier to find a gap in the central reservation and then drive against the traffic until the turn off point is reached. Crossing roads can be as dangerous; there are zebra crossings but why they exist no driver seems to know. The best advice I have been given is to cross alongside one of the many cows that wander along the roads looking for grass on the central reservation if the road happens to be a dual carriageway. The cow being revered no driver will touch it. I saw one who did and as a consequence suffered a beating and was almost lynched, though it was not his fault.

Dr Mansukhani had recently retired from the University Grants Commission and therefore knew many people in higher education. These individuals I was able to meet but his religious contacts outside Sikhism were limited. I was wondering how I could deal with this situation when the decision was taken for me. It was necessary for my host to be out of town and in a rather agitated state he discussed with me what might be done. Fortunately there was a plan B.

I had told him of Jamila and George, at that time editor of the *Indian Express*. We phoned them and as if by magic carpet Jamila found her way through Delhi's traffic and I was on my way to her home in Haus Khaz. It was an early rising family even by Indian standards. At whatever time I emerged George was reading all the newspapers in preparation for going to his office and Jamila would be watering her beloved garden. At five o'clock the scents of spring were wonderful and the sight of a humming bird gathering nectar memorable. Once the family had been cared for she gave me lavish attention, in return for which I helped her carry produce to the car from the nearby market or hang curtains and perform other domestic chores at home. Still, she remembered why her white slave was in India and took charge of my education. We visited sites and friends as well as family until her sons came home from school in the early afternoon and everyone enjoyed a siesta. This I had tried to resist thinking that my time in India was limited and precious but before long drowsiness made it necessary. Evenings were usually scheduled for going out, whether to meet a delightful Sufi teacher in a mosque in Old Delhi or son et lumiere at the Red Fort. The softly spoken white bearded and white robed Muslim was the personification of gentleness and one was aware of his spiritual presence and piety. So far I had met no one like him in England who conveyed the spiritual nature and devotion of Islam to such a degree. The devotion of the British Muslims I had so far met was more dynamic, they were, after all, members of a far younger generation.

One has heard of difficulties encountered by non-Muslim women going to mosques but the men we met at the Jama Masjid in Old Delhi were courteous and respectful to Jamila, herself a gentle and respectful person who put them at their ease with a smile, a few words of Urdu and her appreciation of how to behave. Our first visit to the Red Fort was during daylight hours so that we could enjoy its architecture at our leisure. I looked down from the battlements to see a bear being made to dance, a sight now rare but in 1973 there were still tourists who encouraged such cruelty by throwing its owner a few rupees. This, I was told was the spot where the last Mughal emperor had seen two men quarrelling and had been asked to intervene, but he could only reply that his power did not extend that far. When we came back in the evening we brought a young American with us who enjoyed the spectacle not only because it was well done and informative, but because for once his country was not the focus of critical or hostile comments. He relished my supposed torment but if truth be known I had no patriotic feelings about the Raj, my education concerning the imperial history of British India might be just beginning but I already knew that although we had given India the English language and a railway system and had unified it as never before, our rule had been profitable to one section of British society that represented by Clive and Curzon. During research related to *A Sikh Family in Britain* I had also discovered the story of the Partition of India and our hasty evacuation of the country.

Staying with Jamila and George was comfortable and restful. It was easily possible to become institutionalised, to draw an analogy with long stays in hospital that I later experienced. Occasional visits to such places as the modern Birla Mandir, a fine Hindu temple, or to see Muslims like the Sufi already mentioned, or even to the market, could easily justify staying in Haus Khaz for the next week or two. However, Jamila had other ideas. She packed me off to the station to book a return journey to Agra on the Taj Express which I caught at a reasonable time on the following morning. In the queue while booking my ticket I had fallen into conversation with two young men who told me that they were returning to Agra, where they worked, on the same train that I was. They said they would look out for me and provide an escort. Good as their word they were waiting for me at the station. Seating me near the window they pointed out interesting places en route. Although the train was an express it did not move so quickly that it was impossible to focus on the places indicated and the land being flat it was easy to pick out temples and villages some miles away. At Mathura they suggested that I should go there some time and see the many sites associated with Krishna; a good Hindu guide would be needed who could provide details of the mythology linked with the area. Surprisingly soon we arrived at our destination, Agra, where my friends took me to their home in the cantonment and gave me some refreshment before sending me off to the Taj with a guide who was known to them and could be trusted to be helpful. In fact, I was booked into a tour that included Fatehpur Sikri, the large fort and palace vacated by the emperors because the water supply failed. It is an important place to visit for it is not only the open prison where Shah Jehan, the husband of Mumtaz Mahal, spent his last days but also poignantly, one can stand where he did looking across the Jumna river to her tomb. The Taj itself is magnificent standing as it does at the end of a garden which should also be explored. Modern research suggests that it was planned by a Sufi mystic to resemble the Garden of Paradise. It is, of course, the monument that catches the eye and holds the attention. What might Wordsworth have been moved to write had he seen it?

Earth has not anything to show more fair
Dull would he be of soul who could pass by
A sight so touching in its majesty;

Oh I know it was the River Thames that held him spell bound but surely buildings, temples and palaces provided a context. How might he have responded to the Taj?

Some feminists cannot escape associating it with the fact that the emperor was so infatuated with his wife that he could not be without her and took her on all his military campaigns and other journeys, so it is scarcely surprising that after some thirteen pregnancies and almost giving birth while travelling, she died. In the twenty-first century this appears and is a strange way of demonstrating affection and devotion but five hundred years ago it might seem no worse than British officers who brought their wives to India to die of fever or left them at home desolate while they consoled themselves with local women wherever they went. Our feminist daughters, it must be said, when I had the joy of taking them to the Taj, did not feel that their visit had been spoiled by the tragic circumstances that prompted the construction of the mausoleum. Sad that it took so tragic a death to inspire such an architectural feat! Worse is the savagery of Shah Jehan who, it is said, had the eyes of the architect put out so that he could never again build anything so magnificent.

I enjoyed the best of experiences as it was the time of the full moon and in those days the Taj was open to visitors at night. My friends took me to enjoy the spectacle and then, after a drink and a light supper let me have the loan of their bedroom whilst they slept outside in the court-yard; apart from the midges they probably spent a better night enjoying the cool air of an as yet unpolluted city.

Next day they escorted me back to the station where I caught my train to Delhi. All this time, except for my rail ticket, they had not allowed me to pay for anything, such was their hospitality, expressed in equal measure by Jamila and George, Dr Mansukhani and so many other hosts that I met in India and Britain. It is shameful for me therefore to record that I behaved no better than many other tourists on my return to Delhi. It was now dark and when the taxi drew up at Haus Khaz I felt that the driver was overcharging me. I began to argue. George, who had been listening out for my arrival, came to the garden gate; when he learned what the reason was for the commotion he told me to pay, apologised to the driver and took me into the house. There he pointed out that driving a taxi at night was risky and that fares were put up accordingly, that I was a sahib, and that even if I was to pay over the odds India was still in a state of considerable deficit. He also told me of ways in which he had been ripped off in England. I felt truly ashamed and vowed never to haggle again with anyone in India but to consider that I was only making some small recompense for the predations of my fellow countrymen.

In my absence I had not been out of my hosts' minds. Next day Jamila informed that plans had been made for my visit to Pakistan and a seat had been booked on the weekly Kabul flight that landed at Lahore. She also gave me phone numbers and addresses of relatives in Lahore, her home before 1948, and told me that she was preparing a parcel of clothing for me to take to them.

CHAPTER
8

Pakistan

The one weekly flight to Lahore was on a Sunday. Jamila and George took me to Palam airport and saw me safely through check in. The plane was full, mostly of passengers going to Pakistan and as we journeyed my thoughts turned to Lahore and I became more anxious. It was Sunday and probably banks would be closed. In both India and Pakistan the Raj survived in a number of ways, one of which was the British weekend when all banks and schools closed. This took place at one o'clock on Saturday and lasted until Monday morning. I had no Pakistani currency because it was impossible to obtain it legally in India or England. Jamila and my friend Dr Iqbal who had arranged my stay, could do nothing for me now. Panic was no solution but what was the alternative? As I looked round the plane a familiar face came to my attention and its owner began to smile and wave, then rose to his feet and walked down the aisle in my direction. It was Mr Dharr, a Muslim bookseller from Bradford who was well known to me as I had bought books from him for my own library and the college. He asked me what I was doing and insisted that I should accompany him to a relative in Lahore with whom he was staying. For the first time but by no means the last I realised that plan as one may and must, it is not possible to be prepared for every eventuality in the sub-continent but there is some kind of greater presence that takes over and sorts out things. So it had been when I had to move from Dr Mansukhani's residence, so it was as Jamila and George planned my activities, so it was at Agra and so it was now as we came to Lahore. We arrived on a chilly but fine morning whilst it was still dark. A car was awaiting us and drove us to a house some miles away. It was still dark, so much so that I could scarcely make out the silhouette of the buffalo that was being driven from house to house delivering milk. It was some thirty years ago, when as a child in Bradford, that I last saw a cow being milked and warm milk being delivered to the house, Here, of course, as in India, it was always boiled before being used. The waiting men folk welcomed me graciously and soon I was sitting down to breakfast. Politely they enquired the purpose of my visit and my destination before inviting me to telephone my host and arranging to take me to the station. They did not change my money from English notes to Pakistani rupees, but gave me sufficient for my journey and paid for my train ticket. When I thanked them, they said they were only doing their duty. The word duty has a cold ring to it when used in England, or at least I think so. When Muslims use the word it means much more than a legal obligation laid upon them by their religion. There is warmth, generosity and kindness caught up in it. They walk the second mile with joy. What they meant by duty had been borne out many times in England; it was to be amplified in Pakistan.

My hosts spoke to a group of passengers in Urdu, explaining who I was and asking them to help me, but most of them had left before I reached Salarwala. Two were left, a young man and one who was about forty years old. As we passed through the flat countryside I made notes of things that I saw, mostly houses of unburnt brick, with the occasional burned brick mosque, and took some photographs. The older man who was sitting opposite me, began to eye me with some suspicion and at last took out a service revolver and accused me of being a spy. Fortunately my friend Iqbal had written a brief letter in Urdu and English that said: 'The bearer, Mr Cole, is a friend of Islam, it is your duty to help him'. I passed it cautiously across the compartment. The man read it, put away his revolver, stood up and shook me by the hand warmly. From then on we chatted amicably until I reached my station, where he helped me put my luggage on the platform and made sure there were people to help me. Then he shook my hand again warmly and returned to the carriage.

Four of the Sufi sheikh's followers or mureeds were waiting for me at the station, Mr Dharr had told them which train to expect. All of them spoke excellent English and welcomed me, dividing my luggage between them. The Sufi centre or kanqah was only a short distance away so we could walk to it in a few minutes. As we went along the dusty unmade road another group of young men came towards us. Two were carrying a large cardboard box about three feet by two feet square and six inches deep. They opened it to display a variety of about twenty cream cakes which they invited me to eat. I had the presence of mind to take one and then asked everyone else to help me tackle the rest. After taking a second one I protested that I could eat no more, so the box was closed and we proceeded to the kanqah where Babaji awaited us.

The buildings were single storey, a mixture of kuccha and pukka bricks; the main or largest of these was a mosque of burnt brick plastered over in yellow with the qibla wall facing westwards towards Mecca, unlike the ones I was accustomed to in England and Wales which, of course, faced eastwards. There seemed to be only one entrance to the compound on the other side of which was a separate enclosed area where the women folk lived. One could hear them, and I was aware of them looking at this strange white visitor, but I could not see any of them.

Babaji, the spiritual head of the community and its leader in every way, was an ex-army officer. His English and his organisation were excellent and no one questioned his authority. During the day he might go out visiting or sit working in his office, where he was when I first met him. In the evening he would sit on a low chair in the courtyard with his male followers cross-legged at his feet, giving them spiritual instruction, much like the Hindu gurus I had met and would see many times. If I had been away in one of the villages, he would make way for me and insist that I sat on what I can only describe as his gaddi. Any attempts that I made to refuse were dismissed; his disciples looked on silently, appreciating the honour that was being done to me. I should point out that in his absence the seat always remained unoccupied. Considerable attention was paid to my well-being. I could have had a room of my own, but indicated my wish to sleep with the other mureeds in the mosque and share in the ablutions before prayers. This willingness to be at one with the community was appreciated and well received, it also meant that I learned much more about its life than I would have done if I had allowed myself to be treated as a guest, but they did not impose their customs on me. The first night I was so heavily asleep that I was unaware of the mosquitoes that made a meal of me. When I awoke my right arm that I must have used to fend them off was covered in bites, as was my face down to my cheeks. I had taken no anti-malarial drugs and was relieved not to have caught the disease, as I had once seen my dad shivering on a chair on a hot summer's day by the open back door in Bradford. He caught malaria in the Balkans in 1918. I woke to find the prayer line that had quietly gathered around me; as I heard everyone quietly reciting 'Allah o akbar', I rose to join them. Earlier in the day the time for noon prayer came very soon after my arrival. What should I do? I decided to stand behind the Muslims and remain in that position throughout the cycle of prayer. Afterwards a number of young Muslims gathered around me and one of them asked me if this was the way I prayed rather than theirs? I decided that I could not really explain my situation and decided to adopt their positions as well as their words. This caused me no difficulties as I already knew that 'Allah' is used as the name of God by many Christians in the Near East and I also felt that if I couldn't join in their worship, I had no real right to partake in the rest of their fellowship. Initially Muslim practice had presented a challenge – and a moment of growth. On other occasions when I was travelling to neighbouring villages and a prayer time arrived

I was invited to lead prayer, to act as the imam, when my companions had drawn a rectangle in the sand with a line pointing to Makka; that was a kind invitation that I felt it proper not to accept, but I did remove my shoes and join them in the prayer line inside the area.

The headman of a local village had come in his car to collect me and show me the sights. Suddenly he stopped the car and listened intently. A sound of celebratory singing was coming from part of the village which, he told me, was where the Christians lived. We drove in that direction and on reaching it found a large group of women singing and dancing. He questioned them in Urdu and then informed me that it was an engagement party. Bashfully, a young woman was presented to me who, I was told, was the young girl at the centre of the celebrations. Only the women of the village were present; the menfolk were in the groom's village celebrating with him and his family. It was explained to me that this was an arranged marriage, the young couple had not yet met and would not until the day of the wedding which would be held in this the bride's village. She would then go to live with her husband's family. When they realised that I was Christian the ladies asked if I would like to visit their church which I did, first removing my shoes. It was a cool building constructed of unburnt brick and 'L' shaped. At the intersection of the 'L' was a table on which stood a white cloth with a small wooden cross in its centre. I was told that the women of the congregation sat on the floor in one arm of the 'L' while the men sat in the other. Thus neither of them could see one another, but all could see the focal point, the altar and cross. This seemed pleasingly authentic. Before I left they insisted upon singing a number of hymns in Urdu. Community relations in the village seemed good; we had all been well received, though unexpected, and the headman treated the Christian minority with respect. After a cup of sweet tea we departed.

Not all occasions were of a religious nature. One day I was taken to see sugar cane being planted. Two buffaloes pulled a plough round a field while six men followed pushing pieces of cane into the ground. The headman looked at me and remarked that I must think this was rather a backward way of doing things. Using a tractor the whole job could be done in an hour. And using the newly built sugar refinery in a nearby town, the harvest could be milled in less than a day. But, he went on, what of the villagers? They would have nothing to do and could earn no money. The ways of the West were not necessarily right for them.

One day when I was being taken round some of the villages, a group of young boys gathered around my stationary car and began to shout something that sounded like 'chitta, chitta', white man, white man. My companions spoke to them sharply and the group went away; this was the only example I ever came across of what might be called racism. It was, of course, merely the curiosity of boys who had never before seen anyone with my skin colour.

On the second night of my stay in the kanqah, Babaji introduced me to a young man who was to act as my stenographer. Each evening I would sit with him and he would write down, at my dictation, whatever I had done during the past day. It turned out that he was employed in a similar capacity in the local town but had been summoned at Babaji's bidding to serve me. His employer had released him without asking questions. If Babaji needed him that was enough for him. When I questioned the steno and suggested to Babaji that he might return, it became clear that society did not work like that in Pakistan. What might have happened in the UK had a visitor turned up from abroad and the local bank manager or school master had been asked to release one of his staff indefinitely to meet the local vicar's needs? So it was also with a doctor of medicine who was also a mureed and appointed to be my companion.

Patients had heard that the doctor had come to the kanqah and came to visit him; there were no women or teenage girls who, I was told, would be seen by a woman doctor elsewhere. I was allowed to sit in on some of the consultations. After some discussion and an examination, medicines were usually prescribed. Some were given by the doctor, others had to be obtained from a village dispensary run by the Sufi teacher and his followers. Patients were given a scrap of paper on which the doctor wrote a verse from the Qur'an as well as details of the medication or a few pills which were wrapped in it. It was pointed out to me that he, the doctor, was not the healer, but Allah, hence the verse from scripture. The next day I was invited to go to the town and stay with the doctor for a few days. Dusk comes early in the sub-continent, whatever the time of year; the doctor took me to an empty carriage, checked that I would be alright for the few minutes he would be away and headed up the platform where, being nosey, I saw him talking to a porter who gestured towards a large red arrow. This indicated the direction of Makka. The doctor took out a large white handkerchief which he spread on the platform and said his prayers. As he rose I ducked back into the carriage to await his return.

My room was upstairs in the house where he lived with his mother and sister who was also a doctor. The room was airy with the typical high ceiling found in India and Pakistan, in the centre of which was a fan. The furniture was sparse, a single bed, a chair and table, a couple of pictures, and the usual en-suite bathroom and toilet. Simple but clean and hospitable. We chatted for a brief time until a gentle knock came at the door, which the doctor opened. A hand holding a tray reached round it; my host took it without comment and placed it on the table. It contained our supper. While I was with him, the same procedure was always followed. At the end of my stay, I asked if I might thank his mother and sister for their hospitality, only to be told that he would tell them of my gratitude. From the barred bedroom window I did manage once or twice to catch a glimpse of the sister, a slim woman in her late twenties, dressed in shalwar kameeze, and once her mother who was dressed in black.

Jamila had made arrangements for me to stay with her relatives for one weekend, so after lunch I took my leave of Babaji and made my way to the station escorted by two of his mureeds.

The carriage was like those used on southern railways in England until recently; an aisle running its length on one side and seats facing one another. I sat in the middle as a young man from the local military airfield, going on leave, had the window seat. As usual I looked out of the window and made notes. The carriage was fairly full, but for some time it was as silent as an English compartment until the cadet turned to me to ask whether many people were left handed in my country, as I was. I replied that there were and asked him about Pakistan. He told me there were none, but then I mentioned Purvez, a left-arm spin bowler in the current Pakistan cricket team. He replied that perhaps there must be some. Just as I was preparing to discuss cricket a large man sitting directly opposite me clapped me on the knees with both hands and said: 'You are a Christian; you believe in three gods!'. His tone was one of affirmation rather than interrogation. I replied that I was a Christian and to my surprise found myself defending, or perhaps, more accurately attempting to explain the Trinity for the next hour until we reached Lahore. His view that Christians believed in God the Father, Jesus the Son and Mary his Mother, was one that I had often heard expressed. His charge of tritheism was even more familiar and a number of Jews, whom I knew well, had also expressed it. When I hear of Christians talking about the 'three monotheistic faiths' I am both amused and annoyed; amused because I know that many Jews and Muslims do not regard us as monotheists, and annoyed because of the tendency to exclude Hindus and Sikhs whose religious edifice might be said to be based on a profound concept of oneness. I tried to explain what the Trinity was, Father, Son and Holy Spirit, though I realised that he was not open to being convinced. (It is not difficult to be aware that an argument is going nowhere, with students it may be the glazed eye look, with him it was just the expression and his eagerness to make his next point while trying

90

to hold his tongue as I made my comments. Clearly he was playing to the gallery, that is to all the passengers in the carriage, some of whom climbed on the seat behind me, the rest standing on the seat behind him. As we approached Lahore he asked me what I was doing in Pakistan. When I replied that I had come to learn about Islam he was very pleased and the discussion took on a general flavour, with him suggesting places I might visit in Lahore. At the station he sought assurances that I was going to be met and then he and the other thirty or so passengers, all men, accompanied me to the proposed meeting point at the entrance, those who could taking a piece of my luggage. Before leaving me everyone shook my hand and a few, like the man with whom I had enjoyed my discussion, hugged me. As I stood musing on their friendly kindness my host drew up in a car.

The weekend was interesting in several ways. I met, not for the first or last time, Christians who longed for the Raj to return. They had enjoyed a privileged position and it can never be easy to forsake such things. On Sunday we attended a service in English at the cathedral, the 1662 Eucharist as found in the Book of Common Prayer. The congregation was not very large and consisted mostly of men and women of middle age or older. I could not help contrasting this experience with the visit to the villagers and the 'L' shaped church that I had seen a few days earlier. That seemed more wholesome, more promising in terms of a church having a future in a country in which it existed as a minority. Unlike the early church that had no past about which to be nostalgic it had enjoyed security and some kind of status and possibly prestige and privilege.

After the service I was taken to 'Chiefs' College', where Jamila had studied and the great cricketer Imran Khan's family had been educated. I saw the pitch on which he would learn his cricket some years later. The ground was splendidly green because, I was told, it was flooded twice a week. Among the staff I met a teacher of Islamiat who had published a few books in English introducing teenagers to Muslim prayer and other aspects of the faith. He gave me some copies of this very useful series and I bought others for the library at James Graham. Ramadan was about to begin so he asked to be permitted not to take food at lunch time; his family, he told me, lived in the hills in northern Pakistan, they would sight the new moon of fast breaking a day or more before Muslims on the plain, so if he began his fast on the day that everyone else did he would arrive to find that they had already enjoyed the party at the end of the fast – and he did not want to miss out on a party. In contrast to this teacher was a university lecturer whom I met. He welcomed me but told me to learn Urdu before I next came to Pakistan as no one would speak English. He went on to assure me that all text-books even at university level would be in Urdu, even if it meant translating pages from important science journals. This seemed to take nationalism to the degree of self-disfigurement.

In Lahore I learned of a Christian centre engaged in dialogue with Muslims that existed in Rawalpindi, but whether it was there or back at the Sufi kanqah that I was given the name of a host who would help me, I cannot remember. However, I do know that it was Babaji who made my travel arrangements. He thought the enterprise might be worthwhile and expressed interest in my findings, to be reported to and written down by the steno on my return. He had often expressed pleasure that Iqbal, the friend who had arranged my visit, was active in the area of inter-religious dialogue, it was also something close to his heart. A day or two later I was escorted to the place where I could obtain transport to Rawalpindi. It was outside an hotel cum restaurant where a number of transit vans stood, their drivers vying for custom. The mureeds explained who I was and where I wanted to go and I was told to sit inside one of the vans. Some minutes later I was asked to move to another one and then to a third. It appeared the vans left when they were full so, in a manner that seemed good humoured, each poached the prospective passengers of the other with the result that I was aboard the first van to leave. A few English speakers in the party sat by me and looked after me as they had promised Babaji's disciples. About half way along the journey the van drew into a hotel forecourt and I was told that this was our one refreshment stop; being ready for a cup of tea and the toilet, I followed my companions only to discover that they had gone round to the back of the hotel where there were several mats laid out facing westwards and there they said their prayers whilst I looked on. Only after praying did they turn to a consideration of their bodily needs and once again, they paid the bill. A chauffeur driven car awaited me at Rawalpindi and I was soon in one of the most opulent houses that I have ever seen. Its owner was a high-ranking retired military officer, though as a conscientious objector I have little knowledge of military status beyond the rank of corporal which my father had held in the First World War. Cups, shields and other trophies as well as photographs bore witness to a past spent in sporting activity and membership of clubs; the large and spacious rooms were elegantly furnished. Maids and servants attended to the family's needs; it comprised the officer's wife, two daughters and a son who was away on army duty. The younger daughter was an undergraduate busy at the studies and the parents seemed to spend much of their time socialising, so I was left with the older daughter, a qualified doctor, who was engaged to be married. How different this was from the few days I spent with the doctor who was Babaji's disciple and whose mother and sister I had never met. The daughter enquired about women in England and was very surprised to learn that they might continue to undertake paid work after marriage, though she realised that that might be a way of life for ladies in the villages, however, those like herself who would be married to professorial men, her fiancé was an officer, would only do voluntary work once they were married. The British way of life was of great interest to her; I felt that one day she would like to migrate to the UK or to the USA.

The Christian centre consisted of two middle-aged priests and one young man who remained silent during our conversations in the manner usual for men or women like himself in the presence of his elders. How often have I heard elders of various faiths encouraging their children to express their views when I have known full well that it would have been ill mannered for them to do so. At one gathering I mentioned this and the younger members expressed their agreement while their seniors said that although it might be the custom, we could make an exception on this occasion. I suggested that it might be fine now, but what about when I had gone, wouldn't they rebuke the young. I was met by sheepish grins all round!

The older Christians told me that there was not much dialogue taking place at the moment. Circumstances were not congenial for it. They also conveyed a wistful longing for the days of the Raj and almost gave me to believe that there was a possibility that the British would return. My spirits fell. As I took my leave the young Christian rose and followed me. In the passage outside the room he asked if I could spare him a minute or two. Of course I said I could. He then asked me not to go away thinking that what I had heard was the only Christian voice, he was a Christian and a Pakistani, who had to work out his future in the light of those two realities. Here was reassurance. Perhaps there was a future for Christianity in Pakistan after all. Some years later I was assessing an examination for the International Baccalaureate and found myself reading the paper of a Pakistani Christian. Its representation of Islam was not only inaccurate, it was objectionable and disgusting. Not only did he fail, but the IB may have suggested that he should be withdrawn from the course. If there are Christians who can honestly hold such an ignorant and almost evil view of Islam, might there be Muslims who believe similar calumnies about Christianity? It may not be the task of Religious Education to convert students from one religion to another but, in common with education generally, it is its duty to convert students from shallow insights based upon propaganda and lies provided by missionaries of all faiths, by developing their critical faculties.

It was time to say goodbye to Babaji and his mureeds after submitting my final report that had been typed up by the stenographer and duly signed. On my last night I was invited to walk round the village while my supper was prepared. As I left the compound, a man holding a beautiful cockerel asked me how I liked my chicken; I would like to have replied. 'Alive', but I knew that would not have been understood so I replied, 'In a stew', knowing that as usual in my sub-continental experiences, my expressed preference would be conditioned by decisions already taken in the kitchen.

The next day I had a final look around old parts of Lahore, admiring its buildings and the wonderfully carved wooden balconies and doors. Reluctantly in many ways, I set out for the frontier crossing at Wagah the next day, sad at leaving such a beautiful country and so many kind and generous friends, who like many Indians and Pakistanis replied to my protestations of gratitude by saying: 'Why do you British keep on saying thank you? We know you are grateful; your smile and your voice tell us'; or, 'If we came to your country you would treat us in the same way'. Oh dear. I hoped their illusion would never be shattered.

Wagah was nothing like the scene of daily drama that we may have seen on our televisions screens during 2007 with its strutting peacock-like soldiers eyeballing one another while crowds shout 'Pakistan zindabad' or Ji Hind', to egg them on. The bus stopped some hundred meters from the frontier post; but it seemed more like a kilometre in the hot sun, especially as no porters were allowed. A Sikh officer asked me the purpose of my visit, when I told him it was to study Sikhism in Amritsar, he looked very dubious and made me open every piece of my luggage. I have since discovered that a requirement for being a passport or customs official is to have no sense of humour! This was my first lesson.

9

Back to India

Lahore and Amritsar, once respectively the political and religious centres of Sikhism, are separated by a distance of only some forty kilometres. Even by 1973 they seemed worlds apart. Things had gone well for India since independence whereas Pakistan suffered already from political difficulties that are still ongoing and the expense of its recent war with its neighbour that had resulted in a cease-fire, but not yet a peace treaty. There was another difference; Pakistanis were celebrating twenty-five years of independence when I was there but when I spoke to Indians about the anniversary I was met with rather surprised expressions and a rhetorical question: Why should we celebrate twenty five years when our country is twenty-five centuries old?'

My immediate destination was Khalsa College, a late Victorian building standing imposingly on the western outskirts of the city. Two peons stood at the gate awaiting the arrival of the bus; one of them helped me alight and took my luggage while the other ran into the college to inform my host of my arrival. Hospitality had been arranged by Dr Mansukhani who knew the college and my host well. He was Professor Parkash Singh, an historian. He greeted me warmly, took me to his house where I would be staying and provided me with tea and biscuits before discussing my itinerary. My first request was to send a telegram to our youngest daughter Siân, whose eighth birthday it was. A letter would have taken a week at least to reach Leeds and greetings cards or picture cards generally were not yet part of Indian culture. The telegram would also act as an assurance to Gwynneth that I was safely back in India, for there was always a chance that Wagah might be closed or that something else had delayed me in Pakistan for another week.

My first sighting of the Harimandir Sahib, or Golden Temple, to use the name given to it by the British, was not what I expected. The gold leaf building was exactly as I had seen it in photographs or paintings in the homes of Sikh friends but the rectangular lake that surrounded it was a sea of mud. Periodically, the sarovar, to use the Sikh name, is drained and the accumulated silt removed. This had last taken place in 1923. Sikhs had come from near and far to participate in this voluntary work, known as seva. Some had walked; others had travelled by horse and cart or bus. None in those days owned cars. They cleared the earth in metal bowls which they filled and carried as directed to a dumping ground.

My guide insisted that I remove my socks as well as shoes; previously in Delhi or England the taking off of shoes was regarded as sufficient. He also preferred me to wear a turban which he tied as well as he could instead of a large handkerchief, my usual covering. We walked round the marbled side of the lake in a clockwise direction, receiving God's grace in our right hands, as I was told. The marble blistered my feet and I was pleased when men threw buckets of water on the surface, not so much to cool it as to clean it from the muddy footprints of pilgrims. Later I learned that if I could keep to the black pieces of marble they were cooler than the white but no one told me at the time. Parkash watched me hopping quickly from place to place and spoke about India getting its own back for the Raj. Not always have I appreciated the undoubted humour of Punjabis, this was one such occasion. Unimpeded by the volunteer workers, we made our way passing places associated with Sikh history such as the plaque in the pavement where Baba Deep Singh fell mortally wounded. It is said that during Mughal–Sikh wars he had fought his way from Taran Taran, a town some thirty kilometres distant to the Harimandir Sahib, vowing that he would reach it before he died. Carrying his head in is hand he struggled to the shrine, fighting all the way. This story reminded me of one that I had heard as a child which told of decapitated Indian soldiers fighting their way from the Somme to Berlin and I couldn't help wondering whether the volunteer Indian army of the First World War, largely Sikh, had regarded Baba Deep Singh as a model. We crossed the causeway leading from the parkarma to the Harimandir building passing Lachi Ber, the tree where Guru Arjan sat in meditation, on the way. A Sikh sat reading the Guru Granth Sahib in the central room of the Harimandir and we sat listening to him for a while. Parkash then motioned me to follow him and let me onto a veranda that ran round the building on all four sides. There are four entrances to the Harimandir facing the four main compass directions; these I was told symbolise the belief that it should be open to everyone wherever they came from, and whoever they are. Some Hindu mandirs will not admit people like me supposing them, quite properly, to be meat eaters who will pollute the building. Sikhs should not believe in ritual purity or pollution or in the social hierarchy of the caste system. Symbolism is also expressed through the fact that instead of climbing steps to reach the sanctuary in a mandir, one goes down them in the Harimandir Sahib; only

by being humble can one meet God. We then proceeded on our peram-
bulation passing the tree, Ber Baba Buddha, where the elderly, almost
centenarian Sikh, had helped supervise the compiling of the first copy of
the Sikh scripture, the Adi Granth, whose verses he knew by heart.
Collecting our shoes, we then made our way back to Khalsa College by
rickshaw via Singh Brothers, probably the most famous Sikh bookseller
in Amritsar.

The Darbar Sahib made a great and lasting impression on me and I
have visited it four or five times since first seeing it, though sadly not with
our daughter Siân. When I took her to India in 1985 Punjab was closed
to non-punjabis, not only foreigners, because of the post Bhindranwale
emergency. The focal point, the Harimandir Sahib, is not large compared
with some other gurdwaras, cathedrals or mosques, but it is impressive
and despite the broadcast sound of the ragis chanting from the sacred
book and the hubbub of visitors, there is a wonderful stillness as one looks
at it across the water, and I say this as one who is not normally aware of
atmosphere, even when I stand in the centre of my most loved sacred
space, the cathedral at Durham, though I may be more overawed by it
than the American who disembarked from a coach on Palace Green to
take the obligatory photograph just as I was passing and said; 'What a
glorious God box!'. No wonder Sikhs find it an auspicious place to visit,
as a newly married couple and their friends or relatives who accompanied them did, standing on the pool side and praying towards the shining
building, during one of my later pilgrimages, even though the Gurus
taught that no trust should be put in sacred places or holy days. It is not
surprising that almost every Sikh home that I have visited has a large
photograph of the building displayed prominently in its living room.

That evening I had supper with Parkash and his wife. When we met
I offered her my hand as hand-shaking was now fairly customary in
England with Sikh and Hindu women but not Muslims. Parkash, whose
English was impeccable, tapped me gently on the right wrist saying; 'My
wife will not be touched up by you!' I knew exactly what he meant and
instead I put my hands together and we greeted one another with the
words 'Sat sri akal'. She then withdrew to the kitchen and I was invited
to take my place at the table. Shortly afterwards Parkash's young son,
whom I had not yet met, came from the kitchen with our meal and stood
by waiting on us. He had become an honorary daughter for the evening
and so did not have his supper until we had finished, when he joined his
mother. If he had had a sister, he would have sat at table while she served
the three of us.

Next morning it was suggested that I went to Jallianwala Bagh but that

I left before noon. This memorial garden was the enclosed area where Brigadier General Dyer ordered his troops to fire on a gathering of Punjabis, many of them Sikhs, who were resting and sheltering from the heat on Baisakhi day, April 13 1919. Such assemblies had been declared unlawful by the government, but instead of instructing the crowd to disperse, the General ordered his troops, Gurkhas, to open fire. The fugitives could not escape, there was only one entrance and the soldiers were between it and them. Over three hundred people died, some by jumping into the well that can still be seen, to escape the bullets, marks of which can still be seen in some of the remaining walls. This event, more than any other single act, led to the 'Quit India' campaign and spelled the end of the Raj, though it was not to come for another thirty years. The film *Gandhi* shows the Mahatma and Nehru looking down the well but Sikhs deny that they ever went to the Bagh or showed any real concern for the massacre. Gandhi is not a popular figure among Sikhs.

When I arrived back at the college Parkash had a surprise waiting for me. He had told me that he was going to be busy with something special, but had not said what it was. He asked me to cover my head, take off my shoes and follow him into a small room, which I saw contained a copy of the Guru Granth Sahib towards which I bowed touching the floor with my head before sitting cross-legged in front of it. Parkash sat on a small stool on the other side of the scripture, closed his eyes for a moment and then picked up a silver fan, known as a chauri with yak hairs embedded in it, and waved it over the Book which he then opened at random, and began to read from it. When he had finished, he translated the words for my benefit. These, he said, were a vak, God's words of spiritual guidance; after reading them he closed the Book. As we left the gurdwara, for that was what is was as it had a copy of the scripture installed in it, Parkash explained that he had longed to have a room where he could read it but his previous flat had been too small; now he and his wife could visit Babaji whenever they liked, to read and meditate upon God's word. This had been the surprise and I was grateful and honoured that Parkash had shared it with me. By now daylight and evening were coming together in dusk and as we walked back to the house I could hear Parkash's wife, walking in the garden, singing the evening hymn known as Rahiras in a sweet, gentle, but just audible voice.

I had been told a story concerning Parkash's family that illustrates well the value of the extended family. His father had died leaving him with an elder brother and six sisters as well as the mother. The brother took responsibility for his mother and the rest of the family while Parkash was sent to university to complete his education. Once he had graduated, he found employment so that he could care for the family, and the first brother now went to university, gained a degree and began to earn a living. Each of the sisters completed her education and marriages were arranged for them, beginning with the oldest as is normal in Indian society. Only then did the sons marry and the older one took their mother to live with him permanently. Of course, in no cases did a dowry change hands; the best of Sikh traditions were scrupulously observed.

In the West we often have difficulty getting our heads around arranged marriages though the value of extended families is usually well understood. This story demonstrates its worth and brings out especially the family as a support agency. Old people's home are rare in India though I have visited a very pleasant one in Taran Taran, set up by Sikhs. Elderly dependants are cared for by their children and this fact goes some way to explaining why families are often large and sons greatly valued. Retirement pensions may be enjoyed by teachers and civil servant and business employees but for the vast majority one's children, especially sons, are one's pension. Daughters leave home when they marry and their parents cannot traditionally expect any help from them if they are in need, though affection often overcomes rigid principle. Obligation need not guarantee affection; the elderly can be made to feel that they are a burden on their children, though this may be rare as there is a strong belief in respect for seniority in Indian and Pakistani society. Thirty years on from my initial visit, there are some signs, however, that one of the bad effects of modernisation is a tendency to consider old folks to be a nuisance.

Two factors influence the survival of the system of arranged marriages in addition to tradition. One is the fact that in rural areas boys and girls do not tend to mix after puberty except with their own relatives, so if falling in love western style were the norm many young people might have to wait for a very long time. In cities things may be changing, but village roots are strong then their influence stretches into the towns. By going off the rails there children may be harming their families in the villages, in the same way that what young people do in Leeds or London can have unpleasant consequences for their families in the sub-continent. Secondly, there is also a very commonsense reason for marriages to be arranged as these usually take place within occupational groups. Without going into details, the family of a potter will marry into another potter family and those of a goldsmith into a goldsmith family. Think of the consequences of a goldsmith's daughter entering a potter's family; what use would she be? She would probably be unemployable and if she had been well educated she might start encouraging her new sisters-in-law to question the traditions in which they had been nurtured. It could be even more disastrous if she wielded such an influence upon the young men in her new family that they forsook the occupation that their ancestors had followed for many generations. Who would keep the business going, and who would be left to care for the family in its old age? Extended families and arranged marriages might be described as the cement holding together Indian society.

Not only do an appreciable number of second and third generation children living in the West accept arranged marriages, though 'assisted' may be a better term for young people are likely to have a considerable say in their choice of partners, meeting one another under family oversight, going out together, discussing their joint aspirations, and then mutually agreeing with their parents' suggestion, But I have met couples or unmarried singles who are prepared to say that 'mummy and daddy' know best, as one successful young executive told me. Others may not know about love marriages despite western TV and films and Bolliwood as, for example, a young couple who once gave me hospitality. At breakfast conversation turned to family as it frequently does; when the twenty-nine year old wife learned that our daughters were in their early twenties and about to graduate, she assumed that we must be looking for husbands. My reply, that they would choose their own, shocked her; when she discovered that this was the norm in my culture she expressed the thought that this was a good idea and, putting her hand gently on her husband's knee, said, with a smile, 'And I wouldn't have chosen you!'

When he looked suitably crestfallen, she gave him a slight kiss on the cheek and assured him that she was only teasing. As far as I could discern they were very much in love! Their two young daughters who attended an English medium school could surely look forward to fulfilling lives that would be the envy of many westerners.

Of course arranged marriages can go wrong as in western royal circles recently, not only in the novels of Charles Dickens. In Asian societies a family head living in Pakistan or India can prescribe the chosen partner for a nephew in the UK or America, because of some local agreement that will further the needs of the family, not taking into account the fact that the bride or groom who has been selected will be unsuitable for someone brought up and educated abroad, who may know little of the mores or language of their supposed home culture. Occasionally British-born Asians, including Christians, may ask their families to find an Indian-born wife who will not be used to western ways and might be presumed to stay at home and be little more than a domestic servant, in preference to a girl who wants to party, socialise or go out to work and enjoy a life of her own to some extent. Male chauvinism can be alive and well and living in Slough, Southall or Sheffield, as much as it ever did in Glasgow, Greenwich or the leafy lanes of Guisley.

One important aspect of my stay in Amritsar that had yet to be undertaken, was a visit to Pingalwara. The name means a home for cripples. Puran Singh was born in the Lahore region of the Punjab in 1904 and devoted much of his time to the service of the gurdwara in that town. One day in 1936, he arrived at the gurdwara to commence his duties as a sevadar to find what looked like a bundle of rags on the pavement outside. On closer examination it turned out to be a young man, a cripple, possibly suffering from cerebral palsy, who had been left there by someone incapable of looking after him. Puran Singh began to care for him and they became constant companions. When India was partitioned in 1947, Puran Singh decided to leave the Muslim state of Pakistan for India and took the disabled man whom he called Piara on his back (The name means 'loved one'), which Puran Singh described as a garland around his neck. He came to the Khalsa College on the outskirts of Amritsar, where I was to stay some twenty-five years later, which was then a crowded refugee camp. Eventually, most people were resettled or found their way to relatives in the Indian Punjab, the only ones being left behind being lame, blind, or mentally disturbed men and women whose families could no longer care for them. Instead of only having Piara to look after, Puran Singh found himself responsible for many more. He turned to Sikh charitable agencies and until his death in 1992 cared for all who came his way, and Piara. Whenever I went to the Darbar Sahib I saw them sitting on a bench near the entrance, sometimes with other members of his needy family. Through Parkash Singh I was not only able to go round the Pingalwara, I also spent some time talking to Puran Singh as he gave us a conducted tour, though Piara being unable to talk could only smile. The Pingalwara is not far from Darbar Sahib but is separated from the road by a high wall. As we passed through the gateway we were met by a variety of smells, the most pleasing was that of food cooking, the rest were of urine and faeces as many of the patients were incontinent. Some were sitting on chairs or benches, but a large number were chained to their beds for their own safety and that of the volunteers who were either resident or came daily to assist Puran Singh, who had long been given the honorific title of 'Bhagat', meaning holy one. He told me that he depended on charities and various Sikh institutions for support. The Indian government had offered him money, but besides caring for the needy he criticised policies that resulted in environmental pollution and the destruction of forests, not only because of the damage to the country-

101

side, but also the process meant that villagers had no kindling for their stoves. The Bhagat had a strongly developed all-round social conscience and as an environmentalist long before the term had ever been coined. His inspiration in caring for the needy was, he told me, Dr Barnado, whose policy of the ever open door he had embraced. Before we left he asked me to appeal for funds in the Leeds gurdwara. This I did and within ten minutes the congregation raised seventy pounds, an appreciable sum in 1973 considering that it was done with no prior warning and that most of the members were fairly low-paid blue-collar workers. Some of them continued to give regular donations or remembered the Pingalwara on the birth of a child or death of a relative when it is customary to make charitable gifts.

I left Amritsar and the company of Parkash Singh and his family reluctantly but greatly enriched spiritually, their warm and genuine friendship following up on the generosity and kindness of Muslims I had met in Pakistan and the futuristic outlook of some of its Christians, which opened my eyes to a new world. When I returned to Yorkshire and recounted some of my experiences to members of YCCR I was not best pleased when one of them, a Christian priest opined, 'Ah Christ in Islam'; I'm afraid I replied, 'No, Allah in Islam'.

Even my journey back to Delhi was slightly memorable. I was booked on the overnight express that ran from Amritsar to Bombay, reaching Delhi at about 8 a.m. My berth was shared with a heavily bearded Sikh who had already commandeered the top bunk. He had changed into his night attire by the time I arrived, a long white shirt, and as I lay on my bed he unwound his turban, revealing a keski tied closely round his head, which he also removed to enable him to comb his hair and then his beard. After this introduction to Sikh hygiene I considered my own cleaning of my teeth, face washing and putting on of pyjamas was very inferior. The night was fairly sleepless as the train stopped at every possible station and some that were not scheduled, to pick up mail. Delhi was reached by about six o'clock, by which time my companion was already washing himself and enjoying tiffin. He chatted with me until we pulled out of the siding into the station.

After a day at Jamila's telling her about the well-being of her relatives and my other adventures, I was on my travels again. A researcher from Leeds, Roger Ballard, with his wife Cathy and small son, not yet out of nappies for I had brought some from England for him, were living in a Punjabi Sikh village and I was invited to stay with them. The high point of my visit was a Sikh wedding. As usual it took place in the morning, as all Sikh marriages should, but what was novel was the location, the flat roof of one of the houses, with other members of the village occupying nearby roof tops. In the UK I have usually attended them in a gurdwara, though I once did go to a posh one in a Masonic hall in Birmingham! In India I have yet to go to one in a gurdwara. On the previous evening I had been taken to the bride's home to view the dowry, not washing machines or even cars as in later years, but a shiny bicycle, kitchen utensils, as well as blankets and the like. Next day I walked past them onto the roof top which was already full of relatives and friends. I assured myself that this was probably not the first time the roof had been used for this purpose, after all she had a couple of sisters, and that it would be strong enough to take the strain. Looking beyond it, I saw most of the villagers crowded together on nearby roofs and a smaller group a little further away, perhaps they were Hindu or even Christian onlookers or low caste Sikhs. I never found out but I sensed that for some reason they were apart from the main community. The groom had already arrived and was sitting in a cleared space some yards away backed up by his parents and some male relatives or friends. Glancing towards the lane along which we had just come, I saw a rather elderly man of medium height but heavy build, carrying a copy of the Guru Granth Sahib, wrapped in a green cloth, on his head. Before him walked a teenage boy sprinkling water on the ground to ward off evil spirits. Sikhism does not believe in such things, there should be no place for superstition, but village practices do not always conform to the sophisticated norms about which one often reads in academic books. (I've known British Christians who would not wash their hair on a Sunday!). When he had placed the scripture in front of him on the ground, the glass of water nearby, the granthi began the service, the main part of which is the reading of the wedding hymn composed by Guru Ram Das, the fourth Sikh teacher. During the reading the couple walked clockwise round the Book, the man holding a scarf that had been tied round the waist of the bride. The service was brief, the only essentials being the couple and the scripture. It is good to have members of both families acting not only as witnesses but as endorsers of the fact that the families agreed to the wedding and gave it their approval, but they are not essential. The true witness is the Guru Granth Sahib. A few children then read poems that they had composed or sang songs; speeches on this occasion were few and the women folk of the men who attempted to make them quickly persuaded them to resume their places on the ground. The groom led his new bride down the narrow steps and onto a large grassed area where everyone sat crossed-legged to share the community meal of langar, in this case simple and vegetarian. It was a rural wedding almost devoid of any ostentation but for some of the dowry gifts. Whether the girl's family gave money to the groom's I was not able to discover.

The village had no Muslim inhabitants, but it was possible to discern that before Partition it was a mixed community. Remains of Urdu writing could be seen on one or two walls, almost faded or white-washed over, but not quite. A store house at the edge of the village resembled a mosque; it was possible to make out the qiblah wall, towards its western end, and not far away was a large low mound under which, I am sure, some Muslims who had not managed to flee, were buried. However, none of the villagers could or would confirm my observations.

I returned to Delhi for Easter weekend and this in itself had its moments, not so much Easter communion in the Lutyens designed cathedral using the 1662 prayer book, but listening to Stainer's Crucifixion on the radio on Good Friday. When Indians say that theirs is a secular state they are not meaning the word to be understood as it is in the UK, with the suggestion that religion should be ignored but in the sense of Nehru and Gandhi, namely that all religions should be given equal respect, none being privileged or disparaged. We have some way to go even in countenancing this ideal. India accepts the ideal and generally seems to make it real despite militant communalism that expresses itself in violence from time to time.

At last it was time to return home after the most eventful month of my life, before or since. I bought too many presents at the Emporium at Janpath and probably only succeeded in not having to pay extra at the airport check-in because of the persuasiveness of Jamila and George and the kindness of Air India staff, especially as Santa Singh Virdi, Mrs Sambhi's octogenarian father turned up at Palam airport with a small fold up stool and other gifts including a picture of the imperial darbar of 1911 in a cardboard container.

In the area of religion I was now even more convinced that the Hindus I had met had not been living out a delusion for some five thousand years and that Islam was not a satanic parody of Christianity as someone had once told me, or that Sikhism was a human invention intended to bring together Hindu and Muslim in a religiously united Mughal Empire. I could also see that Christianity need not be the foreign religion that many Hindus considered it to be. Fortunately, if accidentally and unwillingly, it was shaking off its dependence on the Raj and discovering that it could blossom as part of Indian or Pakistani culture in the soil of the subcontinent. I was told that western missionaries were finding it difficult to obtain permits to work in the region. This might be no bad thing; the same arguments that are being applied in Britain for the development of home-grown Islam, Hinduism or Sikhism not nurtured by imams, pujaris or granthis from overseas, who do not understand the challenges faced by Asians in Britain, can be made for an indigenous Christianity freed from the imprisoning influence of Constantine and colonialism.

10

Return to Leeds

Save for being greatly enriched in many ways as a result of my unexpected journey of a lifetime, things resumed as normal at college and in the community. As I managed to return for the end of the Easter holiday many people might not have noticed that I had been away, or had been on a family holiday in Cardiff where Gwynneth and the children had gone. My visit made me aware of the deep spirituality and generosity of Muslims and the way in which a society could flourish in conditions of religious diversity. I was determined to encourage and support efforts to enable the faiths of Hinduism, Islam and Sikhism to put down roots in British soil and contribute to our way of life just as Jews were already doing.

One YCCR project was a series of commercial filmstrips. Peggy Holroyde arranged a meeting with the newly appointed lecturer in Hinduism, Ursula King, and we met in her room in the university. She gave helpful advice on the notes and materials relating to Hinduism and a friendship was established which resulted in her encouraging me to undertake research that led to degrees of MPhil and PhD in Sikh studies. However, on the occasion of our first meeting I was impressed by her ability to have her daughter Nina lying in a Moses Basket on her desk, conveniently during the Easter holiday. Neither of our girls had been on schedule!

In 1974 two Sikhs were responsible for a bus strike involving the Leeds Transport Corporation. Community relations issues are usually the result of accidental clashes with authority that is unaccustomed to change and challenge and doesn't know how to respond. Two drivers had exchanged the regulation cap for turbans because they had now been initiated into the Khalsa community of Sikhs and must now live according to its code of discipline, one aspect of which was wearing the turban, though, of course, colour was not important and they were willing to wear green as required by their employers. The union was not over sympathetic to the case of the two Asians but became more active when a Sikh member of the Socialist Workers' Party, (SWP), became involved on the drivers' behalf. While the strike was in progress, Piara Singh discovered a letter written sometime earlier in which the Transport Authority recognised the right of Sikhs to wear the turban. The strike was completely unnecessary. When, at last, the dispute was settled and the drivers were reinstated the SWP asked that the demonstration that had been planned for the following weekend should now be turned into a victory parade; to their dissatisfaction and annoyance the Sikh community said that, instead, a service of thanksgiving would be held in the gurdwara!

The years 1976 was memorable for most citizens of the UK because of the drought and intense heat; for Leeds Sikhs it had further importance. First, it saw a visit from the Namdhari Sikh Sat Guru, Jagjit Singh. I went to meet him in the gurdwara and discovered that his presence led to a number of responses. He sat on a cushion at an angle of 180 degrees to the Guru Granth Sahib. Some people, myself included, bowed towards him as they went to offer mutta tekhna to the Guru Granth Sahib, others ignored him altogether and some Sikhs prostrated themselves before him and did not bow towards the scripture. Clearly he was a cause of some controversy. During conversations with Piara Singh and other members of the sangat, I discovered that some Sikhs did not accept him as a Sikh because, they said, the only Guru was the Guru Granth Sahib; others respected him for his lifestyle; for he kept the Khalsa code of discipline perfectly, taking amrit initiation and encouraging others to do so, having no place for sectarianism, being a vegetarian, opposing the giving of dowries at weddings and being humble. He also represented a tradition in Sikhism that had played an important part in the Indian independence struggle, wearing Khadi, home-spun Indian cloth, long before Gandhi advocated it, and providing martyrs to the cause. It can be argued that most forms of religion in India require a human teacher to give it strength and purpose; for most Sikhs such a person is a sant, one who follows the Khalsa code and encourages others to do likewise. For Namdharis personal leadership is given by the Satguru. Going around Madras cathedral, watching Indian Christians making their bows at various altars and shrines, I couldn't help wondering whether the church might throw up charismatic leaders in India. Muslims often have their Sufi pirs, of course, and I have been told that every Hindu has a guru although I have no way of checking that out, I do know that most of my Hindu acquaintances have such teachers that they go to for advice in every day affairs as well as spiritual guidance. The Satguru was in England during the drought of 1976 and is said to have prayed for our deliverance from it and the coming of rain which happened a few days before his departure. Some national newspapers had photographs of him and described him as the rainmaking

Guru.

Secondly, the Open University launched a new unit; AD208 entitled Man's Religious Quest, which seems to indicate that its preparation was ahead of the feminist movement. The first video accompanying the written and radio materials was supposed to show Sikh worship but in fact was based on a Ravidasi community in the English Midlands. It became apparent that a new video was needed and it was decided to base it on the Sikh community of Leeds because Piara Singh and I could get easy access to it and could act as consultants. Filming took place on the hottest Sunday in the summer of 1976 in a gurdwara in which the congregation was packed as tightly as possible. Although the film crew had been warned that smoking was against Sikh teaching and was not allowed on gurdwara premises, Piara Singh, in his usual tactful way, told me of breaches of etiquette and asked me to have a word with Terry Thomas, the OU tutor. Almost everything conceivable took place on that Sunday. A notable sant, Puran Singh, honoured the sangat with his presence and blessed a young couple whose marriage was also arranged for that day. As with the Satguru it was interesting to note how Sikhs responded to him and his entourage: some performed mutta tekhna, bowing and touching his feet, others bowed and garlanded him and some of his companions, a few adopted rank order; bowing and garlanding some of his followers, but not others. The video, in which the Sambhi family and other important members of the Leeds community feature prominently, was a very interesting study of a British Sikh community in the nineteen seventies and deserves to have a place in the archives of Diaspora Sikhism.

Two other aspects of Religious Education which were important, one which has already been mentioned, the celebration of Christmas, and interreligious worship and faith schools, must be touched on here. The education of Muslim girls was of considerable concern to everyone involved in community relations and education generally. By the late nineteen seventies girls who had attended special nurseries and infant schools dedicated to helping them learn English were themselves becoming mothers and their children were being taught English in the same schools, whereas Hindu and Sikh children were able to enter mainstream education at the age of five if not sooner. What was happening was that either Muslim mothers were not learning English and remaining at home so that when children returned from school it was to a virtually Pakistani community, or from puberty onwards, or even the beginning of secondary education, girls were being kept at home and, often, so as not to cause any upsets, schools and LEAs were closing their eyes to the situation. Sometimes it seems that it was not a case of either one reason or the other but both. When Bradford reorganised its secondary schools in the seventies, it decided to go co-educational but left two schools for girls only. A Muslim alleged that he asked that his daughter might be given a place in one of the schools but the LEA told him that there were no places left and also that he was not in the catchment area. He refused to send his daughter to a co-educational school and Bradford decided to take him to court. The case dragged on until she was beyond the minimum school leaving age when the authority conveniently dropped it. Meanwhile Bradford Muslims decided to establish a school of their own and formally applied to do so. This time the LEA produced a variety of legal arguments against the proposal and it was not accepted. The community and many other people felt that the reasons for rejection were based on racial arguments, not educational only, I found myself providing an YCCR paper on the issue and how a school could be established within the LEA system. It was later republished by the Community Relations Commission. Despite personal educational reservations about faith schools, I felt that if the law allowed church schools then there were no intelligible reasons for the Muslim wish to be rejected.

I have always been concerned that, as well as being able to respond as fully British citizens, communities should be able to retain their own identities, partly for reasons of self respect. Therefore I took what chances I could to discover what they were doing to pass on faith and culture to the next generation as, quite clearly, most LEA schools did not see it as their responsibility and the government did not seem to be concerned. At Elmhurst, the school which our daughters attended, there was a Saturday school for children of West Indian origin. Its headteacher, Mrs. Paul, the first Caribbean head of an LEA school, provided valuable guidance and practical help, and a number of young people in their twenties gave practical support. The curriculum included reading and writing but also the geography and history, as well as music, of the Islands. The challenge that it faced, in common with all supplementary or alternative schools was to persuade children to attend. Though they seemed to be bursting at the seams one was well aware that only a minority of children went to them. Black children, especially, who were alienated from the main school system, were rarely to be found among those voluntarily going to the Saturday schools. On Sundays well turned out children were to be seen in large numbers on their ways to Black churches. Sikh education took place during week day evenings or after day school. It consisted of Punjabi, learning to read gurmukhi, the written language of the community, and play musical instruments. Teachers were often well qualified professionals who worked in LEA schools. A distinctive feature of Sikh provision was the Sikh camp. A week or more in duration. Rather than being under canvas it was usually held in the buildings of another community. Here, games were added to the study programme and children enjoyed an attractive diet. However, the nagging question remained in my mind, what percentage of young Sikhs actually enrolled at the schools? The situation was very different with Muslims, large numbers of girls as well as boys were to be seen going to mosque schools direct from day schools but education was very formal in complete contrast to what the children had been doing earlier in the day, and learning was often the rote learning of the Qur'an, and Arabic. At secondary age the attendance of girls dwindled dramatically. I was unaware of any alternative Muslim schools known as madrasahs in Yorkshire but did visit some in Lancashire. These gave me considerable concern but when I told inspectors they suggested that they knew of the school but were eager to close a blind eye to them. Numbers of children were small, they knelt on the floor supported by their desks as I had seen in Pakistan, few text-books were to be seen, and learning was by rote. The Qur'an and Arabic seemed to be the main subjects, though I did come across a few women teachers, non-muslim, of English. The quality of education appeared to be very poor indeed. How children aged between about nine and fourteen were evading our school system was something I could only conjecture. Once more enforcement of the law regarding school attendance appeared to be lax. Large minorities of Jews progressed well in Hebrew classes and Hazel Broch also conducted a children's service which they led and through which they learned how to participate in the full worship of the synagogue. The equivalent education by other faiths to what Christian Sunday schools offered might well have provided someone with a worthwhile research opportunity.

Congregational worship among Hindus in India might sometimes be regarded as the exception rather than the rule, though one is likely to come across groups of ladies enjoying a Satsang, a get together to join in the worship of a particular deity. In Britain they did not always feel the same urgency as Sikhs, Muslims and Jews to establish places of worship because each house is a temple or mandir. Once in Vrindaban, the mythical home of Krishna, I asked a guide how many mandirs there were in the town. Nine thousand or nine hundred came the reply. It was difficult to fathom this out as Indians are renowned mathematicians and a discrepancy of 8100 is no small matter. When pressed, he answered that it all depended on what I meant by the word temple; there were about 900 of them in this holy city, but it is customary for each home to have its shrine, sometimes in the kitchen, sometimes in a special place, so there were as many as there were houses, and his estimate was about nine thousand. The movement among Hindus in Britain was mainly to have social centres for the local communities, but these also incorporated a religious significance. In Southampton the community rented a church hall for gatherings on Sundays when most Hindus would not be at work, and for special festival occasions but eventually in the nineteen eighties they bought land and had a purpose-built mandir constructed, at the time the only one south of the Thames apart from London. The larger communities of Leeds and Bradford and other cities bought churches or church halls which Christian groups no longer needed. One such in Bradford was a church where I had been awarded a prize about thirty years earlier in a Sunday School Union scripture examination. What would anyone have thought if someone had told them what the future held for their treasured place of worship? It might have been even harder for a congregation in Leicester that I took my students to visit, whose church had become a mandir Above the door were the words, 'William Carey Memorial Chapel', might he, the famous missionary to India, have appreciated the irony of the empire striking back? The havan or fire ceremony is a feature of Hindu worship and especially temple openings; whenever I took our daughters to such occasions I attempted to sit with them near a staircase or window, partly to ensure a possible escape route but also to enjoy the fresh air rather than furnace like heat.

Our family was invited to a special ceremony in the Leeds mandir, the installation of number of murtis newly-bought from India. We were given a precise time when they were to be dedicated and asked not to be late. There is no English word which adequately conveys the meaning of murti, which as far as I know has not yet found its way into our dictionaries. 'Idol', popular among missionaries and in common parlance, and even used by Hindus themselves, and with some relish by Muslims and Sikhs, is offensive. Protestant Christians brought up on the teachings of the Hebrew Scriptures are inclined to regard them as human creations in which the credulous place their trust. 'Statue' is little better for it suggests that the artefact is no more than a reminder of an historical figure, be it Churchill, Cromwell, or Gandhi. 'Icon' may be the most satisfactory term because it does convey the belief that somehow God is present in the figure, which, consequently possesses potency; however, as with Torah, mosque, Guru or church and sacrament, it is essential ultimately, to understand what the word means to the believer in the faith. As already suggested, divinity, potency, eternity, is present in the murti. The story is told of a king who zealously ordered all murtis to be smashed; a guru who heard of his actions went to his palace where he saw a portrait of the king's much loved, late father. He immediately tore it up. When the king entered the room he was naturally angered at the Guru's actions and ordered his guards to kill him. 'Wait', said the Guru, 'what have I done wrong? I have only torn up a piece of paper!' If we can understand this story, maybe we can appreciate what a murti is to a Hindu.

Having been told the auspicious time to be at the mandir we duly arrived early, only to be told, apologetically, that the ceremony had already taken place. The priest who was appointed to perform it decided that it must take place an hour earlier, this being the auspicious time. Nevertheless, our hospitable hosts showed us the murtis and provided us with a delightful meal.

Some months later I took a group of students to an open evening at the mandir; nearby was another young visitor wearing a large badge upon which were the words, 'Jesus is my Saviour'. We must each decide for ourselves how to dress and deport ourselves when we attend, as guests, the home of another faith. I have known students who have told me that they could not go to a mandir because they considered the Hindus to be worshippers of idols. I have always excused them and on every occasion, by the end of the course they have worked their way through to a position where they have been able to share the experience with the rest of us. However, as the Qur'an says; 'There is no compulsion in religion', and whatever the sentence relates to, I feel that it has a bearing of how people of tender conscience should be treated – with respect.

The priest conducted a brief Arti ceremony and then the secretary began his talk. I had discovered already that Hindu priests are usually ritual practitioners, having made the mistake of asking one to speak to my students on a particular subject; he gave the same talk as the week before, and only afterwards did I learn that the secretary or some other member of the community was the person who possessed the necessary knowledge to speak to our students. At question time the young lady with the Jesus badge asked the secretary how many gods Hindus believed in, telling him that Christians only believed in one. He replied that sometimes Hindus say there are 330,000,000 but he then asked her how many people she thought there were in the world. She replied; 'Perhaps 2000 million', to which he said, 'Well, we believe that God is in each of us, but we also have a verse in our scripture that says that God is one, though wise men call God by many names', He continued, 'By the way you may see representations of birds, fish and animals, in our temples, that is because many of us believe that God is in all life forms, and we even call the earth our mother. But we are not happy calling God 'he' or 'she'. The Supreme Being is the creator of gender but is beyond it. I hope I'm not making things too complicated'. 'Is God personal like Jesus?' the girl asked. 'Oh yes', came the reply. I breathed a sigh of relief that we had not got onto original sin versus enlightenment, and stored up in my mind awareness that there was much to learn if we were to come to terms with the new faiths found in modern Britain.

The Hindu and Sikh festival of lights, Divali, coincided with Guy Fawke's Night one year, so YCCR decided to hold a joint celebration with Ravana with the Guy being burnt together on one bonfire. It was a great success though the local media was uncertain what was happening and how to respond.

The sale of church buildings to other religions in England is very complex. The most famous place of worship in this respect must be Brick Lane mosque in east London. In turn it has been a Methodist chapel, then the spiritual home of Huguenot refugees from northern Europe, a haven for Jews who fled Eastern Europe round about 1900, and now it serves a large and thriving Muslim community. Christian Baptist, Methodist, and Congregationalist congregations have also sold churches for which they have no longer a use. Roman Catholic Christians are mostly recent arrivals since the mid nineteenth century and they have usually grown in numbers rather than migrated from one part of England to another, as Jews have done for example. Anglicans constitute a distinctive group. The Church of England is the form of religion established by law in England. Partly for that reason it feels that it has a special responsibility for its consecrated buildings. Early in the nineteen seventies the Muslims of Dewsbury were looking for a place of worship. There happened to be a derelict Anglican church in Saville Town; when I visited it, derelict was about the most charming word one could find to describe it. There were no pews; even the floor coverings had been removed in many places; the plain glass windows had been smashed and there were spaces in the roof from which tiles had been removed. Perhaps homeless men used it at night, I did not return to find out. The Muslim community was interested in purchasing the building, presumably to knock it down and replace it with a mosque. The vicar and, possibly, Wakefield diocese was sympathetic to their wishes, feeling as I did that the Muslims would at least build something respectable and to the glory of God on the site. However, the local white population did not share this view. Their families had worshipped in the church and been baptised, married and buried there. Although they obviously never even visited it now, it was their church! It was not to be sold to pagans. The vicar decided to call a meeting to clear the air. An eminent Christian scholar of Islam, Kenneth Cragg, was invited to provide a brief introduction to the religion, an imam was also asked to reassure the parishioners, and I was to speak about Muslims in the UK. The evening seemed to go well but at the end, the vicar said, 'Let us join in a prayer that we can all share: The grace of our Lord, Jesus Christ, and the love of God, and the fellowship of the Holy Spirit be with us all'. Kenneth winced, looked at me and said; 'What have we been doing all evening?'

The church was not sold to the Muslim community, but about this time an Anglican church in Southampton, was sold to Sikhs, largely through the influence of the Bishop of Winchester, the late John V Taylor, in whose diocese it lay, and who was liberal in his views and much preferred a church to become the place of worship of another faith than be sold and demolished to become a car park or office block. Synod, the elected body of the Church of England, did not favour the extension of such sales, and a committee report in 1996, entitled, Communities and Buildings, endorsed the position.

Rail journeys in England were usually very dull with most passengers hiding behind their newspapers. One day, however, I felt that I was back in Pakistan. The man sitting opposite me was clearly a Muslim and soon, on our northward trip from London to Leeds, he turned round the papers that I had placed on the table in front of me and began reading them. They were student essays on Islam, as chance would have it. He looked at me and asked me if I taught Islamiat and then if I was a Muslim. My reply did not offend him at all, though I have met Muslims who say that only believers should teach their religion; in fact he was rather pleased and commented favourably upon the quality of the essays he had read. (This might have been yet another example of a cultural politeness that I have witnessed many times). He then told me the purpose of his visit which was to lead a mission in the town of Dewsbury. He hastened to add that it was a mission to Muslims, not to Christians. Many Muslims were only nominal believers who seldom prayed and drank alcohol. These men he hoped to turn around to the way of Islam. His honesty impressed me as often I have been led to believe that all Muslims are men of deep faith, unlike one day a week Christians. We had a good conversation and time passed quickly. Wishing one another well we went our separate ways. Much had come from his glance at my essays, something that many people may have taken for rudeness. We need to understand the cultural differences in our society and accept those that we can whenever possible. 'When in Rome do as the Romans do' is a comment made in response to 'immigrant' requests or demands, but it should be remembered that these were words addressed to the North African, Augustine, by the famous Italian bishop, Ambrose, when he discovered that Roman

Christians celebrated Easter on a day different to that to which he was used. It made sense, just as it might if I were in Moscow for Christmas and joined in the festivities on January 6 instead of sitting in my hotel room opening presents on 25 December, but Ambrose did not advise Augustine to compromise any of his beliefs. So, Muslims do not kill animals in public in the UK on Eid, as they will in many Middle Eastern countries, but will take them to the abattoir, as I helped them do in Leeds. Even though it was a Sunday the authorities eventually complied when it was pointed out that the sacrifice was part of the celebration and could not be performed a day or two earlier, when the slaughter house was open as normal, and the carcase put into deep freeze. This I would not describe as a compromise but a proper gesture of friendship.

Hazel Broch, a Leeds Orthodox Jew, regularly made presentations of Judaism for school children and anyone else who was interested, in one of its dozen synagogues. She also organised a children's schul on the Sabbath morning while parents were in the main synagogue. One afternoon I took my students to one of her gatherings where she easily maintained the interest of over a hundred, perhaps two hundred, secondary pupils and adults for over an hour, at the end of which she was still fresh albeit that some of the children were overcome by her vitality. One student, the wife of a Baptist minister admitted that she had been brought up to regard Judaism as a fossil religion; 'some fossil' she said. There was also a friend of mine, a rabbi in the Reform movement, Douglas Charing, who was in charge of the Jewish Education Bureau; he wrote a number of books, some of which I edited, and has made a valuable contribution to the study of Judaism in our schools. Sadly, not everyone has shared the insights of Hazel and Douglas; a rabbi gave a talk in Bradford in which he argued that Jewish children should not learn about any other religions until they went to university and that the same rule should be applied to gentiles. He gave several reasons to justify his position; he wanted children to be secure in their own traditions before encountering others, he was afraid that teachers would give a distorted view of Judaism, and he was not at all anxious that people who were not Jews should learn about his religion. I suggested that the world at large was aware of Judaism through literary characters such as Shylock and Fagin or the attitudes expressed by the National Front political party and that I knew Sikhs in India, for example, who had never met a Jew, but knew their characteristics. Left in a state of ignorance the old views would persist and people might continue to say that 'Hitler had the right idea', as I have sometimes heard it argued. Eventually, when I had told him of Siân's chanting of 'Jew, Jew, dirty old Jew', and other anecdotes, the rabbi conceded that I might have a point about the need for children and society at large to be given an accurate understanding of Judaism and of the Jewish way of life, but remained anxious to protect young Jews from contact with other religions, especially Christianity. This was not difficult to understand as there is a long history of Jewish persecution by Christians who would convert them by almost any means, and at this time, in the nineteen seventies I still had little knowledge of the Nazi death camps so much so that I remember chatting to my neighbour Len one day and suggesting that as his family came over from eastern Europe round about the beginning of the twentieth century, he would have lost no relatives in the nineteen thirties. Quietly, he told me of two aunts in Poland that they never heard of or from after nineteen forty. Douglas Charing informed me of the York Massacre of 1190, telling me that for many Jews it was city they would not visit. At that time I had no knowledge of the expulsion of Jews from England in 1290, my Durham course didn't cover such things. In fact I only learned the full story when I saw a TV programme called The Expulsion of the Jews, probably in 1980. I have some doubts about the annual Holocaust Day memorial if it relates only to the suffering of Jews, terrible though they were, but if ethnic cleansing in the Balkans, black slavery past and present, oppression in Africa and the suffering of Palestinians are also brought to our attention to be held in our minds, the Holocaust Day can be of crucial importance in the life of the UK and the world. Neither did I know at this time that Grandpa Cole was a published author, dad never mentioned a book, nor did my revered and much loved grandfather himself. I learned about it from my ninety year old aunt shortly before she died, in 1989, she knew no details and no copy survived with the family but the book had been published privately and my grandmother had not been at all happy with a venture that ate up their savings, as a Baptist minister his salary was probably only £150 per annum. As I was teaching in higher education in 1989, I was able to make use of the inter-library loan service and eventually received a copy of The Disruption of Israel by G. R. Cole, published by Arthur H. Stockwell Ltd, London, probably in 1927 as this was the date handwritten on the library copy. It was a poem in blank verse and to my shock and horror was extremely anti-Jewish. To quote one line: 'Mammon will e'r the Jews heart melt'. The whole story was one of greed and venality with the selective narrative of Jewish history frequently stating that they were up to their old tricks. Yet, when granddad died there was apparently no copy in the house and in the few years before his death, he never alluded to it or referred to Jews in a hostile manner. Knowing that I was studying for a Diploma in Theology, he gave me many of his books on church history and Christian theology; they were liberal in their sympathies as were the few sermons that I heard him preach. Did he regret, in the light of the nineteen thirties and the rise of fascism, his attitude towards the Jews and change it? Naturally, I would like to think so but I have no proof of any sea change. I have tried to buy his book on the Internet without success and have thought of purchasing all the copies that I could and destroying them all but one, but the chance has not come my way.

It is usually assumed that England has a long history or respectful acceptance of other races and religions. This is a questionable thesis as the history of the Jews in England indicates. After all, the first laws restricting immigration date to 1905 and were directed against Jewish asylum seekers from Eastern Europe. The history of our Jewish communities is salutary. Working with them can also be instructive as I discovered when I was the Christian secretary of the Council of Christians and Jews (CCJ) in Leeds. There was an Orthodox-Reform split; tension when it came to the kinds of gatherings it should support and promote and a certain amount of mutual suspicion regarding motives between the two groups of members.

The Council was also understandably interested in protecting the Jewish communities, as I discovered when we heard of a proposed National Front march along Street Lane and through Alwoodley, probably the most heavily populated Jewish areas of the city. A leading member of the city council and a friend of the CCJ was encouraged to phone the chief constable of the West Riding of Yorkshire and, if there really was a plan to march through north Leeds, to request that it be to another part of the city. Membership of the CCJ was a valuable learning experience and I have always regretted not being able recently to attend meetings in Brighton, our nearest branch. Two things I did learn :the difficulty of finding mutually acceptable times to meet – I once went through my diary offering Friday evening for getting together with the Jewish Secretary! – and the limited range of topics that were acceptable for public meetings. Theological issues were out, simulated Passovers were in, a joint Chanukah-Christmas activity was a little iffy, and if a gathering was to be held in a church Christian symbols were to be removed or covered. I soon became aware of the pressures that secretaryship could impose. When, some years later, I was sounded out about accepting the national secretarial post, I had no hesitation in expressing my wish not to be considered. There were other reasons too, a religious one being that from my experience, though limited, Leeds CCJ represented Orthodox Judaism and I would have wished to work towards an inclusive organisation. Diversity is something to which most religions claim to aspire, but I have found that those who speak in favour of it have most difficulty when it comes to members of one's own tradition or who are akin to it. It's a bit like vegetarianism or even leisure activities, we can live and let live at least, until we invite the person with different dietary habits for a meal, and then there is panic. Instead of going totally vegetarian, rather an extreme prospect, or providing a separate course for a vegetarian guest, we decide not to invite them. (Our outspoken daughter, Siân, kept running into a friend who always said she must arrange to come for a meal. Eventually, Siân said, 'Why don't we fix up something? Is it because I'm a vegetarian?' Sheepishly the friend conceded that that was the reason so Siân replied, 'What about' – and named a few cheese dishes. 'Oh would that be alright?' came the reply and a mutually convenient evening was agreed). The choice of music on a car radio can be equally stressful! The larger Christian denominations can call Quakers or Baptists sects and behind the term can lay an unwillingness to accept their Christian validity, less so today than in the past. Mormons and Jehovah's Witnesses can't be left to live in peace; someway we have to express our disapproval of them, whilst Jews and Muslim cause no comment. Sunni Muslims can be hostile to a Shi'a and even more to Ahmaddiya though accepting Christians in their midst, and I have known Sikhs who find it difficult to accept that Namdhari Sikhs and even goras, that is white Sikhs, mostly American converts, are really Sikhs, but they will recognise Hindus without a blush. Besides wanting to serve a movement that was truly universal in its openness, and with it the questions of what I might do after my appointment with the CCJ had come to an end had to be considered, and the prospect of living in London or commuting from Leeds to London on a daily basis.

Life was treating me well; there was no need to think of change. Gwynneth decided to train as a nurse as there was no longer a need to be available to give the children lunch. In fact, they were now at Elmhurst and there was no possibility of them coming home during the lunch break. This grounded me as I had to be available to look after Eluned and Siân whilst Gwynneth was working. Ursula King at the university encouraged me to study for the M. Phil. which I did and later John Hinnells invited me to write *The Sikhs: Their religious Beliefs and Practices*, with Piara Singh. Next came a Ph.D. At college money was found to employ Carol Mumford, an eminent specialist in infant RE and Peggy Holroyde on a part-time basis. Things could get no better. Then, at the end of the year we were told that James Graham was to close.

During the later years of our life in Leeds, the Yorkshire Ripper was active. At the end of Chapeltown streets were parked cars which West Indian children assured our daughters and me were unmarked police cars. They might be there for a few hours. On two occasions when I had been visiting Asian families in the area, the police followed me but I did not stop until I reached home even though they flashed me down; it was not a district where one halted at the request of unmarked cars. As I was putting my car away in the garage, they asked me where I had been and searched my boot.

CHAPTER

11

Chichester

Sometimes we need a push to move on from the comfortable condition in which we find ourselves. So it happened as far as the Cole family was concerned though I cannot even now understand philosophically why it was necessary, except for the fact that the Leeds situation was changing dramatically and that to cling on to life there would have meant giving up most of the activities which I cherished. Even our next door neighbour, Len, was considering moving from the neighbourhood.

Local government reorganisation resulted in authorities that had supported YCCR withdrawing financial assistance and the new regions setting up their own community relations organisations. I had mixed feelings about this development. On the one hand it could be argued that there were very few people with expertise in the multi religious field and that most of them were members of YCCR and from Leeds or Bradford, on the other hand it could be argued that new talent would be developed through the necessity of coping with new situations. If history does prove anything it is that no one is indispensable.

During my last few months I was engaged in the unpleasant task of running down YCCR as its chairman Lord Wade was ill and I was vice chairman. As a final act a new edition of *East Comes West* was published but without the committee's knowledge. When I complained the Hindu author said: 'White man we do not need you to hold our hand!' Perhaps this was a sign to go.

James Graham was no longer recruiting students; the local authorities that had provided them could no longer offer promises of jobs in their schools and provide training grants. The decision was taken to close the college and take all higher education into the polytechnic, except for the university. Staff had to apply for their existing jobs and, if unsuccessful, for any new ones. I had four painful interviews and was rejected completely. My contribution to multicultural education courses and teaching practice supervision was greatly reduced even before reorganisation; after it my time-table was cut to teaching three hours a week to a female student who insisted on studying Hinduism as part of her B Ed course, two hours to the B Ed members of the Leeds consortium of colleges who wished to take the Hinduism/Islam option, one hour to the Principles and Practice of RE and nothing else. No wonder I completed my Ph D in less than the minimum time permitted! Academically, my future in Leeds lay in joining the Polytechnic School of Humanities and teaching the Spanish Civil War; and in health terms probably suffering a nervous breakdown. Four years was spent in applying for the rare posts in Religious Studies that were advertised throughout the country and attending interviews. Did someone say it was good experience? After the first six I began to doubt it. Escape seemed unlikely. It was at this time that Bob Jackson, head of Religious Studies invited me to give a lecture on the Guru in Sikhism, the subject of my Master of Philosophy research. I fitted it in with our daughters' half term in October and we spent a few days in the area. Bob made me feel wanted. Perhaps I could come to terms with the Leeds situation. Not that it prevented me from searching for a way out.

My most memorable journey was to Beverley in what had been to East Riding of Yorkshire but which had now been merged with North Lincolnshire in the unpopular county of Humberside. When I was a child my uncle Ted, a railway signal man, use to take me on a walk that took in his box at Hessle and show me the site of the proposed bridge across the river. For all I know the Romans might have planned such a crossing; certainly, at some low tides, modern man had walked from one side to the other. Now, it seemed that the politicians in London had persuaded those in the north that the union of those two unlikely regions was desirable with the promise of the bridge. The bond was to be further cemented by the new education authority's decision to appoint an adviser for RE. Hitherto I had not been very interested in applying for such posts, I was certain that HMIs had to be emasculated before they were appointed because they seemed as powerless as eunuchs, though I gather such men could actually wield considerable influence and power in harems and Turkish courts. I knew many HMIs but they all seemed to have achieved whatever they had done before their elevation. To be positive, I saw that a local authority adviser might do much, as my friend Alan Loosemore had in the West Riding, before he became an HMI. The interview was a serious two-day affair and other people present included Alan Brown, who was working in Chichester. I little thought that his later move to a Church of England Board of Education position would result in my replacing him in that city. I gauged that there would be little free time, in fact we were told that annual leave would be somewhere around 28 days plus bank holidays. The then RE adviser in Leeds had described aspects of his duties to me in preparation for this interview and I knew that on one occasion he and his colleagues were required to be in the office on Christmas Eve to conduct interviews, and that when he took a weekend course he was allowed to claim time in lieu within the next fortnight. More often than not his diary was so full that he had to write off the promise. At my interview I pointed out that I was involved with Shap and in examining and doing other things that I thought kept me abreast of developments in RE and so made me of more value to my subject and my employers. A panel member said that he noted that I had many hobbies but I would have to indulge them in my own time and could not expect the LEA to encourage or support them. The crunch came on the second day when I was asked about my views on Agreed Syllabuses. I replied that they could be helpful to primary school nonspecialists and as quarries for finding where to locate particular stories or scriptural passages but that I had never used one as more than a guide over which I exercised my own judgement, that most LEAs lacked the local expertise to produce one and that a national syllabus would be more appropriate. My answer was my undoing or my salvation, the job was offered to Joe Byshe who had recently guided Cheshire in its provision of a very useful agreed syllabus. Clearly an adviser, an Agreed Syllabus and a bridge were the cement intended to bind the new Humberside authority. I returned to Leeds rather relieved and sure that a career as an adviser was not for me, and resumed my study of the *Times Educational Supplement*'s posts vacant section.

Newman College in Birmingham wanted a head of department and once I had been assured that as a non Roman Catholic I would be considered, I applied – only to receive a letter telling me that as I was not a Roman Catholic I was not regarded as eligible. Another three hours wasted in form filling! I chanced to meet the head of department of West Hill in Halifax Market one day and he told me that he was retiring. When the post was advertised I applied but neither he nor I heard anything. Altogether I applied for five posts in Birmingham without success and later discovered that the family was praying that I might not succeed because they did not like the city, having seen it from the car on our frequent journeys from Leeds to Cardiff.

Eventually, John Rankin offered me a place at Chichester teaching what I had been responsible for since 1967, including teaching practice supervision and a course in multicultural education, even though at my interview the Director had told me: 'We don't have any down here', meaning members of religious and ethnic minorities. In fact West Sussex was the most monocultural area of the country, and it still is, except the

Brighton area and Crawley, which soon after our arrival we discovered the county council would have liked to transfer to Surrey as it returned four Labour councillors in an otherwise Tory authority, but someone noted that Gatwick was in the Crawley area and was the county's richest source of income! The county boundary remained unchanged.

All that was missing was my daily contact with other faith and ethnic groups. That was a large part of my life, and that of our family. The girls elected to join the high school rather than the extremely good church school, Bishop Luffa. Eluned entered the sixth form and began new courses; Siân was in the second year of the fifth and had to adapt to a number of changed syllabuses in mid stream. A new set book was *The Merchant of Venice*; one day she came home fuming because of the anti-Semitism she had encountered. The character of Shylock was discussed and her classmates who had never met any Jews asserted that he was an accurate depiction. Siân disputed this view and said she had met many fine Jews in Leeds, especially uncle Len. She was told that Jews are very cunning; they pretend to be kind and good to take in people like Siân who will then come to places like Chichester and try to present them in a good light. Her classmates knew better and were not foolish enough to be open to persuasion!

As for me, the last years in Leeds were quickly forgotten so generously was I received by all my new colleagues. A reluctant academic is how I describe myself and so far as Sikh studies are concerned certainly not a scholar but a populariser; I left the classroom in the arrogant belief that I had something to offer to teacher training and yet by 1979 things had changed so much that John Rankin told me, one day, that if I had not a PhD I would probably not have been appointed to the West Sussex Institute. This not in any spirit of bitterness but simply as a statement of fact; by the late seventies qualifications, not experience, were what mattered as colleges began to hope for university status.

Even hands on contact with multifaith schools was still possible to some degree, not as much as in the best years of my Leeds career but something was far better than nothing. The Institute already sent students to Mount Pleasant primary school in Southampton which had a Sikh head teacher and children from a variety of religious backgrounds and I was given the opportunity of taking them to visit it. We experienced Divali and Eid there as well as the birthdays of Guru Nanak and Jesus in a context where the desire and enthusiasm to celebrate these occasions were already there with no need to persuade reluctant traditionalists to learn new tricks.

Jorgen Nielsen of the Centre for the Study of Islam and Christian

Muslim Relations was invited to take a party of experienced people to a course on multicultural education to be held in the Black Forest region of Germany. Apart from the German professor who had organised it, addressing us as though this was a new discovery that he had made and no one else knew anything about, and winter snow in October, the value of the conference lay, as usual, in making new friends and sharing experiences. A senior adviser from Ealing who was responsible for Religious Education told me that the authority had no adviser in the subject and asked me if I could go into Southall schools for two days every half term. John Rankin, supportive as ever, was agreeable to me rearranging my timetable to accommodate the situation and I embarked upon a series of visits that lasted for about three years until the decision was made to appoint an adviser. Two of the schools were comprehensive and had excellent teachers, Sue Ashton and Joy Barrow. Sue was the antithesis of the stereotypical teacher, modern in dress and pink haired. Joy was more conventional in appearance but an equally effective and innovative teacher and it was she who, meeting me at a Southern Shap conference in Chichester, invited me to visit her school when I was in Southall, and without warning handed me one of her senior classes with whom to discuss the different beliefs that they held or knew about concerning God. The pupils ranged from evangelical black Christians to Hindus, Muslims and Sikhs. Joy went on to put her knowledge of Southall Sikhs to good use by studying successfully for a Ph D in Sikh studies, becoming only the second Briton after myself to have such a qualification. I could happily have returned to her school many times but sadly, my brief was to give help where it was needed and Joy could manage well enough without me. Instead I went to a series of primary schools that had been prepared for my coming but were not enthusiastic to receive me. The head teachers had asked their colleagues to provide me with lesson schemes which I was then able to discuss with the teachers who were freed from their classes for a period. What I discovered in almost every case was no continuity or liaison between one year and the next, no link between one curriculum area and another and very little RE, it being confined to sharing and caring and encouraging children to be kind and good. When teachers told me about their beliefs it was usually to assure me that they had no wish to impose it upon children of other faiths, so they preferred not to mention it for fear of being accused of evangelising. Whenever I suggested to teachers and head teachers that these were the aims that any school community might aspire to being part of a 'hidden curriculum' as some people have put it, it was clear that I had a problem – or perhaps the teachers had, one of acquiring new material and ideas. It was fairly obvious that they were teaching what they had always taught, much of it what I had learned in primary school, as perhaps they had. Schools were suffering severely from curriculum inertia, a disease that had affected me in my Corsham days, as I now realised. The value of my primary education in Dudley Hill was that it prepared me for becoming a teacher by providing me with most of the areas of geography, history and maths, for example, that I would need later, just as my grammar school courses prepared me for being a secondary school teacher, in a way that my history degree certainly did not, save for the important element of learning to think historically.

Continuity and curriculum linkage was difficult to achieve. Mrs. Hibbert had always taken year two and taught the Romans and Canada, where she had a sister whom she visited every year. RE was the story of the Anglo-Saxon conversion of England. The inclusion of Canada seemed to be an excellent idea; children are always likely to benefit when teachers play to their strengths and her class was obviously interested in what they heard about polar bears and beavers and journeys through the Rockies but it seemed a pity to stop there. Cabot and the North West Passage might have provided aspects of history, not to mention Wolfe and Montcalm and the Heights of Abraham that I learned about in junior school. As for RE, aspects of North American Indian religion might have been introduced. However, Mrs Hibbert was not eager to discuss changes even when I pointed out to her that the Romans were being taught by Miss Collins, her colleague in year one. It must be said that the recipe outlined in the above paragraph is not what I myself would necessarily have taught but I mention it as giving some idea of what could have been done in the name of integrated humanities in preference to exploring three different and unrelated topics.

The Romans were always popular, in fact each of our daughters studied them several times at school and Eluned, who took a history course at Caerleon, renewed her acquaintance with them yet again but this time found she was learning new things and that they were really interesting. In schools in Southall and elsewhere I tried to persuade teachers who were set on the Romans to realise that the Roman citizen about whom most is probably known apart from some of the emperors was St Paul and that his career and journeys as a spreader of Christianity would fit well into a Roman topic, as would an introduction to the Mediterranean world and western Europe in geography but not many teachers made a positive response, it would necessitate the learning of new tricks. Teachers, until the days of the National Curriculum, were probably the only group of professionals who were not obliged to rehone their skills; thankfully my dentists, doctors and surgeons were compelled to retrain periodically. Curriculum inertia had benefited me when I taught junior children, I was able to fall back on what I had learned at Dudley Hill but I now realised that it was a serious bar to development, especially in a context of multiculturalism, and threw what support I could give behind the changes that the 1988 Baker Act introduced though the excessive use of targets and testing has never had my support. Strong head teachers and supportive governors should be able to ensure the delivery of the curriculum, backed up by firm LEA advisers. Another of my criticisms was that it was not as responsive as it could have been to the new multicultural society in which we found ourselves. Migration, including where people had come from and why, and what culturally they had brought with them, could have been more explicitly included so that Muslim or West Indian children could have learned about their heritage and the white, indigenous children could have been better informed. A topic on food could have shown how dependent Britain was for so many of its needs, such as dates, bananas, and oranges. The result might have been the promotion of mutual understanding and respect. Often my mind went back to telling the story of Bhai Khanaiya in Chapeltown.

My visits to Southall were not very successful or satisfying partly because I lacked authority and also because they were too infrequent. Some teachers were pleased to see me on my return but others did no homework in my absence. This was a time when I finally decided that being one of her majesty's inspectors or a LEA adviser would never provide me with job satisfaction, and recognised the need for a national curriculum which, in my view, should include Religious Education. The old argument that RE's content should be dictated by or responsive to local needs can no longer be sustained for even in Sussex many of its children will move to other parts of the country and will encounter Christians who are black and members of other faiths and none in their places of work. If schools do not prepare them for these experiences but for a Britain that has ceased to exist they will be doing them an ill service. In fact, it, like the rest of the curriculum, should have a global perspective and context.

It was in 1988 that the first significant Education Act since 1944 was introduced. School worship was largely unaffected, it had to remain daily and wholly or mainly broadly Christian but it was seen to be a separate curriculum area to classroom RE which was now to include, by law, the study of the six principal religions found in today's Britain. Arguments about the time that should be given to each followed but the principle had been finally established. Some authorities produced new agreed syllabuses and handbooks, and the number of in-service courses increased. One found oneself dealing with issues rather than method very often. A group of secondary teachers needed help in acquiring new knowledge but when we discussed school visits I discovered that the challenge went much deeper, they had never taken Muslim pupils to a mandir, and thought it too threatening to contemplate! They were looking for things that were not challenging. They had chosen the wrong subject and even the wrong career. An adviser friend of mine once described RE as feasting with sharks or crocodiles, and so it is, as is the whole of humanities education if one considers it carefully. RE, History and English should challenge children to think, not merely accumulate facts.

The approach that was encouraged with primary as well as secondary teachers was the exploration of the different dimensions of religion. Instead of naming these just now I will suggest classroom approaches. Let us take the example of Christmas, the event most celebrated in our schools and least understood. First there is the narrative, the story that is found only in two of the four New Testament Gospels – that some times comes as a surprise. Only Luke provides an account of the preparation and birth, the journey from Nazareth to Bethlehem, and does it include the story of a little donkey, one of the most popular carols of today? Matthew describes the journey of the Wise Men or Magi, but does he say that there were three? The teacher must look at his class and decide what of the birth stories they are ready to understand. Secondly, there is the history behind the story, how much of that is relevant to their grasp of it? The story element is sometimes described as the mythical, but this is a dangerous word because the popular use of it in such programmes as the Radio BBC Today Programme tends to suggest that it refers to something untrue, such as the NHS is safe in the government's hands. From the story comes the teaching, the doctrine, what the story is saying to the believer. Here we might use the most theological of all hymns associated with Christmas, 'Hark the herald angels sing' or 'Love came down at Christmas'. The birth of Jesus also presents a challenge, what does the event mean in the experience of the believer; one is not including the student in this category and must be careful not to say that it should affect them in any way, but it is essential that they do not take it as a believe it or not tale on the part of the Christian, for them it has been called a matter of life or death and of ethical conduct. There is also a social dimension when the believing family gathers to celebrate the birth. The exploration of this may not be easy in the UK where almost everyone enjoys

Christmas whether they are believers of not. Perhaps it may be able to use material from India, Pakistan or China to sharpen the focus. For those teachers whose interest is in history stories of Medieval Christmases, as in *Redcap Runs Away*, might be employed and those inclined to art might examine some Nativity scenes, including those from other cultures that are now easily accessible. For children to realise that Jesus was not a white man and that he was a practising Jew, is important. When teachers have examined the subject from their mature perspectives it is time to ask them to think what they would use with their particular age groups. Christmas may not be the best time to examine this topic; I remember exploring it with a secondary class embarking upon a study of the life of Jesus. 'Why are we doing Christmas now, it's only September?', came the question. Another popular focus is Passover, partly because there have been videos that teachers can use for their own education or with children but also because it, like most Jewish festivals, contains a high element of drama. With a Hindu puja there is the need to reassure teachers and parents that the exercise is a simulation, not an actual act of worship, so too with yoga, known to hit the headlines in some local and occasionally national newspapers. However, most contentious in my experience has been examining the Christian Eucharist in this way, and especially the idea of simulation. 'It is a sacrament, we cannot pretend that it is just like a picnic!' was one outcry. 'I couldn't do it, I'm not a priest' was another one. A suggestion that a priest might actually be prevailed upon to perform a simulation was still greeted with some dubiety. I have known clergy simulate a Eucharist with considerable pleasure and success, understanding perfectly the purpose of the exercise and participating enthusiastically. Such experiences persuaded me of the importance of helping students and teachers develop their own philosophies instead of providing tips for teachers.

In multi-faith high schools especially, I have always advocated a thematic approach for pragmatic and practical reasons as well as having a genuine preference for it. How difficult it must be to take a religion by religion approach when three or five faiths are represented in the class. Where would one begin and how? With Buddhism as the oldest, recognising that the Hinduism we know of is about as old as Christianity? When I gave out the prospectus for the next five years would I say, 'You will notice that Christianity is given half a term in year five, just make sure you are not sick then, or you'll miss it'? My solution would be to spend the first few weeks in any secondary school discussing the purpose of Religious Studies as distinguished from the intention of the mosque or gurdwara to confirm its members in the faith; helping pupils to learn to leave their own beliefs on one side, to suspend them academically in the classroom, and consider a few examples. Then I would examine the religious map of the world, where religions arose, where they moved to and why, how it is that they are found now in Birmingham, Sheffield, Cardiff, or whichever place the school is situated. Probably the first topic would be origins and historical development, the background that gave rise to such messengers as Jesus, Muhammad or the Buddha, and the religious world they inhabited. Here I would set pupils to work in groups, not all Jews or Sikhs together but with at least one faith member in each group, as a resource but not an authority, to guide and help but not become absorbed in the minutiae as we so often do when we are presenting our own faith. I swear my best lesson on Buddhism was one, using slides, of course, that I was invited to give in a Harrogate school with a time limit of about eighty minutes including discussion and questions. It helped concentrate the mind wonderfully. (Sadly, after discussing what might be followed up in the next few sessions, the teacher told me that it was Judaism next week and a rabbi was taking the session! Five religions in less than half a term, then back to Christianity.) My own task would be that of a facilitator in the learning process. The culmination of this period of study would be the sharing of what each group had discovered with the rest of the class.

Further topics would be scriptures, worship, pilgrimages, festivals, life ceremonies, and the main teachings, to some extent this would be a bringing together of knowledge and ideas already gathered during earlier parts of the study. There are arguments for keeping the same groups so long as they work well together; the leaders in research would change regularly with their own traditions becoming the centre of interest. Finally, I would want to give time to exploring the coming together of religions and their interaction, positive and otherwise, and interreligious dialogue. (This approach has been followed in *Six Religions in the Twentieth Century* published by Stanley Thornes; it first appeared in 1984 as *Five Religions* but has since been enhanced by Peggy Morgan's excellent contribution on Buddhism and a general revision taking account of liturgical and other developments in this century, hence its current title; *Six Religions in the Twenty First Century*).

Life at the Institute was interesting as well as enjoyable. The B.Ed. course attracted a range of students, among them evangelical Christians. John Rankin and I marvelled at the way in which we seemed inevitably to hit on them when handing out artefacts for research at their first session. Believing in their use and the religious anonymity of our students, if they had any allegiances at all, we began our first excursion into religion by giving each student an artefact to research, finding out what it was, what religion it belonged to, how it was used by adherents, and any other information they could glean, including its symbolism and significance. We would go along the row picking an object at random but somehow rosaries and crucifixes, a murti of Ganesha, or a Hindu mala found its home in the hands of the most protestant members of the group. Once over the shock, however, each recipient responded well, often volunteering the reasons for their initial concern and analysing it sensibly and perceptively. The task was a valuable growth experience for most if not all the class as they had never done anything like it before. They also realised that with modifications it was an idea that could also be implemented in the classroom on teaching practice or when they had graduated, and most of the B.Ed. students were school orientated from the very beginning of their course.

Primary school students and teachers are generally pupil focused; they may also be highly interested in the academic subject they are studying, but often this comes far down the line. Their secondary equivalents are usually fascinated by their academic study and may see themselves more as teachers of a discipline rather than teachers of children. I offer this observation for whatever it is worth but it certainly chimes in with my experience. Fortunately, I have seemed to be able successfully to sit comfortably in both situations, as I am sure many other professional teachers have though a severe criticism that I had to make of my Leeds authority when it decided on the three tier system was that no one helped the secondary teacher to respond to the new situation of teaching nine-year olds, those who found themselves with thirteen plus age groups seemed to cope more successfully, and anyway, there were far fewer who found themselves in this position.

Curriculum courses in RE were taken by all students preparing to teach in primary schools. Usually when I had given them a course outline I began with a discussion of why we should teach world religions and not only Christianity. It came as an agreeable surprise to be told: 'Owen, there is no need for you to tell us why we should teach world religions we share your views. Just let us think of how and what'.

It became clear that they had already thought out the issues and were ready to proceed from there. This change, in the early eighties, seemed to characterise the new generation of eighteen year olds; it was previous generations who most needed convincing but even they accepted the principle and only needed encouragement in acquiring skills and methodology.

This is where the Shap courses based on Chichester and pioneered by

John Rankin proved valuable. Not only did teachers spend two whole days and part of a third listening to lectures and meeting in discussion groups as well as socially, they also met members of the particular faith community that was the focus of the weekend. A room was turned into a mandir or gurdwara for example, and Hindus or Sikhs from Southampton celebrated an act of worship and we discussed how it might be simulated in the classroom. Courses being held at weekends it might have seemed difficult to obtain Jewish participation but a well-known Jew, Clive Lawton, came and explained that he was not forgoing his Sabbath, something he would not do, but he was bringing it with him and inviting us all to share in it. Often it is perspective and imagination that is required. Mutual friendship and respect and a desire for the greater good, in this case an understanding of Judaism, can enable the over-coming of what can seem to be insuperable difficulties when they are first considered. It is rather like making a journey, climbing a mountain or beginning a book or thesis, if the final destination is allowed to dominate many would-be adventurers give up in despair, but if the way and purpose are kept in mind progress is much easier.

Occasionally, a course could throw up difficulties, and in these circumstances it was providential to have a residential element as this gave time for members to stay together, reflect, and sort out issues that were causing difficulty. The most memorable situation arose during a course on the place of women in religion and involved attitudes towards Jehovah's Witnesses. As part of a second-year BA course on Contemporary Religion East and West it had become an established practice to invite members of the Haré Krishna movement, the Unification Church and Jehovah's Witnesses to speak to the students. As I had people I knew well from each of the three faiths it was not diffi-cult to persuade them to visit us and for them to understand the rules of the game, which by then the undergraduates knew well. Consequently, in a Shap course on Women, I asked two Jehovah's Witness members to lead a brief session on the role of women within their assembly. All semblance of a religious studies approach disappeared as some course members decided that this was an opportunity to attack their views on the person of Jesus, the end of the world, blood transfusion and religion in school, especially their non-observance of birthdays and Christmas. It was one of those rare, and possibly unique situations in which I have felt it necessary to call a course to order, remind it that the purpose of RE is to understand what it means to be a member of a faith, in this case the Jehovah's Witness, and not to attack it, and to ask for politeness and cour-tesy. It was only with difficulty that I was able to persuade the two ladies to stay for dinner and accept the book tokens that I had given them. Fortunately, they were very magnanimous and have remained my friends.

From this experience and others I am drawn to the conclusion that it is Jehovah's witnesses and not Muslims or Jews who are the touchstone of toleration in the sense of acceptance and respect in our society, followed perhaps by travellers. Why this should be is probably explained by the facts that the Jehovah's Witnesses are close to Christians, sharing a Bible and certain attitudes to Jesus, for example, that they are critical of some mainstream Christian beliefs, and that they do witness openly to their faith. Diversity is acceptable when the other tradition is far removed from our own, not close to it. Humorously, Witnesses will tell me that the best way to get an empty railway carriage is not to wear a dog collar or embarrassingly and lovingly embrace your partner but sit reading the Watchtower. More seriously, I am reminded that they too died in Nazi concentration camps; in fact I have met some of the survivors and heard their stories, and that the first person to die once war was declared in 1939 was a young man being held in one of the camps who was just brought to the front of the gathered prisoners and shot in the head. It is often forgotten that they were one of the few inmates who could go free; all they had to do was renounce their faith, unlike Jews, and perhaps communists.

RE in England must still be taught according to an Agreed Syllabus, as has already been mentioned. The nineteen seventies saw a major change in the form and purpose of these documents which hitherto had attempted to prescribe or at least recommend what should be delivered but now became briefer outlines covering principles and approaches. Handbooks, supplementing the syllabuses with quite detailed schemes of work suggesting how principles could be turned into practice, tended to accompany them. One proposed syllabus, that of Birmingham, before the one of 1975 was finally accepted by the LEA. It was reduced to little more than one printed sheet of A4 paper. It was eventually rejected by the Department of Education ostensibly on the grounds of brevity; as one HMI put it to me waving it as he spoke:, 'Can one really say that one piece of paper is an Agreed Syllabus?' The feeling of myself and others active in the RE world was that the inclusion of non-religious life stances was the real reason for rejection. At this time Harry Stopes Roe, a humanist philosopher on the staff of the university, was actively inter-ested in education and the British Humanist Association brought out a pamphlet entitled, '*Objective, Fair and Balanced*'. It was his influence more than anyone else's that persuaded Birmingham to go the way it did, though Peter Woodward, its inspector for RE must have been sympathetically responsible for winning acceptance. Objectivity, it was argued, must include an examination of disbelief as well as belief, not to provide a lobby for the range of ideas between agnosticism and atheism but to enable students to examine belief systems rationally and critically. This was not the time for such a radical approach to RE, earlier it might have been and later perhaps, for today such openness is generally accepted, though teachers and pupils can find it hard to deal with it. Even in 1978, it must be remembered, the Hampshire Syllabus had to argue 'that it is no part of the responsibility of a county school to promote any particular religious standpoint, neither can an exclusive Christian content do justice to the nature of the subject'.

Religious Education has always been primarily concerned with knowledge, beliefs and practices, though its original purpose was to nurture children in the broad Christian faith of the nation; it may not be surprising, therefore, to learn that school worship always has been and still is a daily requirement in the life of English schools. My own experience of an emphasis on worship to the total neglect of lessons in the subject from 1944 when both became compulsory until I left school in 1951 is far from unique. The 1944 Act endorsed what was already the practice in many schools, When I first went to Dudley Hill in 1936 daily worship was already the pillar of the school day, it regarded the two as inseparable; only in 1988 was a legal distinction made though in practice it had been developing in earlier decades as some RE specialists made it clear at interview that worship was, as it correctly still is, the responsibility of the head teacher and governors, not part of the duties of the RE department. When I began teaching in 1957 I was totally in favour of school worship, so much so that if, at Corsham or in Harlow, there was not a school assembly, I held one with my own class. In Corsham I also ended the day with a prayer. As time passed I encouraged secondary school specialists to go against the law at least to the extent of organising gatherings of part of the school at a time. To provide something that could be meaningful to eleven year olds and sixth formers I was realising was probably impossible, but I still supported compulsory worship even if it might not be daily. This remained my view until about 1970; in 1974 I wrote an article for the Association of Religious Education, 'Against School Worship: A Case for Abolition'. At about the same time Dr John Hull of Birmingham University also began to criticise it. Which of us was first into print I cannot be sure and it must be for others to decide if they so wish. (Some of us lead sad lives!) For myself I want to insist that it was the developing nature of RE and my understanding of worship that converted me to the abolitionist cause, if such a cause did already exist, or to originate it if it didn't. RE in the classroom was no longer confessional, no longer trying to impose belief upon the children we taught; it was critical in the academic sense of not taking beliefs and narratives for granted. Worship on the other hand must include some element of belief. One could not sing a hymn or pray upon the lines of, 'O God. If you are there, do you listen and can you respond?' There must be some belief, however slight, in the existence of the Other and in the belief that communion with that Being is possible. Put briefly, I could no longer accept the practice of being open in the classroom and then suggesting that we could put it aside and worship in the hall. It should be noted that my views on school worship derived from my approach to RE and not at all from the fact that our schools were becoming multi-religious in their composition. There are those who blame the presence of other faiths for a dilution of the place of the Christian religion in society. This is not a view I can endorse or wish by my statements to encourage. In my own case, as I may remark later, awareness of other faith has not diminished my own but rather has enhanced it. My opposition to compulsory worship was also influenced by my own difficulty; personal faith has never been something that comes easily or naturally to me and I cannot endorse an activity similar to the paying of cult that every Roman in Chichester would be required to do on the emperor's birthday. I cannot support something that says faith can be put on or discarded like a tee shirt or a pair of socks. Primary school children will, of course, do almost anything, as I saw on a programme about education in China in the sixties with little ones cheerfully singing the praises of Chairman Mao and the Revolution. Teachers of the youngest children have a great responsibility for their consciences. Freed from a legal requirement to worship daily, schools might develop meaningful assemblies that most staff and pupils can participate in and which explore important aspects of existence. Muslim, Sikh, or Christian insights might be included, as I am sure they are in many schools but the 1988 Act still requires a daily act of mainly Christian worship. It is one of the remaining shibboleths of twentieth-century society or even earlier, and is contributing to our national tendency to repudiate and even ridicule religion. Apart from faith schools there seem to be few secondary educational institutions that feel able to require students to sing hymns! If we did not have a legacy of school worship it is highly unlikely that we would invent it today.

CHAPTER

12

India Revisited

In 1983 I was given a one term sabbatical by the Institute because, I was told, I had never had one before in my twenty-six years of teaching. . John Rankin was also asked to inform me that I would never have another so I had better make the most of it. I immediately arranged to join Professor Harbans Singh at Punjabi University. Patiala, and work with him on the *Sikh Encyclopaedia*. He offered me a small emolument which went some way towards paying for my accommodation in the university guest house. Eluned and Siân were both due to begin courses. At Caerleon, where Gwynneth and I had met, and Coventry. Once their places were confirmed I set out for India, but I did not go directly to Patiala; with the help of a good friend, Professor Mohinder Singh, and Indian Airlines, I planned a month's a tour of Bombay, Bangalore, Madurai, Madras, Calcutta, Varanasi, Agra, and Mathura using one of those tickets that permitted unrestricted travel within the country for a thirty-day period.

Sadly, there was no Islamic element in my tour except for another visit to the Taj Mahal which could be about as Muslim as eating a bagel might be Jewish but there were numerous Christian, Hindu and Sikh aspects. My first stop was the Bharatya Vidya Bhavan centre in Bombay as the city was then called; a British contact had arranged it. I learned about their publication and educational work and was shown the sights of Bombay, and then they set me on my way to Bangalore providing me with contacts in Delhi and elsewhere. The Bangalore stage was essentially Christian, largely by design as I had written from England to ask for accommodation in a Christian institute. The modern architecture of the city was impressive; it had been the British intention to make it the capital of the Empire, at one time, I was told, and the civic buildings were a testimony to a regime that was expected to last for a thousand years. The variety of Christian denominations was distressing, it read rather like the list of Jewish visitors to Jerusalem listed in the Book of Acts chapter two! There were Roman Catholics, Anglicans, Methodists, Church of South India, Syrians and many more; I began to understand what Piara Singh had in mind when he told me of missionaries coming to his village, Methodist one week, Roman Catholics another, each saying that they offered the true path to salvation. He said that he would wait until they had solved the problem among themselves – and then he might consider conversion; though he added with tongue in cheek that he was extremely settled and happy in his own spiritual Sikh world. There can be few places where the scandal of denominationalism was as obvious as it was in Bangalore in 1983. A young Christian convert told me her interesting story. She was a Hindu brahmin living in a village which had a Christian dalit minority population and she began to suffer from a skin complaint, possible eczema, that no one seemed able to treat successfully. A Christian girl told her that their priest had the ability to heal and suggested that she might go to him. This she did and the rash cleared up but she also came to respect him and the humanitarian work that he was attempting to do in the community. Eventually, she said that she wished to become a Christian, a decision that presented many difficulties – her family would reject her, the Christian community dared not give her shelter for fear of how the Hindus might respond. However, she persisted in her intention to convert, was thrown out by her parents and did provide the Christian community with a headache which was solved by the bishop suggesting that she went to Bangalore where, being a clever girl, she could go to college. But this was not the end of her story for at college she met and fell in love with a Christian man of her own age, who was also a brahmin. All seemed to be well, some might even see the hand of providence at work, but his parents were not impressed, first because they thought that they should arrange his marriage in accordance with Indian custom, but also because she did not come from one of the brahmin groups with which their family intermarried. They made further enquiries about her and their son was able to reassure them that she was not only a vegetarian but that she did not eat garlic and onions; apparently this meant that she came from a superior brahmin group to theirs and so the proposed marriage was accepted. The couple intended that the husband would be ordained and his wife would support him in a teaching role.

This was my first encounter with the caste system in Indian Christianity but I was to find that it was by no means rare; I heard of situations in which the higher caste members received the elements of communion first, to be followed by the lower orders to ensure that they would not be polluted ritually by drinking from a chalice that had previously touched the lips of dalits, or that comparatively few men of low caste were appointed bishops for fear of offending the higher caste minority. On my return to Chichester I included caste among Christians in my sessions on contemporary religion in India but many students were unwilling to believe me until I persuaded some nuns, known to my wife, who were nursing at St Richards, to talk to them about Christianity in India and include mention of the caste system – most of them were of low caste, nursing not being a profession suitable for decent women partly because it involved contact with blood and faeces. One morning I was taking a walk past the Christian colleges and other institutions when I heard the sound of singing coming from one of the buildings; upon inves-tigation I found a group of young Christians at worship singing hymns in their local language to the accompaniment of traditional Indian instru-ments. My mind was carried back to Pakistan where I had shared in a similar reassuring experience. Perhaps their belief in a Christianity that transcended imported western denominationalism might find a fertile soil in India. My concern was not for missionary success and conversion but for the proclamation of a gospel that was free from the trappings of the Reformation that surely had no meaning on the other side of the world. On another occasion I happened to glance over a wall and saw a number of Hindus changing their sacred threads; they explained that this was Ganesha Chaturthi, the birthday of the elephant headed god, and that they were renewing their sacred threads. They happily allowed me to observe their rituals.

The temple of Meenakshi in Madurai is one of the most famous in the whole of India and is built in a style rarely seen in the north, partly, it is said, because such temples were often stripped bare of their treasures and destroyed by the series of invaders who crossed the Khyber Pass or the Indian Ocean in search of the country's riches. It was, therefore, one of the places on my itinerary. The flight from Bangalore was short and kind people phoned ahead to arrange hotel accommodation for me. Someone at the hotel knew an English-speaking guide who met me, took me to the temple, left me back at the hotel to have a rest in the afternoon and, in the evening, took me to see the important ceremony when Parvati and Shiva are taken to their respective rooms and allowed to rest, though not until rice balls had been thrown at them! The reason for this act, enjoyed by adults and children alike, was never fully explained to me. A feature of the mandir was the massive gopuram or gateway many metres high and dominating not only the temple but the town and covered by lavishly colourful mythological scenes, frequently depicted on TV programmes and tourist brochures. Almost as interesting to me were the many stalls built into the walls of the temple precincts; presumably the mandir enjoyed a large rent and taxes from the sales of goods sold there, not only tourist items but food, hardware, clothes, all the kinds of things found in markets back home. Churches and cathedrals in Britain often find it difficult to pay their way; here seemed to be a possible solution, and then I remembered that Wood Street Congregational church in Cardiff had already thought of it by selling or renting the site to developers who, in return, built them a smaller church within the complex, much more suitable for their modern needs.

Madras was a city that I liked, possibly because of the breeze blowing off the sea and the sight of the ocean. It seemed clean and fresh and I could understand why so many members of the East India Company liked it well enough to settle and be buried there though I couldn't appreciate the manner in which marriages with Indian women, at one time encouraged, had later been frowned upon or forbidden so that a new caste, their offspring, the Anglo-Indians, had been created. In the days of the Raj their anomalous status might have been acceptable, many of them helped run the railways, but afterwards the new nationalism following independence and, perhaps their unwillingness to accept the change, resulted in much distress. Whether St Thomas is buried in the cathedral or not I know no better than anyone else; (will DNA offer any help, I wonder), but I certainly accept the notion of Roman trade with south India and with it the likelihood that Christian missionaries were to be found in subcontinent long before there is any evidence for the faith being planted in Britain – and Doubting Thomas may be the best candidate. It is pure speculation to ask what kind of a religion Christianity might have become had it gone east into the lands of the Magi and the Buddha instead of the world of Diaspora Judaism but might St Paul have been more influenced by the idea of enlightenment than that of original sin and the heavy burden of guilt that often goes with it, India might have absorbed something of Christianity into itself; some later missionaries to north India actually argued that it did, seeing in Krishna the word 'Christ' and claiming that the bhakti tradition of Hinduism, liberation through faith in devotion to God's love, was really a response to the Incarnation.

St Thomas's Cathedral was fascinating and after walking around it I spent an hour or more watching the devotees, behaving just as they would in a mandir. I arrived at a time when there was no service and apparently no clergy, only individual devotees, mainly female and alone. They may have been Christians or Hindus, all were dressed in bright saris, and most were carrying flowers, were bare-footed and, as far as I could observe, moved in a clockwise direction around the cathedral, beginning at the door and approaching the altar in a manner that was devout but would a Christian lady have passed beyond the chancel rail? Language and the etiquette of not speaking with ladies whom I did not know prevented me from finding out but I know of a local Anglican church in West Sussex where the space between chancel and altar is reserved for clergy and in Patiala I attended a communion service in a Methodist church where ladies did go beyond the communion rail but they removed their shoes which they had not done on entering the church. Perhaps this was another clue that pointed to my devotees being Hindus? Clearly, the more I learn the more I find out that there is still to discover, but that's life. No wonder that many folk believe in reincarnation, though according to the Bhagavad Gita only Krishna remembers his former lives. To return to present reality as it presented itself on that summer morning in Madras rather than speculating, it was pleasing to note the freedom with which everyone seemed welcome to come and go as they wished. The statue, or was it a murti, and grave of St Thomas, came in for particular veneration; one lady prostrated herself, each offered a flower, and so reminded me of the words of Lord Krishna in the Gita, 'Whatever one gives me with a sincere heart, even though it were only a flower, pleases me'. Could the Christian message forget or at least supplement its creeds and rituals in such a manner that women like these could feel at ease?

The cathedral experience had refreshed me after my early morning attempt to enter a major Hindu mandir dedicated to Vishnu, for the first time ever, and it only happened once again. I was refused entry by one of the priests who told a family of Hindus that I had joined that as I was a European, and therefore obviously a meat eater, I would defile the building. The family were all for my insisting on my rights under Indian law, to demand admission but this would have been against every principle of respect that I held dear so I arranged to meet them later and persuaded them to pay their respects without me. The leader of the party was a civil servant whose mother, a widow, had recently died. As the eldest son he was travelling to various sites to secure for her a better rebirth if not complete liberation. This visit to places of pilgrimage might take about six months; his employers realised that this was a filial duty that must be fulfilled and had readily given him leave of absence. My new friends told me of a pilgrimage route round India that is becoming increasingly popular because of affordable rail travel. By train it takes about ten weeks to accomplish the whole journey. However, my pilgrims seemed to despise this easy method and said that tiraths or tirthas must involve effort and some hardship to bring real benefit. Otherwise the exercise could become a sight-seeing tour – they assured me that my own sincerity was not in doubt! They were travelling for the most part on foot. Sites were often located, they said, where water and land met, on the banks of rivers, especially where two or more rivers met, or by the sea, again at the meeting place of land and sea, or on mountain peaks, where earth and sky came together. Mythically, they were associated with deities, and were favoured by devotees of Vishnu, or Siva, for example. My family were going to Vaishnavite centres, but of course they had also been to Varanasi, sacred to Siva. Everyone went there, I was told. Religious history might link a place with an incident in sacred story, such as the place where Siva took the force of the waters of the Ganges on his head to prevent the earth from being smashed to smithereens, at its source. Though God is everywhere and within everyone, there were sites of especial significance and by visiting them piously, their mother's spirit would benefit.

Calcutta was my next destination. On the flight I sat next to a young Hindu business man who was very friendly and spoke excellent English. As soon as we began talking he said that I could not be British because we were a taciturn lot who never spoke to anyone. Family is a frequent topic of conversation in India and he asked me about mine. My lack of sons came up as it usually did and he hoped that God would eventually bless me in this respect. I think he was convinced when I said that my wife and I were very pleased with our daughters but I couldn't be entirely sure; he, for his part was unmarried. Wheeler dealer, though I was sure he was, it was my turn to express surprise when he said that his would be an arranged marriage, his wife being chosen by 'mummy and daddy', who would know what was best for him. The contrast between this man as a professional and as a son was quite amazing and took some grasping. Too soon we arrived in Calcutta where a group of Sikhs would be waiting for me, I would like to have talked longer and accepted his offered hospitality.

Captain Bhag Singh, retired, was my prearranged host in Calcutta where he edited the celebrated *Sikh Review* that I had subscribed to for some years. So far as I know it is the only regular Sikh publication of its kind. Two of his colleagues met me at the airport and accompanied me on the long drive into the city where the much respected editor was awaiting me, ready to provide me with a cup of tea. I met a number of retired military officers serving their communities just as he was, and found all of them well organised; they brought to their voluntary work the discipline and order that had been an important part of their professional life. Infirmity prevented him from giving me hospitality so I was accommodated in a hostel near his office. It is wise to have a talk prepared because almost everywhere I was asked to speak to an invited audience and the subject, Piara Singh had warned me, should be something about Sikhism or one of the Gurus. The subject I might have chosen, Sikhs in

Britain, was likely to be of no interest, they had jumped ship, as it were, and so passed beyond the interest of Sikhs in India. The lecture was to be given in a hall that was part of the hostel, at 3 p.m. The time came and went and nothing happened so, at about 4 p.m., I ventured out of my room to explore the building and see, if possible, where my audience was. I found an almost empty auditorium but was motioned back to my room. About half and hour later my chairperson, a Hindu lady, came for me and I was led to the hall. Later it was explained that lectures began when it was judged that the maximum audience had gathered. Time gave way to the audience rather than the audience giving way to time; was this the first principle of Indian punctuality? I had long known that in a country where 'kal' can mean yesterday or tomorrow, depending on the tense of the accompanying verb, time not to be taken seriously, but this was a new experience.

Varanasi is said to be the oldest city continuously inhabited in the world and the holiest in India, sacred to Siva, so also known as Kashi besides Benares. Professor Mohinder Singh, whom I had yet to meet, had arranged for me to stay with Professor Shamer Singh, of the anatomy department of Benares Hindu University. The ancient propeller driven Fokker touched down on the tarmac at the airport and my lasting memory as I prepared to disembark is that of the intense heat that hit us as the door was opened. Far across the runway at the airport building I could see one turban amid the many saris and suits, it must be my host. In fact it was his cricket enthusiast son, Gurpreet, himself a medical student who has been my close friend ever since we met. He introduced me and drove me to the university along roads still inches deep in water. The monsoon had been particularly heavy in 1983 and floods were common place. As we drove past a wooden shack Gurpreet told me that it was the stall of a seller of cigarettes and tobacco who had lost all his stock, yet, devout Hindu that he was, he could still 'thank Mata Ganga for visiting him and blessing his shop'. How men like this survive in India; I have never discovered, cigarettes are a popular commodity, though not among the Sikhs, but hawkers and peddlers spend the day and most of the night going from place to place trying to sell things that nobody seems to want. Are they endlessly in debt? How can they buy food for their families and new stock for their customers?

The professor and his wife were eagerly awaiting me with a cup of tea and some cakes, of course and we soon chalked out, to use a popular Indian phrase, my programme for the days that I was going to spend with them. They had already made some plans, for me to travel with a medical team to a nearby village which I could explore while they did their work, for an opportunity to meet some London-based British doctors who were part of an exchange scheme with Indian colleagues at the University hospital. They knew my needs, to visit the city and its temples, and go on a boat trip down the Ganges, and to spend some time at the place where the Buddha preached his first sermon, Sarnath, the deer park near Varanasi. Fortunately the floods were receding quickly and life was returning to normal, including the dawn boat ride, at about five a.m., when one could enjoy the spectacle of the sun rising above the river and pilgrims offering puja to it besides doing more mundane things like washing their clothes, a sight that is supposed to have alarmed Oscar Wilde who declared that they were using his clothes to break their stones! On that occasion I saw no half cremated bodies being carried by the river but observed that the cremation ghat was already in full operation with the Dom raja, the powerful overseer of death rituals, attending to every-thing from the stacking of wood to the arrangement of the pyres. I was told that elderly Hindus would be brought to the city to die between the river tributaries of the Ganges, the Varan and the Asi, in the belief that Siva would then give them spiritual liberation, moksha. The next day when I made my own unaccompanied journey around the city I took some photographs from the landward side for which the menacing Dom raja made a charge.

Buddhism ceased to exist in India sometime before the Mughal inva-sions though there are several suggestions offered to explain its disappearance and most of them do seem related to Muslim invasions though not necessarily to Islamic hostility. Unlike Hinduism which is very domestic, though I was finding out that there are many important mandirs, Indian Buddhism was dependent on the community of monks, the sangha, to provide a focus and teaching. Legend, if not reliable his-tory,had it that marauding armies believed that these were places of wealth and sacked them killing the monks or causing them to flee. Perhaps it was not surprising, though disappointing, to find only a small number of Buddhists at Sarnath and most of the visitors, or rather pil-grims, Hindus. This reinforced my experience at Madras where I was increasingly sure that the ladies who had circumambulated the cathedral were Hindus and my memories of the pictures in mandirs in Leeds, Bradford, Leicester and Southampton of Jesus, Guru Nanak, the Virgin Mary, a pope, the Buddha, besides Vivekananda, Gandhi, and the many deities of Hinduism: it was becoming obvious that India is a country where many forms of spirituality are respected. Whilst making a jour-ney by taxi from Delhi to Chandigarh my Sikh driver stopped at a mosque and shrine in a rural area to offer prayers, and another friend used often to visit the Roman Catholic Church opposite his house to offer prayers. These contrasted so much with the British tradition where Christians until the recent development of Churches' Together have seldom set foot in the place of worship of another denomination. Once my farmer uncle was taking me round his large holding and we passed a Methodist church; when I asked him if it was the one he attended he replied very firmly and sharply, 'No'; when I said but I thought you all joined together in the nineteen thirties, he conceded that the others might have done, but they hadn't in Crowle! I have to admit that I did not attend an act of worship in a Roman Catholic Church until I was about forty years old. One just didn't in those days; the Reformation was still much more than a memory. Sadly, from my very limited observations the attitudes of many Christians in India, not those like Jamila, I hasten to add, may be ecumenical but they do not always seem to be interested in interfaith matters, perhaps it is rather like the situation that Archbishop Runcie said he encountered in Singapore where he wished to meet members of other religions but felt his efforts thwarted, though his chaplain succeeded. He was told that the missionaries had said there was no salvation in Islam and other faiths, and now he wished to meet them? Why?

Gurpreet took me to meet the Satguru of the Ravidasis, a group I first knew about through the Open University video wrongly said to be about the Sikhs. He lived some way outside the sacred part of the city, where Ravidas had chosen to end his days, spurning the Hindu story that by dying between the rivers Varun and Asi liberation was automatically guaranteed. Religions should be organisms rather than organisations and so I found these people to be. They had turned from Sikhism from which they hoped to gain improved social status or at least acceptance, and were in the process of moving further towards total independence. In the sabhas, still occasionally called gurdwaras in England that I had visited, the installed scripture was the Guru Granth Sahib, even though it might be the forty-one compositions of Ravidas that are most used. The Satguru told me that many other hymns existed and that a Hindi collection was being compiled. Ultimately, the Sikh scripture would be replaced by their own and the language of the Sikhs would give way to Hindi, thus enabling the Ravidasis to become more than a Punjabi-based movement. Whether they would ever become more than a dalit movement of chamars or cobblers, like their founder, is more uncertain. Apparently orthodox Hindus were bringing legal actions to deprive them of their lands; this they regarded as an act of persecution. Perhaps with money from Ravidasis living in the Diaspora they would be successful in opposing those who sought to take their lands and in completing their corpus of scripture.

My stay with Gurpreet's family was most enjoyable and I was very pleased when, before I left, he told me that he was getting married in Ludhiana later in the autumn and that he hoped I could attend the wedding. One day I discovered that Baljit was also a doctor and came from a medical family, and that the couple had been allowed to spend a few days in Delhi, suitably chaperoned, so that they might make certain that they were suited to one another.

Before heading for Delhi I took an overnight diversion to Gorakhpur, a place associated with Guru Nanak. Among his compositions is a discussion with a siddha, an ascetic named Gorakhnath. The line did not begin with him and continued to the present day; each guru, when he died, being buried, not cremated as is usual in the Hindu tradition, but buried seated in the lotus position of meditation. The men I met, I saw no women, had long hair and only a loin cloth as clothing, they were very amiable and helpful but knew nothing about Guru Nanak and therefore any link with him and one of their teachers. When I met Gorakhnath, the head of the order, he spoke English, and was very mild and charming; my overnight stay was comfortable. Stories of Guru Nanak's life record his encounter with a yogi but do not name him as Gorakhnath or one of his disciples, but the narrative is of a man who ruled a village by fear. Descriptions reminded me of an encounter that I had one day in a Hindu village. Suddenly a rather small but powerfully built and dark skinned man came around the corner of house and almost bumped into me, his hair was long and matted and he was completely naked. The three-pronged stick that he carried in his hand showed him to be a devotee of Siva. He glowered at me fiercely and sidestepping me rather like a rugby player, was quickly on his way. Guru Nanak might well have met such a yogi. The story goes that he came to a village where he came across a crowd of terrified men and women sitting around a man who claimed to be a guru able to tell them what the future held for each of them. He was in a trance and in front of him was a bowl that he used for divining and putting the money and gifts he collected. Quietly, Guru Nanak approached him, picked up his begging bowl and placed it behind his back. Shortly afterwards the yogi regained consciousness and saw that his dish had disappeared; angrily he demanded to know who had stolen it. At this point Guru Nanak said; 'You call yourself a yogi and claim to be able to foretell the future and yet have no idea where your bowl is? What kind of fortune teller are you?' The crowd began to laugh, the terror of the village saw that he was losing his credibility and power over them, and so, with loud curses he picked up his bowl and went on his way. Guru Nanak told the crowd that only God knew the future, he was the Guru who inspired all gurus in whom they should put their trust.

At last I reached the Guru Nanak Foundation in Delhi and met Professor Mohinder Singh and some of his students. He and I became friends immediately and remain close to one another after over twenty-five years during which I have attended a family wedding, and conferences in India and Canada with him. At the latter he slipped on the ice, broke his wrist and adopted me as a servant, fastening his shoes, helping him put on his jacket and overcoat, and tying his turban, very badly. Now, however, he prepared me to give my lectures on Guru Nanak to be given under the chairmanship of the President of India, Dr Zail Singh. Being an honest and humorous man Mohinder told me that a number of eminent Sikhs had asked why Zail Singh was going to chair lectures given by an unknown Briton. His blunt answer was that the road outside the Foundation had not been completed, the surface was only temporary, his attempts to persuade the authorities to finish the work had got nowhere so, at last he hit upon the idea of inviting the President to perform the honours; this he knew would result in the whole area being made respectable, and it did. I had to admire his skill and appreciated his honesty that has always been a treasured feature of our long relationship together with his thoughtful kindness. A few years later I returned to India with our daughter Siân, when he knew of my intention and flight plans he altered his itinerary in order to meet up with us at Frankfurt and accompany us for the rest of our journey.

There were a number of days between my arrival in Delhi and my lectures; some of the time was spent in reading through the printed version of my talk and making sure that everything was correctly recorded, the rest of my time was taken by giving tutorials to his post-graduate students, all of whom were females, apparently business studies were more attractive to young men whose hopes lay in sharing the growing wealth of India. One never met these ladies in one's own room unless the door was left open or, perhaps, two or three of them came at a time; in fact most individual meetings took place in an open area where other people were free to come and go at will. This practice that was also followed at Patiala and anywhere else I went differed entirely from English custom and I couldn't help wondering how Asian students in England reacted deep down to the door closing behind them and to sitting face to face, alone with their tutor. Superficially, they accepted the practice, but probably their parents would not have been happy about it had they known.

I stayed at a university hostel near the Foundation where I met a number of men of different nationalities. The most salutary encounter was with an Indian author who had come to the country from America to collect his royalties. He told me that he would be spending the next few weeks standing outside each of his publishers' doors until he received his dues, and warned me against writing for any Indian publisher, advice that I have heeded scrupulously, though matters are not always that simple. Some years ago I received a complimentary copy of a book on Sikh teachings, one of its chapters seemed very familiar, and then two more. I discovered that the author had used four sections from books written by me and Piara Singh. When I wrote him a letter of complaint he replied that he was unable to understand my objections, we had presumably profited financially from our book and now it was his turn to benefit. We knew there was no point in taking the issue to law, in India especially it is always the lawyers who gain the most even if the long drawn-out procedure ends in one's favour.

The hot afternoon of my lectures arrived when I had not only to contend with the hum of a dozen fans failing feebly to cool the hall but the turning of pages as my audience of a couple of hundred women and men read my address; this was something unexpected and disconcerting largely because I never scrupulously follow my script. A lecture is always written down in full, I am uneasy relying on notes, having heard too many people who have not known when to stop. At least, I felt, they should write down the last sentence – but I feared losing the plot. However, it has always been my custom to ad lib and this I did but after the second occasion I realised that many listeners were hopelessly lost, perhaps they were not used to talks in English, so I had to help them find their place: 'I'm now on the tenth line of page six', or the top of page ten I would say, but the rustling of paper that interrupted my flow was the most difficult experience to contend with. The event seemed successful, though I am still convinced that Mohinder was more pleased with his pukka road and street lights than he was with me! The next afternoon he took me to Delhi bus station and put me on the vehicle that was to take me to Patiala. Reliable as ever, he phoned the university and arranged for me to be met at the gates.

CHAPTER
13

Patiala

It was about eleven o'clock when I arrived at the university gateway, and pitch black; suddenly, out of the silent darkness two men emerged, asked me if I was Professor Cole, picked up my luggage and took it and me to the guest house, my home for the next three months. Once they had settled me in, checked all the lights, made sure that the geezer for the hot shower was working, and flushed the toilet, they asked if they might take their leave and told me that they would see me on the following morning after breakfast that would be served in my room. As they left they warned me always to lock my door and enforced their words by handing me a large padlock. In no time at all I was asleep and only woke up when I heard the sound of a gardener outside my window. Mrs Sambhi had always provided bed tea so I knew what to expect when there was a knock on my door at about seven o'clock. Breakfast followed half an hour later, just as I was finishing my shower. It consisted of cereal with sugar and hot milk; no one ever uses cold milk, tea, and toast with jam. As this was to be my regular start to the day for some twelve weeks I decided that I must discover whether marmalade had reached India; surely the Raj would have got that right! It had, and two days later I had my own special jar.

My two minders of the previous evening arrived and took me to A1, the home of Professor Harbans Singh and his wife, Kailash; their grown up children were now in the United States. I was welcomed as usual with tea, served in china cups, and biscuits and we discussed my duties and general programme which were delegated to his subordinate Professor Kohli in whose study I could sit when I was not busy elsewhere. Guru Gobind Singh Bhavan was a fascinating and inspiring building, built as a hexagon with areas devoted to Buddhism, Christianity, Hinduism, Islam, Judaism, and Sikhism. Its library covered all these areas and others besides, such as Jainism. Difficulties arose at a practical level as I could well understand. Most, if not all, the students were female, because of male career aspirations; they were also Sikh as this was the university's composition, set in the Sikh heartland. There were Christian, Hindu, Muslim, Jain and Sikh members on the staff but no Buddhists or Jews. As I went round the building I discovered that all the married women, lecturers, secretaries and students were observing Carva Chaut, a fast on behalf of their husbands. This entailed refraining from eating certain foods, for example garlic and onions, for a period of four days; it was not as austere as Ramadan or Yom Kippur but its meaning was very serious; its purpose was to pray for the well-being of husbands. Glibly I might think that it was something to commend to my wife, who would say; 'No way!' but I had to bear in mind the historical position of women in the Hindu tradition.

Less than a century ago a widow was regarded as a bringer of ill fortune and might be compelled to live in accommodation separate from the family house in something like a garden shed and be deprived of almost any human company such as visits from her grandchildren, though she could hear them playing outside. She might have a servant and her son might come to see her occasionally but her daughter in law never. Still, today, the lot of widows can be far from comfortable, especially in rural communities. Wives, therefore, had good reason to fast and pray for their husband's welfare. It was interesting to learn that though the fast was a Hindu practice, and apparently mainly Punjabi, Sikhs and Christians also observed it.

On my very first full day at the university a Sikh professor invited me to his home for tea. Without any warning he launched himself into a diatribe against the caste system telling me that all foreigners, like me, believed it to be endemic in Indian society but that the Sikh Gurus had eradicated it from their community hundreds of years ago. Whilst I was pondering how to respond to this unexpected broadside another professor, a sociologist, let himself into the house and asked us what we were discussing. 'Caste', I quickly replied, and having lit the blue touch paper, retired from the conversation. 'Oh', he said to his colleague, 'I suppose you have been telling him that there is no caste in Sikhism'. Without waiting for a reply, he continued: 'When your wife has had to go to the home of a chamar, (a low caste leather worker), she immediately takes off her clothes when she comes home and takes a shower, then she puts on clean clothes. Am I right or am I wrong?' The surprised colleague agreed but argued that this was done only for reasons of hygiene. The argument continued for some time with myself only in the role of bystander which was as well as not being a member of the religion being discussed any view that I expressed would be considered as biased. In such circumstances to enquire innocently is acceptable in the search for truth and understanding but to go further is to put one's status as an observer at risk and to be accused of trying to undermine the religion one is studying.

When it became known that I was in town requests came for me to address or chair conferences. To comment on the great religions presented little difficulty and, in preparation, at Piara Singh Sambhi's suggestion, I had taken several outlines with me. My forward planning proved useless on the very first occasion when it was put to the test. A number of academics came to where I was sitting in the bhavan and told me that they had organised a conference on Jainism and the Sanskrit tradition and would like me to chair the key note lecture that afternoon. They had already discovered that I was free to help them so I could not plead a previous engagement and my declaration of ignorance was politely dismissed as modesty. When I asked them what my duties would be I was simply told: 'to chair the lecture'. With that they took me to meet the two speakers and to enjoy a waiter-service buffet lunch, better than that awaiting me at the guest house, but I had little appetite for it. Two-thirty arrived and we made our way to the lecture hall where an audience of some fifty men and women were awaiting us. The other members of the platform party stood back to let me go first and I quickly decided that the chair behind the table must be intended for me. At least in this I was correct. After welcoming the audience I introduced the speakers and sat back while they delivered their lectures, mostly in Sanskrit with a few connecting sentences in English. By now I had decided to fall back on British practice so when they had finished I asked for questions and discussion for the floor. Fortunately, there were plenty of these; people who had not been invited to contribute formally to the seminar seemed eager to have an opportunity to express their views; unwittingly I had broken the rules of formality that gave the floor little chance to react and they had appreciated it. Quietly, I then asked one of the organisers what I should do next and was told that this was my moment to make my scholarly contribution. It was now four o'clock and the waiters had laid out cups, saucers and biscuits, so I used this lifeline to tell the gathering that the duty of a chairman in England was to introduce the speakers, let them speak, encourage and control amicable discussion, thank the participants, both lecturers and audience for their contributions, and then invite everyone to enjoy a cup of tea. Having achieved successfully all these goals it remained for me only to declare the meeting closed which I now did. Everyone applauded politely and dispersed to the refreshment tables. A few delegates expressed their regrets that I had not offered my own views on the subject, for my part I breathed a sigh or relief and hoped I wouldn't have to use this particular ploy again.

Some years ago I heard that the late Fred Trueman and Tony Lewis had been invited to speak at a dinner given in honour of Bishen Singh Bedi, the famous Sikh spin bowler who must incidentally have come from the same sub caste or clan as Guru Nanak who was also a Bedi. They never delivered their speeches; as Fred put it in his usual blunt Yorkshire way. 'We were just about to give our after dinner speeches when the buggers got up and walked out!' Such is the Indian custom. First speak and then eat and then leave. One evening I was invited to the home of a professor who lived off campus in the centre of Patiala; when we arrived I was introduced to his wife and given a cup of tea after which the two of us sat and talked. Occasionally the wife put her head round the door only for her husband to wave her away to the kitchen where I heard the pressure cooker steaming and resteaming. By about nine o'clock I decided that whether it was polite or not I had better broach the subject of our meal. Next time his wife appeared he told her we were ready and by almost ten o'clock we were eating. Immediately upon the meal being over my host said he would take me to the bus stop; there we discovered that the last bus had left over two hours earlier. There was a factory near the university, perhaps I could catch the bus taking the night shift and be set down at the university, but this too had gone. Could I take a taxi? None was to be seen. How about hitch-hiking? I pointed out that the road was deserted and it was probably not a good idea for me to take such a risk. When all possibilities had been exhausted he suggested very reluctantly and rather anxiously, that I had better go back to his home and catch an early bus to the university the next day, but his wife had probably gone to bed and he did not want to disturb her. I shared his regrets and apologised, half heartedly, for being a nuisance; we returned to his home where a bed was prepared and pyjamas provided. I fell asleep with the noise of his wife's verbal beating wringing in my ears. Long before the Fred Trueman story, this was the way that I discovered Indian dining etiquette!

Working on the Encyclopaedia was a remarkable experience and one in which I felt very honoured to be allowed to participate. Few Sikhs I have met could have contemplated undertaking such a venture, unless they were totally overwhelmed by haumai, or what the secular world would describe as a super ego of self-destructive proportions. Professor Harbans Singh had a number of virtues that made him the man for the job. He was, in my experience, modest, but confident in his ability to see the task to a conclusion; he was a respected scholar so the people he asked to contribute articles would be willing to help him; he had a broad understanding of Sikhism and this enabled him to exercise wide-ranging oversight; he was well liked so that the project was not troubled by jealousy. In fact, when he died in 1998 almost all of the many obituaries described him as a 'gentle man'. No phrase could better suit him. He did not seem to be the kind of man to suffer fools gladly but during my period in Patiala I came across no fools who were connected with the project; on the contrary I encountered only respect and loyalty and a feeling that everyone recognised that this was an important enterprise that the Panth and scholarship in general needed. Harbans Singh was assisted by a retired army officer who brought a high quality of organisation to bear on the project modified by a rare sense of humour and the secretaries whom he supervised worked patiently and efficiently; two of them were men who had met me from my bus when I arrived at the campus.

The method of soliciting and contributing articles was one that I came to know well because I was caught up in the system as the person between the original articles and the finished and accepted product. The use of word processors and computers was as yet unknown so everything was produced in long hand or typed. The professor had clearly in mind a comprehensive list of articles. A letter would be sent to a particular scholar, asking him to provide an entry of, say, one thousand words in length covering the meaning of the term gurdwara, for example, its origins, its place in the Panth, architectural features, and worship. The scholar would be asked to give written assent and to produce his material by a certain day. It was at this point that difficulties arose. Often the deadline was not met, but more frequently the reply, when it came, was probably three or even five thousand words long and accompanied by a note stating that the topic was too important to be covered in only a thousand words. This is where I and other members of the team came in; we would be given the relevant files, containing all the correspondence, and asked to amend the article to the required length. It was then returned to Harbans Singh who, I discovered, rewrote it in part or even in full. I doubt whether any entries in the Encyclopaedia are as the original author or reviser wrote them. He was not good at accepting the finished work of other people. This seemed to be his only weakness but in spite of it the work proceeded and though he was distraught by the death of his wife before all the volumes had been published and he himself died while one of the four volumes was with the printer, still it was completed and the world of Sikh studies is the richer for it. One scary experience that I had which never became known to the professor occurred during a particularly heavy storm that flooded the basement below the Bhavan where all the documents relating to the Encyclopaedia were filled. Files were to be seen floating around the large room and there was a real danger that much if not everything would be lost but for the quick action of Professor Kohli into whose care I had been entrusted on my arrival. He waded into the room and rescued everything, laying them in the sun to dry for the rain stopped as swiftly as it began. At a town, Goindwal, associated with Guru Amar Das, there is a pool where some Sikhs go to bathe ritually and remove impurities. It is called a baoli sahib; rather unkindly as we saw Dr Kohli paddling in the bhavan's basement some of us said, 'Kohli Sahib is in the baoli sahib'. Had he not been I shudder to think what might have resulted from the flooding because there were no duplicate copies of the articles.

Life was not all hard work; Harbans took me round his orangery drawing my attention to the flavours of the different fruits, though they all looked the same to me, and shared the taste of many of them, it being the time for the fruit to be ripe. Probably the experience had no effect on him but I was unable to leave my room in the guest house for most of the following morning. Friends frequently came to visit him and some-times these were unwelcome distractions from the Encyclopaedia but he always behaved in a polite and hospitable manner, as his culture directed. One man owned a school at Massourie, a hill station not far from Simla which he arranged for me to visit during a special weekend. The sight in the direction of the Himalayas was breath taking and not only because the mountains were some twenty thousand feet above sea level or nearly 7,000 metres. When first I got out of the car I had to stand for several minutes waiting for my heart to stop pounding and return to its normal beat. The school turned out to be a boarding school for Sikh boys and girls of all ages who happened to be the sons and daughters of American Sikhs who had converted to the religion under the influence of a yoga teacher, Sant Harbhajan Singh, popularly known as Yogi Bhajan. Sometimes Punjabi Sikhs debated whether they could be true Sikhs as they had no true sense of Izzat or pride but they were and are very devout, initiated into the Khalsa, and keeping its code of conduct meticulously even to the point of their women wearing turbans, something uncommon among the majority of Sikhs. They are also strictly vegetarian in their diet. They are often called 'gora' that is white Sikhs, because they are white, though they also dress from head to foot in white, Punjabi, dress. The children I met were following in the way of their parents, meditating, learning to read and write and speak Punjabi, and follow the Khalsa path. The weekend was given to dramas, in Punjabi of course, based on the lives of the Gurus and other figures from Sikh history, poetry competitions, playing Indian musical instruments, and singing in groups hymns from the Guru Granth Sahib. I often wonder what these young people are doing twenty years on; some must be parents themselves, did they marry within the gora community and are they bringing up their children in the Sikh path? My weekend was enhanced by meeting an elderly Sikh, Lieutenant Colonel Jit Guleria, who shared a room with me and rose quietly each morning at the hour before dawn, amrit vela, to meditate, without disturbing me. He lived in Delhi and remained a close and much loved friend until his death. He had begun his service with the British and had been on the staff of Lord Mountbatten, later had had been in the war against China, but, like many soldiers, he was a very peaceful man. I also gained a further insight into the hierarchical life of Indian society. Part way through the weekend my host, the owner of the school, asked me whether I would like to become its principal. When I pointed out that he had one already he said that he would dismiss him immediately and I could take his place! Such, apparently, is the security of tenure that many people enjoy.

Upon my return to Patiala it was time to meet the Vice Chancellor (VC) of the university. I was about to learn another lesson. It does not take long to realise how each 'inferior' relates to his 'superior' and to observe a whole sequence of relationships. Student is respectful to teacher and a lecturer bows, in attitude, if not literally, to his seniors who adopt a similar reverential attitude to the professor. When I was taken to meet the VC I was surprised to find that my professor, who was received so deferentially by staff in that administration block behaved exactly as they did when we entered the VC's office. Later I was to discover that this senior member of the university would behave in exactly the same way to the state governor whom, I suspect, like most others in the chain, had the power of hiring and firing almost at will. I had seen nothing like it in Britain, except, perhaps, for the way that some subjects kowtowed to the Queen. To ignore hierarchy, even in apparently affable situations, is to be unaware, to one's potential cost, of an important aspect of Indian life. One evening, to provide a different example, I was taken to a restaurant by members of a Sikh family with relatives in Leeds. My hosts got in whisky for themselves and a beer for me, I don't like spirits and a pint lasts me an evening, not so Sikhs for whom the purpose of drinking seems to get drunk. We chatted for some time, the younger brother in the group doing most of the talking, until his big brother told him brusquely to shut up, which he did on the instant. It was about half an hour later before he was allowed into the conversation again, this time he was mildly and hesitantly spoken, not wishing to be disciplined again. When the drinks ran out he was the man sent to buy another bottle of whisky. This manner of knowing one's place was utterly strange to me; I couldn't see it working with my two younger brothers! Naturally we discussed families and there was much interest in the information that our daughters had just begun college, after which my friends assumed, we would be arranging their marriages. That we would not showed a definite dereliction of parental duty. The elder brother told me that he had one unmarried brother who was still studying; he was going to be an accountant, the family had most bases covered professionally, but they lacked a financially qualified person who could deal with the tax man without non-family members knowing their business; so much for choice of career, in this family at least. When the evening came to an end I was taken to their home where I spent the night and enjoyed a very tasty breakfast of parathas and sweet tea, boiled as usual in a pan with tea, sugar and milk added during the process. Unlike Muslim homes where I had stayed the women folk waited upon me while the men chatted.

Harbans Singh encouraged me to make another visit to Amritsar to see the Harimandir Sahib lit up for Divali when the Sikhs remember the release of Guru Hargobind, the sixth leader, from imprisonment by the Mughal emperor Jehangir at that time. The year 1983 was a time of great anxiety and foreboding in the Punjab. Skirmishes were taking place between government forces and Sikh militants. One heard of incidents such as forced encounters in which an army patrol would enter a village looking for young Sikh men, force them to go for a weapon to defend themselves and then shoot them. To discover the truth about the situation was not easy and probably impossible but I met many moderate Sikhs who were siding against the government. The leader of the Sikh agitators was Jarnail Singh Bhindranwale, a religious teacher or sant, who was said to have considerable charisma. At the time that I was in Amritsar he had set up his headquarters in the Darbar Sahib, the outer precincts of the Golden Temple, and his followers, armed with kirpans and automatic rifles, were to be seen moving around its buildings at will. Had I wished to I could have met the sant, for his supporters volunteered to take me to him and assured me that he would grant me an audience; the prospect tempted me as he was probably the best known Sikh of his day. His name was to be found in many British newspapers and shots of him had appeared on TV news even before I had left the UK. However, I knew that, as a white person, my movements were being watched by the secret police, the same one or two plainclothed men would be at my elbow through much of the day, and I was sure that once I had left Patiala such friends as Dr Darshan Singh, a lecturer in the Religious Studies department, would receive a visit from them. How much truth there was about the methods they employed I could not be sure but Patiala already had a reputation as a hot-bed of anti government opposition so I had no wish to put them at risk. The opportunity of a memorable meeting had to be put aside, a decision that I regretted in June 1984 when the Indian army stormed the Darbar Sahib in Operation Blue Star and Bhindranwale was killed with most of his guerrilla or terrorist army depending on one's view of him. Interestingly both sides respected the sanctity of the Harmandir Sahib, the worship focus in the centre of the sarovar; some years later during another siege the men seeking refuge were not so fastidious and used it for their last stand. As far as I am aware the bullet holes still remain visible, hopefully guides will not confuse the two insurgencies and blame the sant for the act of desecration of the Sikh holy of holies.

Dr Darshan Singh and I became close friends during my stay in Patiala. Each of us was separated from wife and family. His wife was a lecturer in English in another university in the Punjab as, although she had a PhD in Sikhism she could not find a post in Patiala or nearby. We met up on most days after my evening meal and went to his flat on the university campus. During later stays I rode on his motor scooter on the way to the newly built house that he had bought in the city. From these visits I discerned much of his character and the way of life of house owners in India. For a long time he had no phone because he refused to pay the bribe required by the men who would install it, and the drainage system was incomplete for similar reasons. Several other defects existed, a witness to his integrity, and I was reminded of what Ugandan Sikhs had told me concerning their preference to stay in Britain rather than go to India which they could have done; the constant need to pay out backhanders deterred them. Fortunately, as a white Briton, I was never asked for a bribe during any of my visits to India. One evening my friend took me to the gurdwara Dukh Niwaran Sahib, associated with the ninth Guru and the largest in the city, a splendid building with a large pool to one side of it surrounded by paved porticoes on three sides. A large group of men and women sat on a paved square in front of the entrance, facing a preacher who held them enthralled for almost an hour as twilight changed to moonlight and the time came for the evening hymn to be sung. There was an intense air of sincerity and devotion which I could appreciate even though I lacked the language to understand what was said. Atmosphere is not something I usually feel but Dukh Niwaran is an exception. Whenever I was in Patiala I made a special journey to that place though it is also memorable for the time that I sat on the front seat of a bus and saw the Sikh driver take both hands off the wheel, place them together and bow towards the building even though the street was crowded. Happily drivers did not salute Chapeltown gurdwara in Leeds in the same manner!

Before Darshan Singh came to the guest house to collect me I often managed to watch the TV news. It featured Indira Gandhi about nine times per broadcast and not much else. I was given to understand that black and white sets were distributed to the villages or sold at a very small charge and could certainly appreciate the reason. The villagers depended for their knowledge of local, regional and national events on TV as they had earlier on the radio. Newspapers remained fiercely independent but few villagers could afford them and most considered them to be an unnecessary luxury when the village had its television set. My term in India prevented me from ever again taking the freedom of the media for granted. To buy a broadsheet like the *Guardian* regularly is a civic and democratic duty. I never discussed the press with my friend George Verghese whose career was journalism and who edited the *Indian Express* when I first visited India in 1973, largely because I seldom saw him; his day began before I was up and seldom ended before supper time; now I wish I had because India has many regional and national papers ranging from The *Times of India* to the *Hindu* and the *Tribune*. All served the middle class so it was impossible for a stranger like me easily to balance one against the other, there seemed to be no 'red tops' as we call the *Mail*, *Express*, *Sun* or *Star*, in Britain.

Even before I ever set foot in India I had formed the view that its police always get their man, they never leave a village empty handed even if the person arrested is innocent. It didn't surprise me, therefore, that most of the people I met tried to have as little to do with them as possible. (As I said, this was one reason that I did not meet Jarnail Singh Bhindranwale). The day came when it was time to renew my permit to stay at the university and Professor Kohli decided that a personal visit was unnecessary, one of the peons could take the documents to the police station. The young man was summoned and told what to do, immediately he began making excuses and the fear in his eyes was obvious and genuine. It was a long time since I had seen anything like it and I can't recall experiencing anything like it again. Not only would he be entering a terrible place but neighbours and relatives might see him and his and their reputations might be ruined because, it would be assumed, he had done something wrong. It was clear from the start that he would have to go for no peon can win an argument with a professor, but he tried hard and left with us in no doubts as to his apprehension. When he returned it was to tell us of his failure the professor and I would have to go to the police station in person. The professor exerted what authority he could and the police officer, a man of senior rank, seemed to enjoy talking to a foreign 'scholar' so the interview went well, though he pointedly remarked that he had noted that I was left handed – from the fact that my watch was worn on my right wrist – just to indicate how observant he was.

A visitor must be politely discreet though cautious indiscretion is sometimes appropriate as it was when I spoke at a conference on academic freedom. First, I met with students in the Union coffee house; Patiala being a Sikh university no alcohol was allowed on the premises or the campus. As I was an academic, women and men could sit together with me as chaperone. I learned that in most subjects there was something akin to a party line, a correct and wrong way of interpreting Indian history or Sikhism, for example. This confirmed what I had already guessed from my own research that the first thing one must do in studying the history of the Sikh Guru period, my area of interest, is to discover the religion of the author or, somewhat despairingly, accept the word of the Europeans, who can be equally biased in their interpretations even before the period of the Raj which dates from 1757. In addition to what I heard during coffee talk I also knew of one post-graduate who had been waiting for a year to be awarded his doctorate because he had written something, less than a paragraph, to which his supervisor took exception. (I was eventually asked to read his dissertation and managed to nudge the tutor in the direction of giving the student his degree). The story that Albert Schweitzer told in his *Quest of the Historical Jesus,* had fascinated and shocked me since I first read it; scholars being dismissed from their posts in Germany because their views were too radical, one being sacked because he had the courage to give a funeral eulogy at the side of the grave of one of the disgraced men, Roman Catholic scholars who would not risk working on the gospel records for fear of excommunication. This was the narrative I decided to share though it was close to the attitude that many Sikhs had taken when Professor Hew McLeod set out in search of the historical Guru Nanak. No one noticed the similarity and my talk was greeted as a breath of fresh air by most of the audience; how much it affected academic attitudes I do not know.

One day Professor Harminder Singh felt he had time to leave his office and take me to meet a sant some miles from Patiala. This was a young and handsome man with a pleasant smile, good sense of humour and excellent, fluent English. We enjoyed a long conversation over several cups of tea, the professor keeping quiet so that I could learn as much as possible. Before we took our leave the sant suggested that we might come

157

on a Sunday when many devotees came for diwan and to discuss various matters with him. Better still, he remembered, there was going to be an amrit ceremony in two weeks' time which he said I might like to observe. After an early breakfast, on the Sunday morning, the professor picked me up in his car and we went to the sant's dera. Many people were already there, gathered in the gurdwara, joining in kirtan and listening to the sant's teaching. He welcomed us and invited us to sit near him. The initiation ceremony began when diwan had ended. It was unlike amrit pahul as I had observed it in Leeds or read about it in books. Family were welcomed as onlookers, there was no attempt to exclude Sikhs who had not taken amrit, so far as I could judge from the presence of men who were clean shaven. At the end of the row of initiates was a boy of about seven years old, dressed in his best suit, not in the 5 Ks and Punjabi dress. Foremost in the ceremony was the sant; he it was who gave the initiates amrit to drink, who threw it in their eyes and sprinkled it on their hair. When the turn of the boy came to receive the sticky nectar, prepared from sugar crystals and water, his mother ran forward to dry his face and hair with a towel to prevent his suit being stained! I had witnessed a ceremony just as formal, for at least one participant, as many baptisms are today in churches in the UK. I also couldn't help wondering how many marks someone who had described what I had seen in a GCSE paper would have been given. Religious ceremonies are not static but in books we tend to idealise them.

Guru Nanak's birthday was celebrated towards the end of my stay. A few hundred women, men and children gathered in a large open area near the university gurdwara but away from halls of residence, classrooms and administration blocks. The Sunday was cool, but warm enough for no one to need to wear winter clothing though most mothers covered their small children's heads with knitted woolly caps that had pieces covering the ears. On this occasion worship was followed by langar but usually in larger gurdwaras and at festive celebrations they take place concurrently. The congregation gathered on either side of the Guru Granth Sahib leaving a small gap so that new arrivals could each pay their respects to the scripture before sitting on the grass. My white skin meant that I was ushered to sit in the front row with a man who turned out to be an American interfaith specialist who had written several books on the subject. Sikhism was clearly not one of his specialisms so he questioned me, asking, among other things, whether the scripture on its dais was the Sikh altar. A mother and her little son aged no more than two came to make obeisance; as is often the case she pushed him to kneel down on the ground until his head was touching the grass, then she made her own bow. While she was doing this the little boy stretched out his hand and took some of the money that we had placed in a dish as an offering to Babaji. When his mother raised her head she was embarrassed to see what he was doing as were most onlookers who were near enough to see him; there was silence until I began to laugh when everyone joined in and even the relieved mother managed a smile. One lesson I had learned in Patiala is that a white stranger, acting politely, can behave in such a way as to defuse potentially embarrassing situations such as that of a small boy being more ready to receive than give. School children sang shabads and read poems in praise of the Guru; a few men gave speeches which were far briefer than the ones I was used to in England; we all said Ardas and listened to the vak, the randomly chosen verse of scripture, the Guru's advice for the day, and then we sat down on the grass to share langar which was served on disposable plates made of dried tree leaves. I knew that in a few days I would be making my way to Delhi so this celebration seemed to be a good farewell occasion. I also knew that this would not be my last visit to a place where I had made many friends and felt very much at home; even the campus, though literally red brick, was attractive and pleasant to my eyes, but I had also learned that eight months away from the family was as long as I could happily take, for during the subsequent four weeks or so I felt very home sick. Although I had kept healthy and eaten well, I also noticed that I had lost weight and had to cut three more notches in my belt to prevent my trousers falling down.

Back in Delhi my plan was to stay a few days with Sikh friends and then go to Jamila's from whence I would go to the airport. Other than shopping I wanted to spend time in the Gandhi Museum. These intentions suffered a fatal blow when, on my first night in Delhi I was chatting with my host and a well-known Sikh scholar and was offered a piece of sausage. Meat I had always refused but this time my friend, Mohinder, pressed me and I trusted him implicitly, so I took a portion. At ten o'clock I began to be ill and spent the next three days unable to move from my bed except for visits to the toilet and one to a local doctor who prescribed antibiotics. Apart from the Delhi Emporium I was only able to attend a Christmas concert with Jamila. It was in English and most of the participants were Americans living and working in Delhi. The gathering seemed to me to be remarkable for only two things, first it was as secular as possible in the western sense of the word, it was non-religious with 'Jingle Bells' and 'I'm Dreaming of a White Christmas', typifying the event. Secondly, there was an awareness of the birth of Jesus but this also became secular. Mary, Joseph and the baby Jesus entered right and sat on chairs in a structure that was supposed to be a stable – at least the adults did – the baby, a doll, lay in his mother's arms. Two dozen children of various shapes and sizes, but all white, entered left and knelt in front of the holy family, taking it in turns to cuddle Jesus until the next child grabbed him feeling that it was his turn. Eventually, he was given back to his mother and the children sang a song. Santa Claus entered left and the children didn't notice him until he made a loud 'Ho, Ho, Ho!' at which point they turned round, charged him and began emptying his sack. Mary and Joseph quickly summed up the situation, she threw the baby in the air and they joined the mêlée grabbing whatever presents were left. Being among the largest of the children they did quite well. Everyone laughed but this was really the end of the concert as the children could be heard back stage shouting and fighting until their parents felt it was time to try to retrieve the situation.

With that memory of Christmas I came home and was well until Christmas Day when, after I dropped Gwynneth off at the hospital, I made my way to church, felt unwell, and just got home in time. The next day a young doctor called; she said she could do nothing more than hold my hand, an experience that she has long since forgotten, and give me a prescription for antibiotics, deciding that I probably had amoebic dysentery.

14

Return to Chichester

Family is everything to me and if I had any doubt about its importance my stay in India persuaded me of it. To be away from Gwynn and our daughters for almost four months was much too long. Even though I enjoyed almost every moment in India and was busy and among friends yet I discovered after eight weeks what my comfortable limit was. However, back in Chichester I resumed my normal teaching duties with my refreshed experiences of India hopefully improving their content and my understanding. The India bug had been well and truly caught and during the next twenty years, whenever I come to a cross-roads, I saw and heard young beggars, mainly girls, in my mind, pathetically saying, 'May you be blessed with sons'. I returned there another ten times and had the pleasure and joy of introducing Eluned and Siân to my favourite country outside Britain.

I recognised that if the Religious Studies approach was to be successful it needed, besides text-books, in-service courses, and committed teachers, to influence A level syllabuses. Hugo Gryn was involved with the development of the newly established World College of the Atlantic at Llantwit Major in South Wales and with help from people like Angela Wood was responsible for them establishing a course in World Religions. I was asked if I would like to be appointed to be teacher in charge of the course and the temptation to seize the opportunity was considerable but as the school was outside the state system of education to which I felt committed I refused. I did not feel that I could train teachers to work in a system that I had myself left. However, I was willing to help appoint the first teacher of Religious Studies, to prepare the syllabus, to take part in the annual conference, largely organised by Hugo, and to serve as examination moderator appointed and paid for by the International Baccalaureate (IB). The syllabus was school based but as time passed other schools and colleges around the world became interested and I found myself by 2007, when I finally resigned after over twenty-five years service but with no gold watch as a reward, setting a paper and moder-ating the assessment of almost one hundred students annually. Now, the course has broadened beyond the six major religions found in Britain today to include Chinese and Japanese manifestations and other Indian traditions, and to be, like other syllabuses, one governed by an examining board. In the earliest days Atlantic College was enthusiastic as it always remained but there were some tutors moderating such subjects as sociology who were critical of courses in religion: philosophy yes, that was acceptable but they could not perceive a study of religion that was not confessional and so a threat to the integrity of students as well as being academically unacceptable. The argument over RE as an examination subject was to some extent a rerun of those I had experienced with Christian teachers who did not believe that faith could be examined, but now my opponents were people who were hostile to religion itself and who refused to recognise that it was worthy of being regarded as an academic discipline. For them belief was the antithesis of reason. Eventually such teachers were talked round or talked out, grudgingly accepting arguments with which they did not really agree but which had the blessing of the IB.

I brought to this work my experience of setting up A level courses with the Joint Matriculation Board in Manchester and that of being examiner in Hinduism and Sikhism, in addition to examining undergraduates in Chichester and later being external examiner to a number of universities, including Wales, Surrey, and Edinburgh. These roles were the most intriguing; the West Sussex Institute at Chichester and Bognor had to have all its courses vetted by outsiders, university teachers, which ensured good discipline. Universities, however, seemed free to set up any courses they liked as long as they could find students interested in taking them. No one at that time questioned the ability of such tutors to teach courses, or seemed to ask for detailed course outlines and syllabuses. Good manners, fear of prosecution, and advice that things have changed radically in the last decade, prevent me from boring any reader with further details, but I did begin to understand how my own university, Durham, in the nineteen fifties, could set questions on the whole of the Middle Ages, for example, when lectures had covered less than a half of the time span.

About this time many LEAs appointed advisers and produced Agreed Syllabuses often supported by handbooks of outlines of work. Eventually West Sussex decided, at least, to have its own agreed syllabus and proposed to adopt those parts of the new Hampshire Syllabus that it found acceptable, mostly the sections on Christianity and ethics. John Rankin, a member of the local council, got wind of the idea, contacted the Hampshire adviser, David Naylor, and West Sussex was told that it must accept the entire syllabus, not bits of it. There was also a move to appoint an adviser and some councillors expressed surprise and consternation when they discovered that he or she would have to be paid more than the bishop, though without a palace, car and chauffeur, of course. A suggestion was made that a retired clergyman might be appointed! It was some time before a satisfactory syllabus and a very capable adviser who related well to local teachers and did much to advance RE in the authority, was appointed.

If we did not already have faith schools I doubt whether we would be inventing them in the twenty-first century. My own attitude towards them has been at best ambivalent. In Newcastle and in Leeds we decided not to send our daughters to them; in Chichester they chose, of their own accord, to go to the county school, as it was then called. Yet, in the nineteen nineties I found myself accepting the position of chairman of the Education Committee of the London Diocese. My decision might take some explaining. I served on an education committee of the British Council of Churches with a number of extremely competent teachers who were employed by the London diocese and was invited by its Director, the Reverend John Osborne, to lead several half-day courses on religions including arranging visits to a Buddhist vihara, Brick Lane mosque and the famous Bevis Marks synagogue. This was also a time when the only real opposition to Mrs Thatcher's government seemed to be coming from the churches. When John Osborne invited me to become chairman I was prepared to put away my reservations and support educational excellence that in no way seemed elitist, narrow, or sectarian in the worst sense of the word. While he and Archdeacon Tim Raphael ran the Board I was happy to serve with them and was fully accepted even though my reservations were understood, helping make appointments to the advisory staff in addition to chairing committees. It was a pity that I lived so far from London and therefore could not be more involved. This said, I must confess still to having doubts about faith schools. Some do not seem to have worked out their raison d'être in the twenty-first century and government policy has not helped. Roman Catholics made tremendous efforts in the last century and perhaps before, to establish schools having such aims as a primary and secondary school in every location where they had an appreciable membership; to be told that they must take a percentage of children from other faith backgrounds was insensitive in the extreme and smacked of a disease widespread among politicians, namely an ignorance of history and an inclination to be doctrinaire. Anglicans might be more open to the presence of other faith in a school because of their history and philosophy which was to provide education for all in days when scarcely any schools existed. Today their major challenge may be that of a plausible admissions policy; one knows of many children who attend church and become confirmed but then treat it as a passing out parade, their aim of winning a place in the church secondary school having been achieved. I would not like to be a vicar or headmaster of a church school between December and August during the application and appeals period!

It is not uncommon even now to find Jews who recall persecution in Germany or elsewhere and who expect it to occur in the UK eventually. Assimilation failed in Germany where some Jews did not know they were the children of Abraham until the Nazis brutally informed them. Separate schools are a means of maintaining a distinct identity; to ask Jews to admit other children is to contradict their ethos and purpose. So it is with Muslims who may also be fearful of losing identity and being infected by the inferior morality of the British society in which they live. (In Leeds and Bradford, for example, their neighbours were often prostitutes and addicts to alcohol or drugs.) Then there is the religious part of the curriculum. It has taken a long time to persuade Christian teachers even in maintained schools to teach in an objective, fair and balanced manner a religion that they do not hold, and for them to help their pupils to study it in the same way. This was the greatest difficulties I found in A level or IB examining, yet faith schools are expected to do this. Not being an OFSTED examiner I cannot comment on the success with which they manage it but having visited some Muslim schools that claim to teach Christianity I have found that the view of Jesus that is put across is that of the Qur'an where he is a respected prophet and the messiah but not the divine Son of God. I am aware also of trained secondary school Muslim RE teachers who effectively and successfully teach Christianity and other faiths, but they have had postgraduate specialist training that most primary teachers and others in faith schools lack. For Christians to present the Jewish interpretation of the Hebrew Scriptures, emphasising the significance of the Torah, rather than that implicit in Handel's *Messiah* also requires skill. Suspension of belief is not easy but it is expected as though it were automatically achievable. Of course RE is not the only subject that faces this kind of challenge; many historians who cover the rise of Hitler have to overcome a natural bias especially if they come from continental European backgrounds. If politicians in France have difficulty understanding the Vichy regime and the role of their compatriots who collaborated with the Germans, or ministers of religion can encourage their congregations to learn about other religions but at the same time instruct them to 'remember that they are searching after the truth which

Jesus revealed to us', as I have heard said from pulpits, it is not surprising that faith members in classrooms experience difficult challenges. My final concern regarding faith schools has to do with the autonomy of the pupils who are its products. From their birth my wife and I recognised that there would be time when we were no longer at the sides of our daughters to support, guide and advise them. We had to enable them to become themselves, not clones of us. The success of our achievement is for them to judge but it is not easy to be autonomous when politicians, media adverts, religions and peer groups, are all inviting us to do rather than think, to let them make up our minds for us, to make us conform. The best schools, faith based or secular, achieve the aim of autonomy; but what of others, is it actually an aim to which they think they should aspire? Religions and states have been slow to embrace nonconformity of any sort and it is still regarded with suspicion by some democracies and religious groups who only promote kindred spirits; their big tents have carefully guarded narrow entrances.

However, even if these reservations can be adequately met, the fact remains that there are not, and cannot be sufficient schools for every Jew or Muslim to attend one; it seems much better that nationally we should combine our efforts and insights to create community schools that mirror the reality that one day this country must achieve. Meanwhile, of course it is necessary to help teachers respond to the mix that they face every day, one that can be as volatile as a lava flow. Some years ago a head teacher was confronted, as she regarded it, by a Sikh ten-year old suddenly turning up at school wearing a turban one Monday morning. At the weekend he had undergone his turban tying ceremony being at the age when he had learned to tie it himself. The head suspended him from school. The LEA became involved and required her to lose face by readmitting him. None of us likes this, especially head teachers who are usually figures whose authority is not questioned or challenged. With hindsight it is easy to suggest that the parents of the boy should at least have informed the school what was going to happen and at best invited the headmistress to the celebration. On Monday morning she could have made valuable use of the event in assembly, discovering what similar occasions other children had in their own cultures whilst endorsing Mandeep's growth in the life of his family and community at the same time. Instead, I am informed, she resigned unable to face humiliation. Sadly, after a half century of an Asian presence in Britain lessons do not seem to have been learned. A Sikh child may be refused permission to wear the Kara by a school that regards all bangles as ornaments; failing to recognise that of all the symbols a Sikh wears this is the most universal.

It is sometimes described as God's handcuff binding the Sikh and God together and, worn usually on the most used wrist, (on mine it would be the left), it should remind him, or her, not to act in an evil way. Similarly, if a Muslim girl begins to cover her head or wear a full jilbab, even when swimming, a common sight in many Muslim countries, schools should be responsive to their growing sense of identity. Of course, there are still some parts of the UK where the presence of such children is new, LEAs have duty to help their schools accept them. Incidentally, as a matter of fact, it is far more likely that a cross, often regarded as acceptable, is worn as an ornament, than artefacts or clothes pertaining to other religions. Writing as I am in 2009 I am surprised that issues dealt with forty years ago are still being addressed and that there seems to be no reservoir of acquired knowledge. For example, an MP can say he likes to look a woman in the eyes when he is speaking to her, yet I have always been told that no Muslim lady should look a man in the eyes unless she is related to him; she should lower her gaze, this applies too to children, when a teacher says, 'Look at me when I am talking to you', she is going against his parental cultural upbringing and encouraging him to be rude.

I had never previously been to Israel or crossed the pond to the USA but I did both in the eighties. Rabbi Douglas Charing, a friend from Leeds days, asked me if I would like to go to Israel for a week at the cost of £100 for flight and half board. Of course, I needed no second invitation but cleared things with college and made my preparations. The visit almost did not take place so far as Alan Brown and I were concerned; we found ourselves on the same south coast train service with plenty of time for the three-hour ElAl check in at Heathrow when we discovered that a derailment at Purley was delaying all trains into London from our area. British Rail was very helpful but our chances of reaching the airport on time seemed to be receding with every minute. However, Alan phoned the ElAl desk and we pressed on arriving with about fifteen minutes to spare. Customs and security were dealt with amazingly quickly and we found ourselves on the plane and departing on time! And usually the process took three hours, as I have just said! I found Israel like a curate's egg, good in parts; or like a game of two helves to utter another cliché, the Christian holy places in Jerusalem and Bethlehem left me cold, they were too full of commerce and denominational divisiveness for my taste. When people asked me whether I couldn't feel that pilgrims had been praying there for centuries I had to say, 'No', just as I had at Durham Cathedral years earlier. Only one place has had that kind of effect on me, a medieval manor house near Kidderminster, owned by the Roman Catholic Church; it had a dozen or more holes for hunted priests to hide in during Elizabeth I's reign. I expected men and women in Tudor clothes to enter the room at any moment. *There* was atmosphere! The Garden of Gethsemane, one of the lovely churches at Nazareth, crossing the Sea of Galilee, were all satisfying experiences but the richest of all was the visit to Masada, the place where Jewish fugitives held out against the Romans for three years, it really stimulated my imagination, but historical rather than religious. Yad Vashem, the memorial to Jewish victims of the Holocaust, the experrience was moving for different reasons but I couldn't help being even more upset when I saw photographs of Nazi troops burning Jewish homes, knowing, as I did, that Israelis were destroying Palestinian houses while we were in Israel. Call me old fashioned but the sight of Israeli teenaged women in army uniforms carrying automatic rifles also disturbed me. These, and the finest bagels I have ever enjoyed, bought at one of the Jerusalem gates, are the memories that have made the biggest impact on me but I am glad that our visit was organised by a Jewish educationist and not a Christian pilgrimage agency, the impact of that would have been too much for me.

The eighties and early nineties was my decade of tourism, thanks mainly to the Unification Church led by the Korean Reverend Moon and, therefore, often known as the Moonies. As I was a very unimportant person on the global scale I did not come in for much criticism but men who might be described as representatives of Christian churches did. The conferences, however, were well organised and thoroughly academic in content and no one ever tried to convert me to the Unification view-point or use me for propaganda purposes. The young members of the movement, whom I met, were all friendly and sincere and one of the greatest values of the conferences was meeting men and women from all five continents. Piara Singh and I were both invited to a conference in Chicago, after which we were free to visit members of the Sikh community. One Saturday we were invited to the service at a house in the rich part of Chicago and arrived to discover that Diwan was in the basement. This made my friend rather anxious because it should be held in a room with no access to the floor above. To walk over the scripture in this way is thought to be extremely disrespectful, (I recall going to the home of a friend who had died when we lived in Leeds; his son telling me he had some Hindu calendar pictures for me which he would give me at the end of the ceremony, only for him to apologise because they were in the loft and he couldn't fetch them while the scripture was in the room below. I would have to wait for a week until post-mortem ceremonies were completed.) Furthermore it was clear that the room served as a bar throughout the rest of the week, the bottles of wine and beer were not curtained off during Diwan. The granthi or bhai sahib brought the Guru Granth Sahib from a gurdwara in the next town and installed it so that the service could begin. Teen-age girls, wearing short-sleeved blouses and knee-length skirts or short trousers entered the room and sat on the floor with their feet towards the holy book. Diwan was brief, well under one hour in length, and when it was over we were invited to take langar, the communal meal, on the patio upstairs besides the swimming pool. We sat at tables on picnic chairs and were served by two Polish servants, a man and his wife. At least the meal was vegetarian if not simple. I was surprised that Piara Singh did not explode before we were back in our car! On the next day, Sunday, we went to the gurdwara from which the bhai sahib had come. Everyone sat respectfully on the floor in an upstairs room. Langar was served from pails as in Leeds or the Punjab, and was simple vegetarian food, dahl and chapattis washed down with water, not even mineral water, and we sat on the floor. Normality was restored; this was how things should be; Piara Singh was a happy man. As for the rich Sikhs of the previous day none of them was to be seen at the Sunday gathering. Recently there has been some tension between Sikhs who assert that langar should be taken seated on the floor as it usually is in India and certainly was in the days of the Gurus, and those who are happy to sit at tables. Being something of a moderniser my sympathies have tended to lie with the eating at tables group, that is surely what a Guru would do in the West in the twentieth century, but the Chicago experience showed me very clearly the other side of the argument. From tables it is easy to move from community service to waitress and waiter service, to a richer meal, and to a point where the equality principle of langar is lost, though this need not be so if the underlying precepts of Sikhism are kept in mind.

Shortly before I was due to attend a conference in San Francisco I received a phone call from the Unification organisers suggesting that I left a few days earlier so that I could enjoy Thanksgiving with my hosts. I am glad that I did. The lady was a Scottish Christian; her husband was a Punjabi Sikh. They were joined for the celebration by a Peruvian Roman Catholic and her Jewish husband, and by a Mexican Catholic and her Arab Muslim spouse. This showed me what the future might be like in the UK though not for some years, perhaps. When I returned to England I had to complete a course as visiting lecturer in Oxford; I knew that many of my class were evangelicals and enjoyed, rather naughtily, telling them of my recent experience. They politely said little but I doubt they agreed with me that this might be the way of the twenty-first century world.

One day a letter from Archbishop Runcie arrived, inviting me to represent Sikhism on a consultancy committee that he was convening. It came as a complete and welcome surprise not only because of personal vanity but as an indication that the archbishop was taking the existence of other faith in British society seriously. It was a bit of a shock, however, to discover that most Sikhs seemed very little interested in the appointment and my employers only mentioned my honorary position in the local paper about a year later. At least this brought me back down to earth. It was our responsibility to keep the archbishop informed about matters concerning the community, in my case mostly turban issues but the meeting I remember best had to do with his 'smorgasbord' lecture on Religious Education in which he had criticised multifaith RE as nothing better than this Scandinavian delicacy which, I assured him, having twice been to Denmark, was tasty, interesting and thoughtfully prepared. He seemed to think it was no better than a thoughtless throwing together of scraps of food nearing their sell-by-date, a mish-mash. From that we went on to a more serious discussion of the need for schools to cater for all their children in curriculum terms, reverting to the dietary allusion, rather like introducing children to one another's dishes and wider options such as vegetarian, vegan, fish and herbs and peppers not in order to make the Hindu vegetarian eat beef but to be aware that some people did and to understand that they were not not necessarily wicked for doing so!

My study of Sikhism had suggested to me that an adequate and convenient English translation did not exist. UNESCO had produced some passages and Sikh scholars had served their community well in providing others as had Max Macauliffe, a British civil servant at the turn of the nineteenth and twentieth centuries, who wrote a six-volume study entitled the *Sikh Religion* but the scriptures follow each biography of the Gurus. More was needed, perhaps a translation of the gutka, the hymns used daily by Sikhs in their personal devotions. I also perceived a need resulting from children of the Sikh Diaspora world-wide not being able to read their own scriptures in the original language. The standard length of the *Guru Granth Sahib* is 1430 printed pages, a little longer than English translations of the *Hebrew Bible/Old Testament*. How was such an objective to be achieved? It so happened that a Sacred Literature Trust had recently been established under the patronage of the Duke of Edinburgh and had published material from Zen, Jainism, Sufism, the Australian Aborigines, Christianity, Judaism and other forms of spirituality and that Kerry Brown, an American with a close interest in Sikhism and Dr Narinder Singh Kapany, a scientist and business man who was a pioneer in the discovery and development of fibre optics, were interested in

Sikhism being included in the list. He was also the inspiration behind the Sikh Foundation based in San Francisco. I was invited to be the Consulting Editor and Professor Nikky Guninder Kaur Singh of Colby University was engaged as translator and also asked to provide the introduction. Once the content was agreed upon Nikky began her work. Periodically she would send passages to me that she had translated and I would disseminate them among a group of linguists and scholars such as Professor Christopher Shackle of the School of Oriental and African Studies in London. Dr Kapany would also look at them, I would collate the passages drawing Nikky's attention to areas in need of revision, of which there were not many and gradually, if somewhat laboriously, the volume was completed. Now, at last, there was an accessible corpus of Sikh teachings. When it appeared in 1996 not only was I pleased to think of its potential value within the faith and beyond, but to have collaborated with the daughter of my friend, Professor Harbans Singh of Patiala. How proud he was of her work! It was the most worthwhile thing that I could do to serve a religion and people that I so much respected.

John Rankin retired to devote himself to LibDem politics and being mayor of Chichester, which he was twice. Not being contentious, as he put it, he chose Amnesty International as his mayoral charity! I agreed to replace him as head of department but could do little more than ensure that my colleagues kept their jobs when management was looking to make savings by cuts in staffing. One of the Religious Studies tutors began contributing to the English programme but we all remained in post. In 1992 at the departmental review I shocked the Director and his deputy for the one and only time in my experience. At the end of a successful session I announced my intention to apply for early retirement on the grounds that I was not satisfied with my teaching. I had been reduced to writing one new lecture a year if I was lucky and often found myself looking through last year's notes to check that I had all the pages and that they were in order. Occasionally, I might be able to read the first page or two in order to refresh my memory. Quickly, John Wyatt and Barbara Smith recovered their composure. A few days later they told me that they had agreed to my request and I suggested that Clive Erricker of Winchester should be head-hunted to be my successor but my advice was ignored. I, for my part, began to teach part time.

There followed a period of intense enjoyment. The Institute had to pay for the completion of certain courses and the marking of examination papers and, to my satisfaction, these earnings exceeded the £5000 deal that I had suggested that Barbara. might pay me for doing them. Our daughters married during that summer and autumn and I was able to enjoy the occasions and what led up to them without being concerned for the welfare of a department. There were some curriculum courses to teach and King Alfred's College, Winchester, also invited me to do a thirty-six hour, one term in duration, Hinduism module. The Institute opened a centre at Crawley for the training of primary school mature students and Friday was devoted to work in English, History, and Religious Studies, consisting of an academic input, method sessions and school experience. My colleagues, Hugh and Ray, were congenial companions and the course proved very successful; in many ways it was reminiscent of teaching at James Graham. The mature students were enthusiastic and critical, the schools we used were welcoming and multiracial, and I could invite visitors and make visits to a local gurdwara, church and Friends' Meeting House. Teaching practice was usually a group activity, with each of us tutors taking about a dozen students into a school. One of them might conduct a lead lesson after which the class would divide into groups to pursue various topics. Sometimes my colleague Judith Evans who had been one of our in-service students and been appointed to the staff of the college, invited me to participate in one of her in-service course. It was for head teachers, usually formidable characters. My subject was the aims of RE. One of the members took exception to almost everything I said. Criticism I was used to but this had something acerbic and personal about it. If I had said, 'Today is a Tuesday', which it was, I felt she would have disagreed. When I had finished my session I left to teach another class but at lunchtime returned at Judith's invitation and found my self sitting next to this lady whose disposition towards me had not improved. At tea time I met up with Judith in the common room and shared my disturbed feelings. She told me that the headteacher had asked why I was giving a talk on RE. Judith said that I was her mentor but this gave no satisfaction. 'But why was a Hindu talking to us about RE?' Judith replied that I was not a Hindu to which the lady responded by saying; 'But you said he was a guru.' 'Yes, my RE guru', Judith answered. It was summer and being dark skinned after working in the garden as well as having black hair, I could be taken for a Hindu. In fact, once at Patiala, someone asked me whether I was a Kashmiri brahmin, as I had the name Kaul! Without knowing it I had experienced racism, I suppose. Not a bad thing. Perhaps I could sympathise more with those for whom it was a daily experience. Why shouldn't a Hindu or Muslim or Jew teach RE? At the time of writing Cornwall's RE adviser is a Jew. In those days it was rare. Now it is fairly common, thank goodness. It seems unthinkable to ask a teacher or student about their beliefs and it may well be illegal outside some faith school situations.

Personally, I have met good atheist and humanist RE teachers; it is their understanding of the subject, their integrity and respect for it and the children that they teach that matters. On the other hand one could point to convinced believers who should not be allowed near a class of children.

Our daughter, Eluned, was living in Perth, Australia, with her husband and as I was now employed part time by the Institute I could rearrange my teaching commitments to enable Gwynneth and I to visit her at a time when it was mutually convenient, which happened to be our autumn and Australia's spring, the time of thousands of species of wild flowers. Perth had a Muslim school which I was able to visit at the time of morning assembly and for much of the rest of the day. I was very impressed with an institution that seemed Islamic and liberal, preparing children for life in a the Western hemisphere, the place where it is ideologically located, though Indonesia and China may soon be more influential than the USA and Europe

Similar health was to be found among the Sikhs whose gurdwara I twice visited during morning worship. It was, of course, on a Sunday morning in a hired hall but as many objects and pictures that might have caused a distraction were removed and the Guru Granth Sahib was placed in a focal position upon a dais. What I appreciated was that some of the hymns that were used had been translated into English so that the children, most of whom could not read Punjabi, were able to understand the teachings of the Gurus. Ardas, the final Sikh prayer, was also transliterated so that everyone could join in saying it. Addresses too were in English. Here, I felt was a community that was thoughtful of the needs of its next generation and helping them to live as Sikhs in a strange land. It was so very isolated; they told me that they went to Madras rather than Sydney to buy things for weddings because India was easier to reach and nearer.

As I considered these two minorities I couldn't help wondering what life must be like among Christian communities that were also small and isolated and struggling for survival. All had a sense of belonging to a larger group, the umma, panth or church, but only Christians seemed to have a network which, through its ecclesiastical organisation, it belonged to. Will Sikhs and Muslims develop something similar? Even in the internet age it will probably be needed.

Throughout the nineteen nineties and well into the first decade of the present century I served on ecumenical or Anglican national groups that produced documents on such diverse inter-religious matters as worship, the sale and use of church buildings, a guide to school relationships, and being a Christian in a multifaith society. There is much of value in all

these documents and the first thing that must be noted is how little attention has been given to them by government departments and ministers.
This might be understandable if they had been written by so called woolly
minded liberals like myself but, for the most part they were conservatives
and with regard to that on worship I actually suggested that the booklet
might include the kind of warning that is placed on cigarette packets to
the effect that; 'Interfaith worship can damage your spiritual health'!
Perhaps it is not surprising to discover that the religion that celebrated its
unity by the sharing of bread and wine, which are now tokens of division, cannot easily pray with other people of faith. My own view on this
matter, for what it is worth, used to be that such worship should be for
a clear purpose, for example to celebrate a civic occasion or the death of
someone like my friend Ivy Gutteridge of Wolverhampton who, with
her husband, had served her city and Christianity well over a period of
many years. Now, I am more relaxed. If such a coming together seems
natural then it is prompted by God.

I also took two primary method courses in RE and also a thirty-hour
module in Sikhism as part of a newly established MA course. This was
probably the most attention given to Sikhism anywhere in the UK at the
time. One student was himself a Sikh which added to my interest, especially as he knew little about what might be described as its doctrinal
aspects but much about the religion as he and his family lived it. When
we came to discuss such matters as the importance of the turban and uncut
hair, ceremonies or diet, other members of the group were often
confused as, coming from Christian backgrounds, whatever their own
views, they could not understand that his attitudes were determined more
by his social group than personal beliefs.

Piara Singh was in the early stages of cancer when Sussex Academic
Press invited us to write a completely revised edition of *The Sikhs: Their
beliefs and practices* and, at about the same time, we were asked to prepare
a manuscript on *Sikhism and Christianity* for Macmillan under the series
editorship of Glyn Richards, something that we had long wanted to work
on. *The Sikhs* went well and the edition that we prepared was much superior to its Routledge parent. Sadly, my friend did not live to hold a copy
of the printed book in his hand, but died on 30 November 1992 in the
knowledge that it was completed. The comparative study was a different
matter, we assembled his material on Sikhism but he died before I could
produce my section on Christianity and link the two parts with critical
or appreciative reflections. The result was a book with which I was and
am disappointed. My advance copies came to Australia where Gwynneth
and I were staying with Eluned in 1993, and I was able to give one to

Peggy Holroyde who had introduced us some some tthirty years earlier. At least the gesture pleased her. I fear that my hopes of revising the parts for which I was responsible are unlikely to be realised. At least we achieved our aim in one respect; whereas other books in the series were being written by one person, presumably Christian, ours was a properly comparative study though not as interactive as it might have been. There are many Sikh and Christian friends today who could succeed where we failed; I hope they will make the attempt. During the 1980s the Reverend John Parry, on behalf of the United reformed Church, organised the first Sikh–Christian Consultation to be held in the UK. He later researched a PhD on the encounter of the two religions historically. Through these important meeting I got to know Charanjit Kaur Ajit Singh and her husband Ajit, and renewed my acquaintance with Joy Barrow. Of course, my friend Piara Singh was also part of the core membership of the group. I would not dream of pointing the finger at John but as a theologian possessing a rare experience of dialogue, he might be the person to build on the attempt made by myself and Piara Singh.

In 1996 I spent seven weeks in hospital suffering from pneumonia. Its cause was a mystery and the antibiotics needed to cure it proved elusive. Besides watching Richard Hadlee from the TV room win the one-day cricket trophy for Nottinghamshire the main event of my stay was a supreme epiphany moment in an epiphany life triggered by the tragic death of my long-time friend Rabbi Hugo Gryn which I heard of while I was eating my breakfast and listening to the 9.0 a.m. news one Monday. I had met him once or twice during the summer and knew that he was not well but the announcement, coming as almost a postscript to the news bulletin, came as a complete and devastating shock. Gwynneth brought me in my copy of *Forms of Prayer* that he had helped produce and I read passages from it as I recalled our many good times together. He was only sixty-six and heavy smoking for the twenty or more years I had known him had proved too much on top of all his other exertions such as his youth spent in Auschwitz. Feeling depressed by this news and my own illness I happened to listen to Thought for the Day, as was my custom. That Thursday morning the speaker was another friend of mine, Clive Lawton, who based his talk on some words of the *Torah*, 'Today I have set before you life and death, . . . Choose life' (Deuteronomy 30:19). These words came as a rallying call and challenge and I decided there and then to shrug off my illness and escape from St Richards Hospital as soon as possible. It was a rare experience, one that confirmed me in my belief that underneath are the everlasting arms, even when I am too doubting to put my trust in them.

Teaching and committee work gradually came to an end and more time was spent in the study writing, but there followed three further visits to India and two to Canada to stay with our daughter who had settled there with her husband, and a contribution to the excellent Victoria and Albert Museum exhibition on the Arts of the Sikh Kingdoms. Recently I was asked to give a statement to the High Court on a case involving a Punjabi Welsh Sikh girl who had been excluded from school for wearing a kara, which, it was claimed, was a piece of jewellery. It is sometimes upsetting to be made aware of such situations and to realise that the issues of two generations ago are still alive today. We should be able to move forward. Our nation is multiracial and multireligious and we should be able to cherish it and celebrate it without Jews or Muslims, gays and blacks, feeling a need to look back over their shoulders anxiously, or whites seeking to maintain their status when all that matters should be quality of character as we all struggle for the equality of each and share a vision of unity and cohesion in the midst of enriching diversity.

Every class of children that I have taught or observed a student teaching seems to have had two or at the most four members who were intent on being disruptive. Then, out of the thirty, to use a round figure, there were another six to eight who waited to see whether they got away with it. The silent majority of somewhere around a dozen was ready to swing in behind a firm teacher or those taking the class out of his or her control. Finally, there was the half dozen who would always behave reliably, not necessarily goody goodies but pupils eager to learn. One such a boy was ten-year-old Peter Ford, who used to catch the same bus home as I did in Corsham but waited for it at a different stop. I happened to ask him what he did until the bus came. Hesitantly, he enquired whether I really wanted to know and when I replied that I did told me that he looked for houses with interesting knockers, rapped on them and then ran away. But, he assured me, he only chose unusual knockers! One day, after morning play time, I returned to the classroom to find the contents of a full bottle of milk on the floor. The class knew the rule that whoever caused a mess cleaned it up and no one would be in trouble. Accidents happen. I asked who was responsible and was met by total silence. 'Very well', I said, 'unless someone owns up before afternoon playtime we shall all have to miss our break, myself included'. As I was about to organise the clean up operation, Peter Ford, looking very sheepish, admitted that he was the culprit, which threw me, for a moment, because I knew that he was the one person who must be innocent as he was out of the room with me helping me to collect a pile of books. Society is very much like a class of children, a minority will attach itself to a racist or anti-Jewish party and if it is not firmly but justly dealt with, others will follow including some members of the silent majority who find it to their benefit and advantage. A nation's leaders must look to supporting its Peter Fords.

We decided, Gwynneth and I, to stay up to see in the New Millennium, though it was not our custom to greet the New Year in this way. It proved unremarkable. The party of the great and the good did not impress and the promised fire-work event of the River Thames on fire did not seem to materialise. Our millennium hasn't really improved. The destruction of the Twin towers on 9/11 was dreadful to behold on television as I saw the second plane live, flying purposefully into the tower; but much worse was to follow when, a few days later I learned that the husband of my one goddaughter, Elizabeth, was a casualty of the event and that she was seven months pregnant with their child, who turned out to be a son, William. Though the whole 9/11 episode may seem minor in comparison to the Somme, D Day or Anzio, one has to remember that this was the first time in recent history that America had been attacked on its own soil, and that the previous occasion had been when the Native Americans dared to rise against white rulers who had ignored their treaty obligations. Added to this insult and threat, there was no directly identifiable enemy who could be dealt with in an act of retaliation.

Much of the late summer and autumn of 2000 was spent in hospital having a double heart by-pass. Benign hand shakes developed which may or may not be Parkinson's disease, the jury is still out. Then, in 2003, I had a revision of my left hip which was infected during the operation or very soon after. Eventually, I became virtually immobile and a second revision took place in 2007, this time accompanied apparently by MRSA. Having provided this update on my health, and with an expression of gratitude to Gwynneth for caring for me, I will pass on to more important matters.

The second war on Iraq came. Ever since the Suez war of the nineteen fifties I have reconsidered my pacifist position whenever it has been challenged by such hostilities. The year 2002–3 was no exception but this time I was more convinced than ever before that my stance was right and the war was unjust. It seemed to me that Bush and Blair had decided what they were going to do and then found reasons to legitimate their actions so a whole nation was put at risk in an awesome bombing offensive and no one seemed aware that democracy and unity in the region of Pakistan, Afghanistan and Iraq depends on the power of a tyrant who can keep the local war lords in check. Eight years on and we still are not certain of achieving a peaceful solution to the area and meanwhile have alienated many Muslims in those countries and beyond, including the UK. The unfolding crisis made me feel the need to identify myself with fellow pacifists. At a Good Friday sermon in our cathedral I heard Paul Oestreicher preach and discovered that he was an Anglican and a Quaker. There and then I decided to follow in his footsteps.

I had just decided to close this chapter on my decision to become a Quaker, when I received a most pleasing email from a delightful former Ph.D. student. When dad was preaching he sometimes amused me, and himself, I think, by saying 'Finally, and with this I close'. Hands reached for their hymn books but I knew that it was rather like Paul's; 'Finally, beloved', a warning to the amanuensis to sharpen his quill, or whatever he used. Today, Opinderjit Thakur, nee Randhava, informed me that she had been appointed to a Religious Studies post at Wolverhampton University, in a city famous for its interfaith activities. At last I have found a home for my remaining library. Opinderjit caused me some anxiety when she told me in the last year of her research into Sikh identity that her marriage had been arranged. It took place soon afterwards and within a few months she became pregnant, true to Indian tradition. However, by the end of the year she also had her Ph.D. Now she has two daughters who will, I hope, prove the same joy to her as ours are to us. And on that note I will finally close the chapter!

15

At My End Is My Beginning

What lies ahead in terms of religious autobiography is impossible to say. Certainly, it will be less in quantity than those of sports people or pop stars who write their autobiographies as the age of twenty two. It is now time to reflect and I will begin with Religious Education.

An education department colleague, at his retirement bash, told us that he did not want to hear any more about Education. I cannot and would not say the same about RE. I have lived and breathed it since 1954 when I discovered its existence. During my days as a Gas Board navvy I often thought that I should be thinking great philosophical thoughts as my pick hit the clay and gravel of the trench I was digging, but I could not. Working in my garden here in Chichester, I often solved a teaching issue or planned an article on some aspect of RE whilst I dug or weeded. There is no point in suggesting a new name for the subject; we have gone through Scripture, RI, and RE, and it is clear that to offer a different name would not necessarily result in the subject being better taught or taken more seriously. It will remain the Cinderella subject, until governments recognise its potential to help children develop a critical understanding of diverse beliefs and values, skills essential for any citizen in our society, and give it support. Ironically, legally, no one need study and no one need teach RE, exercising the legal right of withdrawal on grounds of conscience. Perhaps post-1988 changes have had one result; by widening the religious areas to be covered it has been made a subject that only trained specialists can teach. Heads can no longer expect a Methodist local preacher who is on the staff to give a few periods to it. I have often likened this attitude to that of a head, who knowing that a colleague frequented a pub occasionally, might suggest that he could therefore teach Chemistry. RE's content and pedagogical demands are such that it is no subject for the well meaning amateur. Though it may be weak, the chances of it dying are very slight unless powerful anti-religious politicians form an alliance with people of faith who demand that it should be taught only in religious schools in an attempt to win back the large numbers of children who no longer go to church, mosques, gurdwaras and other places of worship. Politicians as a whole do not yet realise that it does not exist to provide fodder for pews or check the rise in unwanted teenage pregnancies. When I use the term RE I actually mean the study of beliefs and values, many of which will be religious but which will also include Humanism and Atheism. It covers a realm of meaning without which no one can be considered educated. The breadth of this subject, together with its aims, to inform but not persuade sixteen or eighteen year old young people that they must or should adopt a particular life stance, is important if they are to grow up to be critically aware of their human responsibilities and environment and capable of responding to global challenges. The curriculum as a whole should have this kind of purpose. RE should not be the only subject concerned with meaning and values and respect for the world we live in, but it does have its own special contribution to make. At recent general elections in the UK one has heard people seriously asking why they should have any responsibility for the poor, sick, or disabled. RE is no more an antidote to greed and selfishness than the churches have been, but it should provide such citizens with the critical ability to consider the implications of what they have just said. Such RE should be more than knowledge based, it should explore the impact that the Qur'an and Bible are intended to have upon the believers who base their lives on them, it should examine the significance that the Passover has for contemporary Jews, and what a journey to Varanasi means for Hindus or the pilgrimage to Lourdes means to Christians. In my experience as an examiner, candidates can answer the what, where, and when questions well, but why presents problems. Empathy is not a skill that is acquired naturally or easily. One of my most vivid memories is of a two-session study of the Hajj. The first week I described and explored the journey using slides and eye-witness accounts, but on the second week a Muslim friend who had recently been to Makka described his experiences, using the same slides. The Journey of a Lifetime came fully to life as the class entered into the experience as much as any non-Muslim could. Nowadays, such events are well covered by video and DVD but sometimes the spiritual experience and significance is not conveyed, especially that of Christian rituals because, perhaps, the film makers think that what they are describing is well known, but this is often untrue. Most children have only a poor understanding of what Christmas or Easter mean to believers, and have never entered a church for worship. Perhaps the one value of faith schools is that they enable pupils to understand what the major events in the church calendar mean. There is still a reluctance to go to the heart of religions because there is a fear that, as teachers they are trying to encourage children to accept our own beliefs, if we have any. This may be especially true when the class is thought to comprise children whose heritage is Christian and the teacher is Christian. Such feelings can, and should be overcome as soon as the child enters school at five or transfers at eleven or thirteen or enters a sixth form college. This is a teacher-pupil relationship matter that cannot be implicitly or explicitly addressed too often. Christianity is certainly the most difficult religion to teach about in our schools because it is so often assumed that we are all Christians, or were, and should be, and if the child is a Sikh it may be thought that she may be expecting the teacher to try to convert her as Christians did her family in their village in India. Islam can be just as challenging in a Muslim school which accepts the requirement to teach according to the 1988 Act. It is easy to adopt the cop out approach that I once overheard a nonspecialist who had to teach some RE make; 'I just teach them all Buddhism, they are not Buddhists and they know that I am not so no one is offended'. But such a teacher is presented with one insurmountable difficulty, just like everyone else, the 1988 Education Act still requires a daily act of collective worship and it should be 'wholly or mainly Christian', to quote the Act itself. Escape to Buddhism or any other religion is only an illusion! The 1988 Act distinguished between RE and worship for the first time, but still required both. Only the abolition of worship in our schools can ensure the true delivery of RE as a subject like every other in the curriculum. My strength of feeling concerning worship is partly because faith has not come easily to me and I do not believe that it can be turned on and off like a tap and do not want to give the impression that it can be; at its worst it is manipulative, as was the forcing of Chinese children to sing songs eulogising Chairman Mao which they would do with gusto, at best it dilutes an important faith activity beyond recognition as it bears no resemblance to the worship of any Christian group, and by law it is forbidden to do so. Freed from the worship requirement the whole school, whatever its composition, can focus on such human issues as poverty or refugees with each group free to bring its own insights to be shared. Even Ramadan or Easter can be included, as fasting and diet are considered together or Easter in art, music, poetry are examined, with, of course, time being given for the exploration of what the different events mean to those who practice them. Even then I doubt the wisdom of holding such gatherings daily as the Act requires, or as activities of the whole school.

Religious Education has a very low glass ceiling. I am not the only person who became a head of department without serving an apprenticeship to a more experienced teacher in the subject, and when I was looking for promotion found that only a handful of denominational school offered allowances of more than £200. Financial or leadership opportunities lay in moving out of the classroom to become a deputy head or a lecturer in a training college.

Finally, however, on the subject of RE, I would leave the last word with my colleague and friend John Rankin, 'RE should be fun'; and add, because I cannot really allow him the enjoyment of ending this section; 'as all education should be'. Governments who place obstacles in the way of this goal being realised should be challenged on a daily basis.

My experience of Religious Education has been confined largely to a multifaith society that is part of multicultural Britain but for over twenty years I was moderator of the school-based World Religions syllabus and examination of the International Baccalaureate. This was based largely on the six major religions found in Britain today but has now been enlarged to cover most of the living religions of the world. I would want to argue that such a study should have its place in the curriculum of every democratic society. Religion has done much harm in the world but has been the source of considerable good; it is far too important to be excluded from its classrooms to be left to sectarian interests such as missionary groups. One size fits all cannot be the answer any more than it was the kind of answer to the kinds of democracy imposed by European governments upon the nations of Africa, but if we are ever to enjoy global harmony education rather than the bomb and the bullet should be looked to provide the basis. There are democracies where the broad study of beliefs and values is encouraged but more can be done if social cohesion in the midst of diversity is to be achieved, even in the UK. Perhaps the United Nations could add the universal study of beliefs and values to its list of educational goals.

Is there a religious gene? Is the need for faith so deeply embedded in our make-up that we must believe in a religious instinct? If there are beings similar to ourselves on other planets but far too intelligent to disclose themselves to a human race that would immediately wish to colonise them, as it did the indigenous races of the Americas, we might have an answer to our question, if we found that they had no need for a belief in God. I fear that would be considered a grave deficiency and we would immediately organise missions to convert them and persuade them that their ignorance was not blissful but literally damnable. But before we set out into the ether we might ask ourselves which if any religion is true on our own planet.

Presumably, we must begin by assuming that our own religion is true, or authentic might be a better word to use. We may doubt certain aspects of it, its attitude to women, to homosexuality or war, for example, but we can probably cope with these so long as we can accept its essence and the other features do not stack up overwhelmingly. If we were to become disillusioned with the religion as a whole and saw its tenets as a denial of human rights, equality, and integrity, presumably we would have to discard it though possibly only after making a resolute effort to maintain our allegiance, as one finds all too frequently with the followers of political parties, or football teams. Cunning arguments are invented all the time to convince us that the unacceptable is wholesome, often by ourselves. We need look no further than Nazi Germany or Stalin's Russia for examples.

The first position that we may hold is that my religion is true or authentic but the rest are false. This has been the view of many Christians down the ages and has led, on the one hand, to religious wars and persecutions, and on the other to intense missionary activity. Some Muslims share this view but something that I have learned over the years is how rare it is among the disciples of eastern religions. Jews, of course, do not share it either, even if they do believe that they are the chosen people, that is a nation chosen by God to be witnesses, not a privileged race. All followers of the Noahide code, namely the belief in one God and the necessity to live moral lives, are acceptable to the Almighty. The exclusivist position is held by those who believe that Jesus was sent by his father to atone for the sins of humanity and that only those who share this belief will enjoy eternal salvation. It is a view well summed up in the still very popular hymn;

> There is a green hill far away,
> Without a city wall,
> Where the dear Lord was crucified,
> Who died to save us all.
>
> We may not know, we cannot tell,
> What pains he had to bear,
> But we believe it was for us
> He hung and suffered there.
>
> He died that we might be forgiven,
> He died to make us good,
> That we might go at last to heaven
> Saved by his precious blood.

There was none other good enough
To pay the price of sin.
He only could unlock the gate
Of heaven and let us in.

When children and some adult Christians are asked to explain the meaning of Jesus' death they can do no more that quote these words. Of course there are many verses in the New Testament that have informed and inspired Mrs.Cecil Frances Alexander (1818-1895), but it is a view that receives little support from Jesus himself, certainly in the Synoptic gospels. Its effect on mission can be clearly seen from these words composed some years earlier by Bishop Heber,(1783-1826):

Can we, whose souls are lighted
With wisdom from on high,
Can we to men benighted
The lamp of life deny?
Salvation, O salvation!
The joyful sound proclaim,
Till each remotest nation
Has learned Messiah's name.

This is a verse of 'From Greenland's icy mountain', a hymn rarely sung today but still illustrative of the belief that humanity must become Christian if the world is to be saved spiritually. Am I being harsh or unfair? In the late nineteen nineties we took a party of students to Coventry, a city rich in religious diversity. Many of us began our visit by attending evensong in the cathedral where we were invited to sing the hymn, 'Thy kingdom come O God', which includes the verse:

O'er heathen lands afar
Thick darkness broodeth yet;
Arise O morning star,
Arise and never set.

More recently, in radio broadcasts, I have heard the words modified to:

O'er lands both near and far
Thick darkness broodeth yet,

This is scarcely an improvement if we think about it seriously.

183

Can one really be surprised that some of the parishioners of Elveden in Norfolk, where the last Sikh Maharaja, Duleep Singh, is buried with other members of his family, asked whether the church should be reconsecrated when they came across a Sikh praying in it? It is said that the influence of religion and especially the Church of England has declined in recent years. Perhaps this is good if it has led to a decline in racism based on religion, though as I write there is a proposal before Synod to take more seriously the evangelising of Muslims.

Secondly, I may believe that my religion is true, the result of divine revelation, but that all other religions are human searches for that truth. In my experience this view is preached by ministers who have little knowledge of other faiths but are eager to create harmonious interfaith relations. It seems to be a fairly popular position. The uniqueness of Christianity is safeguarded and some place is given to the sincerity of other people of faith. They may still remain to be persuaded of their error but deserve some respect. This solution raises the question by what criteria I can make this assertion and convince the outsider? In some ways it might be seen as even worse than telling members of other religions that their religions are false because it still tells Muslims or Sikhs that they are the victims of an illusion.

A third position may be to say that my religion is true but others may be ways in which God has prepared for the authentic message. Classically, this has been the attitude towards Judaism. It was revealed by God but somehow lost its way and, consequently, when Jesus came, most Jews failed to recognise him. Some Christians noting the word 'Krishna' in Hinduism, and movements devoted to the worship of a loving deity, have spoken about the presence of Christ in Hinduism. This notion can convey to view that such religions have some authenticity and even a place in the divine plan of salvation though now they belong to religious archaeology and history. Their time has gone. The apostle Paul made use of the idea at Athens when he drew his audience's attention to the 'unknown God', and the writer of the Letter to the Hebrews began it by declaring that God, 'who spoke to our ancestors in many and various ways by the prophets has, in these last days, spoken to us by a son'. At its worst the position may be stated in the claim sometimes made, that Islam is a demonic parody of Christianity, a view that I have not come across recently.

A more sophisticated and developed form of this argument is the belief in what has sometimes been described as progressive revelation. This was popular among Christian biblical scholars who noted how from the wrathful, polytheism of the early Hebrews gradually emerged the belief in the one God of the whole world, demanding justice and mercy and finally, in Jesus, to become the God of love. Most recently this idea has been put forward by Baha'is who trace the progressive development of religion through Buddhism and Hinduism, Zoroastrianism, Judaism and Christianity to their own teacher. Herein lies its sophistication that it provides an authentic place for other faiths that are always treated with respect.

Even more authenticity and respect might be given to each religion if we share the attitude that every one of them leads to God or is divine in its origin just as there are many paths to the top of the mountain, as my Hindu friends say. The view seems popular among many Unitarians and Quakers I have met but less so among Anglicans and Roman Catholics.

At the opposite end of the spectrum that affirms that my religion is true and the rest are false is one that assumes that all religions constitute the sum of Religion. Why there are so many religions is a question that has puzzled believers from time to time, though less so, it seems, today than in the past. On the one hand, plurality is an interesting phenomenon to be accepted, on the other it is a fact to be ignored, anxious, perhaps, that it is can lead to a kind of relativism that threatens to diminish the status of one's own beliefs. It might even be used to argue for the existence of a religious instinct or gene. We might suggest that in different environments God has been disclosed in different ways. Each may be authentic or contain an element of truth but perhaps emphasising varied ideas as the result of particular insights or experiences. Paradise is more likely to be a garden for those who live in hot desert regions than for those whose environment is a rain forest, perhaps. The feminine aspect of God may be stressed by those who feel that the patriarchal nature of the divine has been overemphasised. The whole is the sum of the parts or more. The Christian hymn that is now quoted in full below seems to be based on this belief. It does not seem well known today and in fact, I could only trace it with the help of two Indian Christian friends, Jamila and George Verghese, though I certainly sang it as a child or teenager in the church where my father was minister.

Gather us in thou love that fillest all;
Gather our rival faiths within thy fold;
Rend each man's veil and bid it fall,
That we may know that thou hast been of old.
Gather us in – we worship only thee.

In varied names we stretch a common hand,
In diverse forms a common soul we see;
In many ships we seek one spirit land.
Thine is the mystic life great India craves;
Thine is the Parsee's sin-destroying beam;
Thine is the Buddhist's rest from tossing waves;
Thine is the empire of vast China's dream.
Thine is the Roman's strength without his pride;
Thine is the Greek's glad world without his graves;
Thine is Judea's law with love besides;
The truth that censures and the grace that saves.

Some seek a father in the heaven above;
Some seek a human image to adore;
Some crave a spirit vast as light and love;
Within thy mansions we have all and more.
Gather us in – we worship thee alone.
(The last line is a refrain to each verse).

The hymn writer, George Matheson, suggests that God is concerned for all human kind and always has been.

The only view, of those cited above, that Matheson implicitly rejects, is the exclusive Christian belief that Christianity alone is authentic and this may be a reason why, I understand, the hymn has not been included in any anthology since Percy Dearmer's and Vaughan Williams's *English Hymnal* of 1925. It is certainly not in *Congregational Praise*, the collection I used in Durham. This hymn must have introduced me to the word Parsee, if not Buddhist, but it was many years before I found out the meaning of them and I did not bother my dad to explain them, I pondered them, and the hymn, in my heart or not at all.

Last year, 2008, I was asked for a contribution to the parish magazine and decided to set out my beliefs. Here I can use more than the 350 words I was allowed then. They are the result, most importantly, of seventy-seven years of living, of fifty-five years studying and teaching about religion, and a forty year relationship with people of other faith. Many of the men and women who have influenced me have already been mentioned and the others know who they are so I will simply note their love and generosity of spirit rather than name them, and move on to discuss the issues.

My original beliefs were conventionally Bradford nonconformist. Socially, I was implicitly brought up to respect everyone so that homosexuality, the place of women in the church, class issues of rich and poor, were matters of which I was not aware. I accepted all people without question. As Easter approached each year, I sang:

There is a green hill far away
Without a city wall,
Where our dear lord was crucified
Who died to save us all.

The only difficulty that I had with the words was that of wondering why a green field needed a city wall. Scott's Field at the bottom of our garden didn't have one, and I saw none surrounding those in Toftshaw Bottom, or on Bierley fields. But as usual I kept my curiosity to myself. That Jesus died to save us all presented no problems and I probably sang the hymn with gusto in chapel and Sunday school. At university I came across the famous hymn of Charles Wesley that begins:

And can it be that I should gain
An interest in the saviour's blood?
Died he for me who caused his pain
For me, who him to death pursued?
Amazing love! How can it be
That thou, my God, should die for me!

Once again, I accepted the general principle of salvation through the death of Jesus and the blood of his sacrifice, but I became increasingly uneasy with the idea that eternal life was denied to those who did not accept the forgiveness of sins made available by his death. I once considered becoming a missionary but my intention was to educate the 'little black babies overseas' that I had heard of in Sunday School rather than save souls. Christian Union sermons were often based on John 3:16: 'God so loved the world that he gave his only son that everyone who believes in him should not perish but have everlasting life', or from Pauline passages that stressed original sin, our universal inheritance from Adam; these seemed adequately to explain my own shortcomings and those of the world in which I lived.

It was when I met other people of faith that these views were challenged, men such as our neighbour Len Abramson, a mensch if ever I knew one, or Piara Singh Sambhi and his wife, Avtar, who kept the faith even though their small daughters had been killed on a zebra crossing as they went to school. In them and many others I found the presence of

God at work. My academic studies made me question this traditional teaching in other ways. I discovered that Jews did not accept the idea that the sin of Adam and Eve affected the whole human race from that time onwards. Ezekiel warned that: 'only the person who sins shall die; (18:4); and in verse twenty he adds: 'A child shall not suffer for the iniquity of a parent, nor a parent suffer for the iniquity of a child, the righteousness of the righteous shall be his own and the wickedness of the wicked shall be his own.' Reminiscent of Jeremiah (31:29), he denies the validity of the proverb; 'the parent has eaten sour grapes and the children's teeth are set on edge' Jeremiah also said that all should die for their own sins (verse 30). The whole of chapter eighteen of the prophecy of Ezekiel is worth considering, it ends with the words: 'I have no pleasure in the death of anyone, says the Lord. Turn then, and live.' On the Day of Atonement, Yom Kippur, Jews may gather in their synagogues for the whole day, but each adult must accept responsibility for his own sins, no one else can take his place. The concept of Messiah may not feature strongly in contemporary Jewish thought, Christians have tended to make it an embarrassing issue, but the purpose of the Messiah was not and is not to deliver people from their sins but from oppression. Handel's *Messiah* could not have been composed by a Jew. We have a long way to go in altering our attitudes to Jews, I don't expect us to change our name from Christian, which carries with it the belief that the Messiah has come, in the person of Jesus, but I am careful to avoid the word 'Christ' especially in interfaith gatherings. It means little to Christians today; perhaps they think it was his surname as the child did who was asked to name Jesus'parents and replied: 'Mr and Mrs Christ.' Some friends active in the world of inter religious dialogue assure me that there is nothing in the Lord's Prayer with which a Jew could not agree. That is not surprising as its author was a Jew, but for two thousand years it has been the property of his followers who claim that he was the Christ, (Greek for Messiah), and that is sufficient reason for Jews to find it unacceptable.

How then was I to look at the Genesis story of the Fall and the teaching that: 'as we all died in Adam so we shall all be made alive in Christ' (I Corinthians 15: 22)? When I came to read the first three gospels again Matthew, Mark, and Luke, I found very little support for it. Jesus seemed seldom, if ever, to put himself forward as a saviour figure. The words: 'Come to me all you who are weary and carrying heavy burdens and I will give you rest. Take my yoke upon you and learn from me for I am gentle and humble in heart, and you shall find rest for your souls. For my yoke is easy and my burden light', (Matthew 11:28), could have been spoken by any compassionate rabbi. The lawyer who asked Jesus what he must do to inherit eternal life, and who gave Jesus the opportunity to tell the story of the Good Samaritan, was a Jewish teacher or student of the Torah, not a lawyer in the modern sense of the word. Jesus, in good Jewish manner, answered his question with a question: 'What is written in the Torah, what do you read there'? And the man answered by quoting the two greatest commandments to which one famous rabbi said the other 611 were merely commentary. (The passage occurs in Luke's gospel 10: 25 to 37). I realised that Jesus was endorsing his own scriptures; so very often I had been given to understand or explicitly told by Christian preachers that the commandments of love originated with Jesus himself, when actually he was quoting the Torah, Deuteronomy 6:4 and 5, and Leviticus 19:18.

Where did this leave me? Easter has always been for me the great festival. Christmas may not have been celebrated for some three hundred years after Jesus' birth and for me it has never had the attraction of Easter, but what now could I celebrate? I realised that there were other interpretations of the crucifixion available to me. Even the medieval church had not pronounced that only one doctrine should be accepted. It lay to hand for me in the great hymn of Isaac Watts that I had also been singing since childhood,

When I survey the wondrous cross.
On which the Prince of Glory died,
My richest gain I count but loss
And pour contempt on all my pride.

Forbid it, Lord, that I should boast,
Save in the death of Christ, my God;
All the vain things that charm me most;
I sacrifice them to his blood.

See from his head, his hands, his feet,
Sorrow and love flow mingling down,
Did e'er such love and sorrow meet,
Or thorns compose so rich a crown?

Were the whole realm of nature mine,
That were an offering far too small;
Love so amazing, so divine,
Demands my soul, my life, my all.

I can only echo the words of a theologian whose name I cannot remember who said, looking at a cross: 'God loves like that'. So, I was able to remain within the Christian family and value the death of Jesus as the supreme act of love as I have discovered the love of God also in Judaism. Jesus and the prophets of the Bible were also Jews, in Islam, especially in the teachings of the Sufis but also in the Qur'an, and in the bhakti tradition of Hinduism as well as Sikhism. Their discovery endorsed my personal experience.

However, I still felt a need to explain the belief that Jesus undid the effects of Adam's sin, even though I no longer accepted it.

Imagine being an advertising agent given the task of trying to sell Jesus and his most important followers, Peter and Paul, to a sceptical world, both Jewish and Gentile. Three criminals all legally executed by the Roman authorities. The key figure, Jesus, was a trouble-maker in Palestine who threatened the *Pax Romana* and was justly put to death at the instigation of the Jews, even betrayed by one of his own men. Care is taken in the gospels, not only to bring out his innocence but also his interest in restoring his fellow Jews to the moral decency that the priesthood was neglecting. He kept the Sabbath and worshipped in the Temple whenever he was in Jerusalem. His wish was to reform Judaism to the very end of his life, possibly he even quoted a psalm, twenty-two, at the moment of his death. The cleansing of the Temple (Luke 19 but mentioned in all three synoptic gospels), should be seen in this context, not as an act of violence, an embarrassment to pacifists! It is impossible to tell what happened at the Resurrection, but Christians believe that it was inspiring event that transformed his followers who had deserted him (Mark 14:50). But how could they persuade the public? Partly by their courage but also by claiming that Jesus' death was abnormal and had cosmic significance. Some genius concluded that his fate had been part of a divine plan, not just the story of a good man who came to a bad end, there were plenty such examples in human history, and that whoever believed in him would be given spiritual salvation by God. Its originator may have been Jesus, we cannot deny that completely but from the evidence of the synoptic gospels it seems unlikely. I have in mind, however, the story of the encounter that two disciples had with the risen Jesus on the road to Emmaus, and especially the clause: 'he interpreted to them the things about himself in all the scriptures' (Luke 24:27). It would have been a fascinating experience to be an eaves dropper on that conversation. The complete form of the death of Jesus as undoing the effects of Adam's sin, however, is to be found in the writings of Paul whose preaching was intended to present Jesus as an innocent man who was executed illegally and raised to life as an act of vindication. Quite rightly, the first letter to Corinthian Christians asserts that if Jesus had not been raised from the dead the message he proclaimed would have been in vain, as would be his faith and those of all who shared it (I Corinthians 15). It was much more important for them to believe in and experience the Resurrection for themselves than it was to accept the theology as it was the experience that gave the message its authenticity.

Perhaps a word should be said about Peter and Paul at this point. Christianity is based on the lives of three criminals, not one. Peter and Paul were also executed by the Roman authorities after being repeatedly imprisoned, and in Rome of all places, the centre of the Empire. The documents of the Bible are not historical in the main in the same way that those I studied at Durham were, but many of them related to actual events. The Acts of the Apostles, seem, most importantly to tell the stories of Peter and Paul before they reached Rome. What happened to them afterwards did not need to be recorded, it was already known to the Roman Christian community, but each of them reached the city accompanied by rumours that had to be dispelled or accepted as true. One purpose of Acts was to remove both the smoke and the fire of gossip should any opponents of the new religious movement seek to discredit them.

In recent times my attention has been focused for the most part upon the religions of the East, especially Hinduism and Sikhism, and, to a lesser extent, Buddhism. In these I found no trace of a doctrine of original sin but an essential belief that, in our natural state, we are ignorant of the fact that the spiritual or God permeates us and the whole world. Our problem is that we are self centred instead of God oriented and aware that we are actually God filled. There is a Hindu story that tells of a priest who performed rituals for money which he then hid in a river bank near his home. When he died he was reborn as a water rat so that he could be near the object of his desire. In his rat form he realised that gold was of no use to him, he couldn't spend or eat it. When he became a man again he remembered his former life, learned his lesson and lived a God focused life; when he died he attained liberation, moksha, with no more physical rebirths. For Hindus, I discovered, there are many paths to liberation, from severe austerity, going on pilgrimages, to trusting in divine grace being some of them. The story is told of an ascetic who stood on one foot outside Siva's cave for a thousand years. Eventually, the god noticed him and asked his purpose. He said he hoped that Siva would see his pious austerity and grant him moksha. The god told him that he could not yet, but must stand on one leg for a much longer time. Rather exhausted and somewhat frustrated the man asked whether there might be another way of achieving liberation. Siva replied, reluctantly, that there was; he should utter the Name of the god, Ram, with total sincerity and devotion and he would gain moksha instantly. This the man did. Of course, it is a somewhat playful story told by those Hindus who believe that God's grace is freely available to all who put their trust in it. A loving God is as much a part of Hinduism and the essence of Sikhism as it is of Christianity. This discovery shocked me.

In Islam too I found compassion and mercy, loving aspects of a demanding God who was nearer to us than our jugular vein. In the poetry of the Sufi mystics was an expression of divine love as great and strong and compelling as I had ever experienced. Sheikh Nizam explained the path he taught when he wrote: 'Love is the bond that binds hearts, the basis on which to build. If love is the foundation, your building will with-stand all earth-quakes and storms, and you will build it as high and wide as you please without it being in danger. Therefore our way is the way of love. Leave what is keeping you from that path and turn to follow it with perseverance, follow the path all the way to your destination.' He also advised: 'Go sweep the room of your heart. Make it ready to be the dwelling place of the beloved. When you depart he will enter it. In you, empty of self, he will display all his beauty'. Had he this story of the Prophet in mind? As he went to the mosque to pray each day, an old woman threw her rubbish upon him as he passed under her window. One day this didn't happen, and the second, and so on for a week. The Prophet enquired about the lady and was told that she was ill. Each day he cared for her until she recovered. The woman asked her neighbours who had looked after her. They told her; 'The man on whom you threw your rubbish'. Children are told this story of compassion and encouraged to be like the Prophet as much as possible.

Rabi'a, a female Sufi, wrote, famously;

Two ways I love thee: selfishly,
And next, as worthy of thee.
'Tis a selfish love that I do naught
save think on thee with every thought.
'Tis purest love when thou dost raise
the veil to mine adoring gaze.
Not mine the praise in that or this:
Thine is the praise in both, I wis.

Rumi said: 'Never does the lover seek without being sought by the beloved. When the lightning of love has shot into this heart know that there is love in that heart. Mark well the text: He loves them and they love him (Qur'an Sura 5:55).

This knowledge, combined with the kindness, friendship and generosity I found in so many people of other faith who were not Christians made me think seriously about my attitude to their religions. The conclusion that I reached was that good was within all of them and that of God is present in everyone, not only Christians. I heard a Sufi in Delhi say that he was a Muslim Universalist, that is that he followed the path of Islam but accepted the authenticity of all others. I became a Christian Universalist. What has this meant for my Christian views and beliefs?

Evangelistic missions have been a cause of increasing unease. For many years I doubted the appropriateness of transferring western culture to Africa or India in the name and guise of religion and recently I have been pleased to see that many missions and new Christian communities in India share this view. (Sadly, I have never set foot in Africa). 'Mary' or 'Clarence' have given way to Jamila or Ranjit, musical instruments indigenous to the culture have replaced the organ though not the harmonium which I sometimes suspect was brought by Welsh missionaries and left by them. Hymns are composed in local languages and sung to Indian tunes. However, I also reached the position of doubting the propriety of sending missionaries at all, as opposed to teachers or medical workers to raise the quality of care where necessary. We seemed to be denying the authenticity and worth of Hinduism or Islam and, even more seriously, asserting the superiority of Christianity over these faiths. It was not possible any more to sing any missionary hymns. Even,

> The light of the morning is breaking,
> New people are learning to pray,'

though I liked the tune it was sung to, Crugybar, and Elved, its composer, was a Baptist minister friend of my grandfather and a crown bard of Wales! Soon after I began studying Hinduism and meeting Hindus I discovered that they had been praying for at least some five thousand years, possibly before the time of Abraham. These hymns may be sung now less frequently than in the past and maybe Christian civilisation, which Gandhi declared would be a good thing, has become more humble after two world wars and the dropping of atomic bombs on a non-Christian culture, though the current Iraq war does not support this hope. If we could carpet bomb Hamburg and Dresden, I have no doubt that

we could have nuked Berlin had the need arisen. Other hymns are equally
pernicious; only this morning I was invited to sing;

> Tell of his death on Calvary,
> Hated by those he came to save,
> In lonely suffering on the cross
> For all he loved his life he gave.

If that could not be used as a reason for Jew bashing in less temperate
times, consider the Advent hymn, perhaps sung less now than in the past,
composed by Charles Wesley.

> Lo, he comes with clouds descending,
> Once for favoured sinners slain,
> Thousand thousand saints attending
> Swell the triumph of his train.
> Alleluia!
> Christ appears on earth to reign.

> Every eye shall now behold him
> Robed in dreadful majesty;
> Those who set at nought and sold him,
> Pierced and nailed him to the tree,
> Deeply wailing
> Shall their true messiah see.

In my opinion this hymn should be expunged from hymn books for
it anti-Jewish sentiments. (Its out of date cosmology. suggesting that
heaven is above the clouds and its simplistic teaching about the Second
Coming. are lesser reasons for its exclusion). It was recently sung during
a Songs of Praise BBC TV broadcast in advent 2008.

A Good Friday collect from the Book of Common Prayer that I heard
used not long ago reads: 'Have mercy on all Jews, Infidels and Hereticks,
and take from them all hardness of heart and contempt of thy word; and
so fetch them home, blessed Lord, to thy flock so that they may be saved
among the remnant of the true Israelites, and be made one fold under
one shepherd'. In a modified version it was retained in the Alternative
Service Book of 1980 because, it is said, Canon Peter Schneider, a prominent figure in interfaith Anglicanism, being ill, was unable to produce
something different in time to meet the printer's deadline. Common
Worship, published in 2000 and used in many churches, does not include
the offensive collect.

The issue goes beyond liturgies and preaching. There is a need to recognise and accept the presence of people of other faith at a national level. I was present at the installation of Archbishop Carey at Canterbury and the five other major faiths to be found in Britain were represented but like children in past times they were seen and not heard. This seems to be the norm for all civic and political national occasions but it is no longer acceptable. Prince Charles has said that he wishes to be known as the 'Defender of Faiths', an important statement, (so long as one remembers that God requires no big brother for protection). He was reminded that he will be head of the Church of England and expected to be defender of that particular faith. Excuses will be found to keep the religions in their present position but if the will and vision are present a positive change can be made. I know, from talking to members of the faiths that they do feel slighted rather than honoured by a situation that invites them to be present but requires them to be silent. It must be remembered that they are voters, pay taxes, and that some have laid down their lives for this country; they are fellow citizens, with the same rights and duties as Christians. In a multi-religious society they must be recognised fully.

The love of God is unconditional and the presence of God is in everyone whether it is recognised, accepted, and cherished or not. Nowhere does Jesus seem to deny this and claim that eternal life depends on accepting him, except in the words, 'I am the way, the truth and the life. No one comes to the father except by me'; (John's gospel 14:6). In considering these words I must remember that they come from a book that is extremely difficult to interpret. In one verse the story is of a man, in the next of the Logos, the eternal, divine word. It is full of symbolism and should not be taken literally, in my view. Together with its sublime insights is a pernicious anti-Semitism. (My few Jewish students have found it the most difficult and painful to read of the four gospels by far). Sometimes, when the author uses the word 'Jew' I cannot help feeling that he is almost spitting it out with loathing. The wedding at Cana in chapter two has nothing to do with Jesus attending an actual marriage, though I like to think he was the kind of man who would make a welcome guest. The old wine has run out and all that is left is water for Jewish rituals of purification. This he takes and the new wine is superior to the old. The new wine is the message of Christianity. In the next chapter Nicodemus, a pious Jew, comes to Jesus by night, (he is in the dark), and is told that God gave his only son so that whoever believed in him should not perish but have eternal life (3:16). More challenging to those who would interpret John literally is the story of the raising of

195

Lazarus in chapter eleven. It is full of drama; we are told that only recently the Jews have tried to stone Jesus, (in chapter ten), and that he delays his visit rather than going urgently to his friends' home, so the man is clearly well and truly dead. Jesus then raises him, to what? In John Tetley's ballet based on the story, Lazarus becomes a peep show and ultimately pleads to be put back in the tomb. If the essence of John's gospel, and *the* Gospel, is that Jesus is the bringer of eternal life, what is the benefit of such resuscitation? The Fourth gospel may have links with history as we know it; much is made of the word 'Lithostroton' used to describe the place where Pilate tried Jesus, for example, but there is an urgent need to be more radical when reading the Bible and especially for Christians, the gospels. The chickens are coming home to roost for those who taught an over simplistic literalist view of the Bible, especially in Africa. From the missionaries came interpretations that are now being turned against those who accept homosexuality. Might this eventually lead to a demand for the restoration of capital punishment, for homosexuals were to be stoned to death, (Leviticus 20:1)? After all, it, like slavery, is nowhere condemned in the Bible. If Christianity is a religion of love and not of law it is the love principle that must govern its morality not the acceptance of proof texts.

My world view leads me to the belief in a need for a new relationship between humans and the world, the future lies in harmony and cooperation instead of the presumption that we are supreme and may do what we will – cut down forests, provoke climate change, hunt animals and fish to extinction. I once came across an Indian book for children called; *The Earth our Mother*, which argued that we should treat her with the care, love and respect that we show to our parents.

It is also imperative to establish a new relationship with God, one of adult maturity rather than childish reliance. In the Bible we read that he makes wars to cease and in the Book of Common Prayer we ask, 'Give us peace in our time', but as with famine and flood, ample advice has been given to us concerning the way we should conduct ourselves. As the Hebrew Bible puts it; 'He has taught you, O mortal, what is good, and what does the Lord require of you but to do justice and love kindness and walk humbly with your God' (Micah 6:8). If we heeded God's advice by doing these things life would be transformed. If we do not there is a good chance of us condemning ourselves to extinction and we cannot depend on divine intervention as in the past – and do we really believe that God sent plagues upon the Egyptians and condemned them to be drowned as they pursued his people? What kind of a God is that? There is a Jewish story that the angels joined with the Hebrews in singing and dancing as they watched the Egyptians perishing but they noticed that God was not enjoying the revels. Gabriel asked God why, and received the reply, 'How can I rejoice, the Egyptians are also my children and they are being killed?' Some years ago a family friend miscarried and sent not for the doctor but for the curate because she felt that the tragedy that had befallen her was some sort of divine punishment. Not long ago I heard a Christian say, on the radio, that forgiveness can only be gained at a price. She cited the story of King David and Bathsheba. David committed adultery with Bathsheba and had her husband murdered. God forgave them but because of their conduct the child died (2 Samuel 12). Is that an example of divine love? Such disasters as tsunamis and the eruption of volcanoes or infestations of locusts are to be explained by evolution, and cancer or Alzheimer's disease should be attributed to genetics. Why things are as they are we do not know and never shall so long as we describe them as 'acts of God'. We are now in a position, if half the money and most of the ingenuity that is used in finding new ways to kill one another, is devoted to finding solutions to most of these issues. Others, of course, will take their place, that is part of the process of growing to maturity, but it is infinitely preferable to acting like teenagers who steal a car and drive it without skilled knowledge. God's love is like that of a responsible parent. The children have been given guidance, now it is up to them to act responsibly. It is tempting to think that the death of Jesus deeply affected the Father if the Christian view of their relationship is valued. The concept of a dying and rising god is not exclusive to Christianity, it is especially present in the story of Mithraism, its great fourth-century rival, but totally missing from that myth, using the term in a proper religious sense, is the reality of suffering and the idea of vulnerability. The death of Jesus provides a new aspect of divine love. The concept of unconditional love is found in many faiths but here it is anchored in a specific historical act, for those who accept it.

Belief in God's unconditional love has a number of consequences and challenges. First, I cannot believe in hell. As a child I used to think that it was a hot place at the centre of the earth and was anxious for coal miners, such as my father had been, because he had told me how hot it could be underground and I had visions of them cutting through a coal face to find themselves in the Inferno. Later, of course, I had a concept of hell as a state of being rather than a place but now I cannot reconcile it with my belief that God is the source of unconditional love. More likely it is a political and religious creation of human beings designed to keep people in fear and order so that they might be obedient to church and state. It seems to have less of an influence than in times past and sadly, those who cling to the belief most are victims of cruelty who want to believe that the sufferings they are enduring in this life will be inflicted upon their torturers into eternity. One feels that their heaven must have a window in it to hell so that they can watch the sufferings of the damned. So what happens to the evil doer? Henry Horatio Hobson, in *Hobson's Choice* asked whether there would be lawyers in heaven. My answer must be 'yes' and worse – Hitler, Himmler, Stalin and Mugabe and a host of other undesirable people must also be there. Transformation is necessary if we are honest, and possible if we trust God. My problem is what happens to the honest atheist like my friend Harry, who once said to me, 'Owen, life is not fair. If there is an eternity as you believe, then you will be able to tell me that you told me so! If there isn't I shall not have the pleasure of saying the same to you!' The integrity of every Harry must be respected in the state of unconditional love, it may be by annihilation. I cannot share the patronising and disrespectful view that they will come to their senses when they experience the divine love. By the way, in heaven there can be no windows on the world. Jesus himself spoke of a great gulf or chasm that existed between this earthly existence and the next (Luke 16:26), and it would cause me no happiness and perhaps much pain, to look upon my children and grandchildren in either their joys that I could not share or their sorrows that I could not help them overcome.

In a world of love what are we to make of evil? It cannot be personified by an evil being, the devil or Satan, or the serpent in the Garden of Eden because this would seem to suggest the existence of two opposing powerful forces, even if, ultimately, good, in the form of God, wins the struggle. When the Christian prays not to be led into temptation it is the expression of a fervent wish not to commit selfish acts that harm our neighbour. I try to solve the question of evil to my satisfaction, by thinking of love gone wrong, turned inwards upon itself, selfishness in the form of pride, greed, seeking after power, lust, the wish to control other people or the natural world for our own ends. It seems to be our natural, unenlightened state. Ambition, of course, has its place. Unless we seek the best for our children and community, there will be no development, no attempt to grow better crops or heal diseases. We might still be living in caves. But surely there is a way to do these things without harming our world at a human or agricultural level. Evil is not buying a bigger house or a more expensive car, unless my gain is at someone else's expense. Few, if any of us, attain the state of selflessness in this life, but it is the goal that we must aspire to, otherwise we shall be content with greater and greater imperfection day by day.

What do I mean by heaven? I prefer to write about the state of eternity, then we may be able to set aside all childish images of reward and reunion with those we have 'loved long since and lost awhile', though I find that phrase very appealing and part of eternal bliss. Eternity is a spiritual state to which many of my Indian friends give the name 'Anand', bliss, and believe that the liberated soul will be reabsorbed into the loving God from whom it originated. One of them told me that he would not meet his much loved, recently dead brother, in eternity. The Abrahamic religions believe in some form of survival of an identifiable personality. Life, in each case, has the purpose of helping us to embark upon a spiritual journey homewards, but God alone knows why we are here at all unless it is to experience and develop love. In eternity we shall recognise one another and enjoy the rapture of being in the divine presence but there will be no past or future, only the eternal present. Memories of our faults and virtuous acts will be expunged so there will be no room for guilt or place for pride. As I have already suggested, it will be a state completely separate from our earthly existence so we shall not experience either the joy or pain of our descendants' lives but we shall know them when we meet again but not ask them how many GCSEs they got, or why the wasted their legacy, if we had one to leave them, on a Ferrari! There will be celestial music, the eternal sound that emanated into the scriptures of the world. The anahad shabad, the logos, became the scriptures of India and the Torah, New Testament and Qur'an. And is there not an element of eternity also in the music of Mozart or Schubert? There will also be the eternal music that rocks the universe and called it into being.

Coming back down to earth, perhaps not before time, my argument about the place of women in the Anglican church should not be about Jesus choosing men to be his apostles, or that all of them were Jews, but that in Paul's letter to the Philippians chapter two we are told that Jesus emptied himself of his divine powers and lived his life on earth as a servant. Somewhere I have read that he emptied himself of all but love. It may be a Methodist teaching. He accepted his role as a Jew among Jews in a country occupied by Rome, whereas, if we say he could have chosen women or Gentile apostles had he so wished, we must admit that he could have become incarnate as a Roman emperor, a Jewish woman, or a brahmin Hindu. His ordinance of self denial meant he became a man of his time, subject to the knowledge and ideas of his day, a man of his heritage, a Jew. To have chosen women or Gentiles would have been to take a step too far, to be so provocative that no one would take him seriously. In a very different world he would be facing the issues that the church and society are facing today. He was too wise for that! (Becoming human did not mean that he had to become stupid). But if the doctrine of the Trinity and the person of the Holy Spirit are taken seriously then theoretical possibility could become reality as his followers and humanity were, and still are, led into new developments motivated and inspired by love, feeding the hungry, healing the sick, establishing racial and gender equality, and so on. We might ask who decided that a small Galilean, Aramaic sect, should become a Greek-using, in its speech and the books, eventually called *The New Testament*, Gentile-admitting, community, that was soon appointing Gentile bishops? If the Holy Spirit could accomplish this, who is to say that today women might not be chosen by the same Spirit to become bishops? Or has his work and influence come to an end? Sadly, all too often, the inspiration of Jesus, the Qur'an, Guru Nanak, and others, has been countered by followers who are too small minded, too ready to turn God's love into selfish power play, prepared to stifle the Divine Spirit. It is as though the Divine hits the earth running and human self-interest trips her or him up. To use another image, God may rub the lamp but we quickly try to push the geni back into the bottle and make sure it is securely corked. However, God is not mocked and rendered ineffective, the Divine Love is expressed wherever the bereaved are comforted, the hungry are fed, the thirsty are given drink and the lame helped to walk. Faith in action, as the Letter of James puts it, is the love of God at work in the world, whether it be through Gandhi or Tearfund, a Christian relief agency, or the Red Crescent, the Muslim equivalent of the Red Cross.

Meanwhile, the faithful pilgrim need not be frustrated by establishments and organisations, though, as for John Bunyan's Pilgrim, they can be obstacles. A Sufi told me of a man who was travelling in the desert and saw someone coming towards him. In terror, he said, 'It is my enemy'. As the person drew nearer, the fearful traveller relaxed and said, 'No, it is my friend'. As he came nearer still he said; 'It is my brother!' and ran forward to embrace him. This has been my experience as I have met other people of faith. I commend it warmly, hoping that what I have written has not been a collection of silly musings but the story of one who has tried to keep the faith and grow into it, in the midst of faith. The story is not ended; the best is still to come.

Glossary

Anglican Church: alternative name for world wide forms of the Church of England.

Agreed Syllabus: document drawn up by an English LEA based on recommendations agreed by four groups representing the Church of England, other denominations and religions, teachers organisations, and representatives of the local authority, to provide the legal basis for what is taught in LEA schools within the authority.

Amrit ceremony: initiation rite by which Sikh men and women are admitted into the fellowship of the Khalsa.

Arti: important Hindu fire ceremony.

Babaji: affection term of respect used of a Sufi teacher, or Hindu and Sikh holy man.

Baptist: a believer in baptism into the Christian church only on confession of faith, usually as an adult; as opposed to infant baptism.

Bevin boy: conscript who worked down a coal mine as an alternative to military service. Named after the cabinet minister who devised the scheme.

Bonfire night: 5 November. Commemoration of plot to blow up the English King and Parliament in 1605.

Chapel: place of worship. Often used by denominations other than Anglican or Roman Catholic in England and Wales.

College of Education, often just mentioned as 'college'. An establishment devoted to the training of school teachers; eventually reorganised and renamed as Institutes of Education or polytechnic departments. Now universities.

Community schools: secondary schools controlled by local education authorities.

Comprehensive school: non-selective secondary school.

Congregational: a Christian protestant denomination independent of other churches other than by loose ties of common belief and association.

County school: name formerly given to a community school.

Curriculum or method course: an activity in which non-specialists in a subject are taught how to teach it, (e.g. history, music, R.E.). usually for students intending to work in primary schools.

Department of Education: the central government body responsible for education. Variously renamed since 1944. Now known as the Department for Education and Skills (DfES).

Diaspora: a community dispersed beyond its original homeland.

Eleven plus: examination taken a ten or eleven years of age to decide whether children were suitable to be educated in selective secondary schools.

Faith school: a religious foundation usually or largely free from LEA control.

Five Ks: symbols worn by many Sikhs whose initials in Punjabi, begin with the initial letter K.

Gideon Society: a voluntary, charitable organisation that donates copies of the Christian scriptures to such places as schools or hospitals .

Grammar school: a secondary school within the maintained system of education entry to which is determined by success in a selection examination at ten or eleven plus years of age.

Guardian: a broadsheet daily newspaper with liberal views.

Guy Fawkes: a member of a Roman Catholic plot to blow up the English Parliament in 1605. Though he was hanged, drawn and quartered his effigy is burnt on bonfire on this date.

Head teacher: person, male or female, appointed to be in charge of a school in England or Wales.

Her Majesty's Inspector (HMI): person appointed by the Department of Education to inspect standards in Schools.

Ilkley Moor: a well-known Yorkshire beauty spot.

Kanqah: a Sufi settlement.

Local Education Authority (LEA): the body that controls education in given geographical or political area.

MRSA: an infection suffered by people after operations.

Mul Mantra: important Sikh affirmation of belief.

Mureed: a follower of a Sufi teacher.

OFSTED: Office for Standards in Education (in the UK).

Polytechnics: Higher education institutions created in the 1970s; now universities.

Primary school: school for children aged five to eleven years.

Public school: a fee-paying school independent of local government control.

Pudsey Bear: a yellow teddy bear with a red bandage that features in the annual BBC charity appeal, Children in Need.

Raj: term used to refer to British rule in India.

Ramadan: Muslim holy month of fasting.

Robin Hood: legendary twelfth-century outlaw and hero who is said to have lived in Sherwood Forest and robbed the rich to give to the poor. May be buried in the grounds of Kirklees Abbey in Yorkshire.

Sanskrit: ancient sacred language of India.

Secondary modern school: school to which children who were not selected for a grammar school at the eleven plus examination were sent.

Secular: in the West, a belief that religion is unimportant or irrelevant to existence; however, in India followers of Nehru and Gandhi define it as treating all religions equally and giving none a place of privilege.

Three tier system: division of education into three age groups; 5-9, 9-13, and 13 to the time a pupil leaves school.

Two tier system: division of education into two age groups; 5-11 and 11 to the time a pupil leaves school.

Yom Kippur: Day of Atonement, a day of community repentance when Jews fast for the whole period and attend the synagogue.

Yorkshire Ripper: nickname given to Peter Sutcliffe who murdered a number of women, mainly in the Bradford–Leeds area of Yorkshire in the late nineteen seventies and early eighties.